Fatal Treasure

Fatal Treasure

Greed and Death, Emeralds and Gold, and the Obsessive Search for the Legendary Ghost Galleon *Atocha*

Jedwin Smith

WILEY

John Wiley & Sons, Inc.

Published by John Wiley & Sons, Inc., Hoboken, New Jersey
Published simultaneously in Canada

Illustrations used by permission. Illustration credits: pages 7, 41, 178, 192, 216, and 226 courtesy of Mary Martin Photography; pages 10, 23, 53, 121, 139, 161, 164, 187, 197, and 232 copyright © and courtesy of Pat Clyne; pages 33 and 126 courtesy of Don Kincaid; pages 64, 91, and 233 courtesy of Jedwin Smith; pages 97, 136, and 140 courtesy of Syd Jones; page 115 courtesy of Damien Lin/ Paradigm Productions; page 236 courtesy of Andy Matroci.

The author gratefully acknowledges the following for permission to quote from:

"A Pirate Looks at Forty," words and music by Jimmy Buffett. Copyright © 1974 by Universal-Duchess Music Corporation (BMI). International copyright secured. All rights reserved.

"The Ballad of the *Atocha*," "The Conch Republic Song," and "Tourist Town Bar" by Michael McCloud.

For general information about our other products and services, please contact our Customer Care Department within the United States at (800) 762-2974, outside the United States at (317) 572-3993 or fax (317) 572-4002.

Wiley also publishes its books in a variety of electronic formats. Some content that appears in print may not be available in electronic books. For more information about Wiley products, visit our web site at www.wiley.com.

Library of Congress Cataloging-in-Publication Data:

Smith, Jedwin.
    Fatal treasure : greed and death, emeralds and gold, and the obsessive
search for the legendary Ghost Galleon Atocha / Jedwin Smith.
      p. cm.
ISBN 978-0-471-69680-3 (paper)
    1. Nuestra Señora de Atocha (Ship) 2. Treasure-trove—Florida.
3. Shipwrecks—Florida. I. Title.
G530.N83 S65 2003
909'.096348—dc21

2002153118

10 9 8 7 6 5 4

Mel Fisher was a dreamer, a visionary.
The men and women who dived into the sea
to pursue his dreams are supreme realists.
This book is for them.

Contents

Foreword

I think at some point in his or her life everyone dreams of finding buried treasure. In *Fatal Treasure*, Jedwin Smith has done a wonderful job of telling the story of Mel Fisher, who made that dream a reality. While I believe it would take an encyclopedia to tell the whole story, Jedwin's book has captured its essence. It made me laugh and it made me cry. It made me cheer for victory and it made me angry.

Finding a Spanish galleon that sank in a hurricane over 350 years ago is no easy task.

Most of all, *Fatal Treasure* made me remember a lesson my father taught me: Believe in your dreams, never give up, and you can make your dreams come true.

I hope you enjoy this book as much as I did.

As Mel always said, today's the day!

Kim Fisher

Acknowledgments

My goal in writing *Fatal Treasure* is simple: to tell the story of the men, and of the few daring women, who shucked most of the trappings of modern life for the chance to reach back in time and touch history. In doing so, they have given substance and validity to the dreams of Mel Fisher and to his ongoing enterprise, the *Atocha/Margarita* Expedition.

I will forever be indebted to Don Kincaid, Donnie Jonas, Pat Clyne, K. T. Budde-Jones, Syd Jones, Andy Matroci, Kenny Lingle, Tom Ford, and the late Bleth McHaley, who not only passed along their hard-earned knowledge but also shared with me their secrets, desires, frustrations, and sometimes their tears, along a nautical course that was often as skewed as it was perilous.

Also, this journey could not have been possible without assistance from the entire Fisher family, especially Mel, who always found time for me, mainly because he considered me good luck. Kim Fisher extended me the same courtesy. I thank Kane Fisher for allowing me to get close; I thank Deo Fisher for sharing her love and compassion. However, at no point have I considered the family or the company—to the extent that one can ignore the bigger-than-life presence of Mel Fisher, even from beyond the grave—to be the main focus of this book. Accordingly, it was undertaken with no agreement, explicit or implied, with either the family or the company, and neither tried to influence any part of my work. The manuscript was read by many of the participants, however, and their comments about factual elements were duly noted.

I am eternally grateful for the hospitality extended to me by all—including today's *Atocha* divers, especially my brother Jim and his wife, Mary Martin—for the things they have taught me about the sea and its bottom and the mysteries that lie there, and for their diligence in trying to ensure that I got my facts straight. But most of all, I am grateful for their friendship.

I also am indebted to several landlubbers, most of all my wife, June, who continues to allow the little boy within me to roam, to dive, and to seek life's treasures. I could search the world over and never find another jewel like her.

I also would like to thank my agent, Marilyn Allen, and the good folks at Wiley, especially my editor, Tom Miller, whose diligence made me a better writer. As always, I thank Lanny Franklin for keeping me in touch with history. I also want to extend my gratitude to my colleague and good friend J. Stanford Fisher. This adventure was compiled at his urging, and he dutifully scrutinized its telling chapter by chapter. I also wish to thank Elizabeth Mangum for putting me in touch with the poetry of the sea.

Prologue

I was scuba diving with Donnie Jonas in search of the lost treasure, and as I slipped through the blue-green waves, I felt as if I were being smothered. Panic was immediate. Treasure took a distant second to my discomfort as pressure built up on my eardrums. I must have swallowed my fear because suddenly the pressure was gone. Then I began to struggle with my regulator, which tasted like burned rubber, as I fought to breathe.

The sand bottom came up quickly, materializing out of nowhere. As if caught up in a nightmare, I plummeted, reaching out with both hands to stop my journey. My flippered feet hit bottom, jarring my backbone. My knees buckled from the weight of the compressed-air tank on my back and the weighted belt on my waist. Suddenly I was sitting on a cushion of sand. Instinctively I looked up for help. There, 53 feet up, was the safety of the *Magruder*; its hull nothing more than a faint shimmering shadow. But the reassuring sight of Jonas, who now flashed a thumbs-up sign of recognition, quelled my claustrophobic terror. No longer afraid, I breathed evenly and slowly. I motioned to Jonas that all was okay. And then, side by side, gliding with the current, we slowly moved toward the tomb of the *Nuestra Señora de Atocha*.

On this day, the sea once again relinquished its hold on the riches and glory of 17th-century Spain. And by the grace of God, I would share the moment of glory.

Jonas and I moved toward the *Atocha*'s worm-eaten timbers, which lay at odd angles, poking like prehistoric fingers from

1

beneath the sand. Some jutted upward, others were in a cross-hatch pattern. Here was the final resting place of a great ship and its 260 passengers and crew. Pausing briefly at the side of the tomb, we then swam upward and hovered directly above the timbers. Barracudas and snappers kept us company.

At that moment I could not help but reflect on the tragedy of what transpired 364 years ago. I remember trembling, then dived to the timbers and reverently ran my hands over the worn beams. My fear of the depths of the sea was immediately forgotten as I touched history and was overwhelmed by it.

I have no idea how long I spent peering at the wreck. I remember trying to swallow a lump in my throat and clearing my eyes of tears, then working my way with Jonas to the glistening sand to the right of the timbers. There, suspended inches above the bottom, I began the search. Pebbles and shells came into view, as did a four-foot-long barracuda that hovered inches from my mask. I watched Jonas comb the sands and tried to imitate his search.

Time was forgotten. My fear was replaced by the tranquillity, the deafening silence of a world few have seen. My mind raced with the events of history, and I found peace.

And then the green stones.

Jonas pointed out the first of them—a tiny pebble that glowed green in the white sand. Then another and another. Twenty meters to my left, near the ship's timbers, Jonas plucked emeralds at a furious rate. To his left, Kim Fisher was doing likewise. Kim was on a roll; five days earlier he'd discovered 40 feet of intricately crafted gold chain, a 10-pound gold disc, and three gold coins near this spot—almost $1 million in New World plunder. And now we'd found emeralds. Handfuls of them.

In the blink of an eye, I acted like a child at an Easter egg hunt—scurrying about, mindless of everything else. I just had to find another emerald. And another and another. This might explain why I had become a writer to begin with, a newspaperman with the bad habit of plunging in headfirst, no matter the consequences.

Now, despite the warning by Mel Fisher and his divers and my respect for the sea, I was consumed by greed. I forgot to check my air gauge; I breathed too deeply and too quickly, until there was nothing left to breathe.

I was reaching for my eighth emerald, another big one, when the invisible hands squeezed my trachea. In desperation, I clutched at my throat to pry away the enemy's fingers. But no one had hold of me.

Instant panic. *Shit, I'm out of air.* The surface seemed as if it were a mile away; Jonas and Fisher were shadows in the distance.

I swam to Jonas's side, tapped him on the shoulder, and then ran my finger in a slicing fashion across my throat. Jonas's eyes widened; one hand reached for my pressure gauge, which registered empty; the other pressed the mouthpiece of his life-saving regulator to my lips. And then, far too slowly it seemed to me at the time, we cautiously made our way to the surface.

I was lucky. The *Atocha* is not always so kind.

I

Invitation to the Party

There's a schooner in the offing, with her topsails shot with fire, and my heart has gone aboard her for the Islands of Desire.

—Richard Hovey

Until May 25, 1985, Mel Fisher was a name I had never heard and *Nuestra Señora de Atocha* just four more words of Spanish I did not know. But then it started to rain that Saturday afternoon as soon as I made a right-hand turn off Truman Avenue onto Duval Street in Key West, Florida. By the time I had gone two blocks it had become a downpour, and I was lost. My life has not been the same since.

I was a reporter employed by the *Atlanta Journal-Constitution* and I had taken the day off from the story I was working on up the road at Sugarloaf Key that would immortalize two Atlanta members of Ducks Unlimited who were making their first venture to fish the Florida flats. It was also my first experience with the Keys and its laid-back lifestyle of wind, water, and seemingly carefree idleness. I was hooked.

For three days we caught tarpon, bonefish, and permit, an extremely flat fish the size of a large frying pan—a fish that looked more like a stone to be skipped across the ocean than something that wore your arms out as you tried to reel it in. Three days of easing through the flats in a shallow-draft skiff watching black-tipped sharks and jacks and manta rays slide beneath the boat. Three days without worry or life's daily rat race while being fried by an unmerciful sun. I am Irish American, light-skinned and full of freckles, among other things; another hour out on the water and I would have blistered. This was why I decided to play tourist and visit Hemingway House.

But then I got lost in the rain and pulled into the only vacant parking spot I saw. When the sun finally returned, I found myself parked in front of a massive, multistoried stone dwelling adorned with a quaint sign: "Mel Fisher's Treasure Museum." Hemingway House would have to wait.

Long-lost treasure excites me every bit as much as the next person. Maybe me even more, because I am still a child wrapped in an aging man's body. Years earlier, when my family and I lived on Merritt Island off Florida's east coast, visiting Disney World was standard fare. Part of the bargain I made with my wife and daughters was a ticket swap: they got my "It's a Small, Small World" coupon in exchange for their "Twenty Thousand Leagues under the Sea." To me, Disney World was an endless ride on Captain Nemo's sub. The only thing that would have made the day even brighter would have been the opportunity to slip into the hard-hat suit and walk among the fishes.

That is what was going through my mind when I walked up the concrete steps of Fisher's museum and paid my three-dollar admission. It entitled me and six other tourists to be ushered into a small room with hard-backed chairs, where we viewed a 54-minute *National Geographic* documentary, which explained a number of things: who Mel Fisher was, what he did for a living, and why this museum was here.

"What kind of man pursues a dream against tremendous odds for over 16 years? What kind of dream is powerful enough to hold someone in its grasp for all those years?" asked Martin Sheen, who

The Mel Fisher Maritime Museum, which I stumbled into by accident.
My life has never been the same.

narrated the video. And then Sheen said: "Mel Fisher has been
called a hero and a huckster, a visionary and a schemer, an inspi-
ration and a con man."

The *National Geographic* video explained that Fisher was a former California chicken farmer who got interested in scuba diving
during its infancy in the 1950s. One thing led to another, and
Mel searched for and discovered Spanish treasure near Florida's
Sebastian Inlet before moving his family to the Keys in 1969 to
search for the *Atocha* and her sister ship *Santa Margarita*, two of
Spain's most bountiful treasure galleons that sank somewhere
near here during a 1622 hurricane. In the ensuing years, Fisher's
divers found the *Margarita* and its $20 million in gold, but only
bits and pieces of the *Atocha* treasure. Both the state and the federal governments wanted to confiscate all of these riches under
the guise of protecting our national heritage.

The video also explained that although the U.S. Supreme
Court eventually awarded ownership of the *Margarita*'s and *Atocha*'s

gold and silver to Fisher, it was a hollow victory because several people had drowned during the search.

It was impossible not to be enthralled by the Fisher saga. Treasure, death, government conspiracy—it was all there.

Yet this was the first that I had ever heard of it. I was enduring Marine Corps boot camp when the Fisher family first arrived in the Keys. I had been covering innocuous National Football League games when Dirk Fisher and the others had drowned in 1975. I had been a war correspondent, trying my best to stay alive while covering the civil unrest in Beirut, Lebanon, just 18 months earlier when Fisher's divers had made their last big discovery, 23 pieces of ornate gold jewelry found near a place called the Quicksands somewhere out there in the Straits of Florida.

I was kicking myself at the end of the movie, upset that I had missed reporting on the events I had just seen, when we tourists were escorted into an adjoining room. If anyone doubted the veracity of the just-viewed video, the contents of this room made you a believer. Its walls were lined with glass-enclosed cases filled with gold bars, gold rings, gold chains, and silver coins, stunning displays of the *Margarita* and *Atocha* treasures. I remember my knees growing weak and finding it difficult to breathe as, almost in a trance, I ambled from one display to another, pulled along by the desire to run my hands over the gold, daydreaming about actually being at the bottom of the sea and helping discover such riches. Then I heard first the soft chuckle and then the words "Pretty neat stuff, huh, kid?"

Mel Fisher stood before me and I almost swallowed my tongue.

At six-feet-five, he appeared larger than life. He was wearing a gaudy Hawaiian-print blue shirt. A gold doubloon dangled from a thick gold chain around his neck. He draped an arm around my shoulder and said, "Have I got a deal for you, kid." With that, he escorted me to a card table where there was a large skillet cake. Fisher pointed to his coin and said that for only $10 I could pick out a slice of cake, which might or might not have a Spanish silver piece of eight inside it. Win or lose, the $10 also entitled me to become a member of the Mel Fisher Maritime Heritage Society. The coin alone was worth $600; somewhere in the cake were three of them.

"Tell me which slice you want and I'll serve it to you myself on this here gold plate that we brought up off the *Margarita*. C'mon, don't be shy," Mel said. "The odds are in your favor, kid. Hey, today's the day."

A fool and his money are soon parted. Despite having no desire to become a member of any society, Mel Fisher's or not, the lure of possibly getting a fabulous return on my money was too much to pass up. And even though the smooth-talking guy looming over me was reminiscent of a carnival barker, I immediately liked him. I identified myself as a newspaperman in search of a good story.

That's how the adventure began. To use the lexicon of the deep-sea divers I would one day work alongside, I was "invited to the party." It was the day before Memorial Day, and Mel Fisher once again was flirting with financial disaster. As was often the case with his operation in the mid-1980s, more money was going out than was coming in. So he had rolled out the cake and its hidden coins under the guise of a Heritage Society membership drive in hopes of defraying some of the back wages he owed his office staff and divers. Mel did not share any of this with me at the time. Instead, he ushered me through a labyrinth of narrow, dark hallways to an immense, dimly lit room, where he introduced Duncan Mathewson, his archaeologist. Mathewson reminded me of a college professor: deeply tanned with wind-blown hair, Clark Kent glasses, and sporting a short salt-and-pepper beard. He was also the first person I had seen wearing slacks in three days. We shook hands and exchanged some rudimentary small talk. Then Mel asked: "So what would you like to know?"

Mel Fisher smiles as he examines the cache of gold bars, chains, and disks discovered under the sand and silt near the *Atocha*'s gravesite.

"Everything," I replied, which prompted them to laugh.

Mel shook his head and sighed, then lapsed into silence. While he was taking his measure of me, I did likewise of him. Fisher did not fit the image I had envisioned of a treasure hunter. No peg leg like Long John Silver. No cool hat or snappy dialogue like Indiana Jones. Instead, when he spoke, he sounded as if he had just been awakened from a nap—eyes focused on something beyond his reach, mumbling softly or speaking in half-finished sentences and filling in the gaps with the rattle of soft chuckles. A *Miami News* reporter once described Fisher as looking like your slightly dyspeptic uncle, tall and soft and stoop-shouldered, squinting out from bifocals at a situation not entirely of his own making.

He was a chain smoker and a heavy drinker. He also was usually a man of few words, although that was not the case on this day. Even though he talked at great length, he preferred speaking of his wife and family and his divers, but was embarrassed elaborating about himself. In the following months I would learn that it was not uncommon for him to turn away from a conversation in midsentence and disappear. He was easily bored, even when the subject was treasure.

Finally Mel said, "So you want to know everything, huh? Well, I ain't got *that* much time, kid. We're still looking for her. Been looking for her for 16 years."

I told him that was part of what baffled me. According to the movie I had just seen, it seemed as if he had a fairly good idea of where the *Atocha* sank. So why was it taking him so long to find her?

"You just don't go out in a rowboat and find something. It's not like you drop to the bottom and find a treasure chest open here and a cannon over there," Mel said. He paused, obviously measuring my intelligence or lack of it. Noticing my glazed expression, he said, "Guess you've never been at sea, never done any diving, right?"

I told him I had done neither. Mel responded with a tight smile, then spread a huge chart on the table and pointed to thousands of little red-inked circles that had been added to the chart. The red circles represented anomalies, anything different from the bottom's natural structure, he said, then went into great detail about the nuts and bolts of conducting a treasure hunt at sea. Over the past 16 years, Fisher's search boats had dragged a magnetometer behind their boats, running prearranged courses back and forth across the Straits of Florida—east to west, from the Marquesas Keys to Rebecca Shoal; north to south, from New Ground Reef to Cosgrove Shoal. By his own estimates, his crews had magged close to 140,000 linear miles of ocean by 1971 alone. A magnetometer, Mel explained, made it easier to detect ferrous metals at the bottom of the sea. When the mag recorded a hit— a metal reading on the ocean bottom—it was duly marked on the chart; hence the red-inked circles I was looking at. Sounds simple enough, he said, except that virtually the entire area he and his crews had been searching used to be a World War II naval air corps bombing range.

"So, sure, we know the *Atocha* went down somewhere in this area," Mel said, running his hand over the chart. "We know she surely struck the outer reef, which tore out her bottom, but we don't know exactly which part of the reef she struck. And even though we know the general direction the storm carried her, that she was being pushed slightly to the northwest, all we know for certain is what the artifacts have told us—the *Atocha*'s anchor, all of them pieces of eight from an area we call 'The Bank of Spain,' stuff like that. Other than that, there's the information the Spanish handed down when they went looking for her and the *Margarita*."

Mathewson, noticing my obvious confusion, picked up the story at this point. The Spanish were brilliant when it came to salvaging their ships, he said, seldom leaving a stone unturned at depths up to 70 feet. In the case of the *Atocha* and the *Margarita*, however, never had salvage been of such paramount importance, for when they sank, so plummeted the fortunes of Spain. Spain's power came at the point of a sword and from the mouth of a cannon. It was continually at war, and the gold and silver pillaged from the New World was the only way to keep the war machine running. Spain desperately needed to recover the *Margarita*'s and *Atocha*'s riches.

"The *Atocha* manifest says she was carrying something like 40 tons of silver and 160 boxes of gold—bars, bracelets, stuff like that," Mel chimed in with a magnanimous grin. He let that thought dangle for a few moments, then said, "We're looking at something like $400 million in treasure on her alone. Any day now we'll be bringing it to the surface. Today's the day."

Mathewson said he might as well start at the beginning. I glanced at Mel, who smiled and winked at me.

King Philip IV was his name, Mathewson said. Philip was only 16, a little headstrong and not overly bright. In 1621, when his dad died, Philip inherited a kingdom that stretched from the Philippines to the New World. Just like Great Britain two centuries later, the sun never set on the Spanish Empire, due in large part to its concept of diplomacy: Invade and conquer, then systematically pillage those stomped beneath their boots. Naturally, transporting the treasure back home to Spain was somewhat of a problem. Then again, the Spanish were the greatest seamen of their day, and their warships, the multigunned galleons, pretty much ruled the waves.

In concept, the *Atocha* was such a galleon. Built in 1620, the three-masted ship sported 20 cannons and was capable of displacing 400 tons of cargo. She proved to have been shoddily constructed, however. To meet the King's deadline, the vessel was completed in haste. Not only were the ship's deck timbers not secured by nails, but also the number of spikes in crucial joists was reduced from five to two. She developed leaks in her bow during her maiden voyage. But when she set sail for Seville with the *Margarita* and the 26 other ships of the fleet on Sunday, September 4, 1622, six weeks behind schedule—a delay that had pushed her sailing into the heart of hurricane season—the *Atocha* was deemed capable of withstanding anything nature could offer.

But then Spanish bureaucrats compounded her structural problems with greed, grossly overloading the grand vessel. Besides the normal abundance of cargo, 15 tons of Cuban copper and 12 tons of royal tobacco, the greater part of the *Atocha*'s hold was filled with 40 troy tons of registered treasure: 1,235 silver ingots, 250,000 silver coins, and 161 pieces of gold in various bars and discs. This recorded wealth does not include the scores of boxes of personal riches from the 48 passengers, 38 of whom were considered royalty. In addition, friars had 35 boxes of unrecorded wealth loaded aboard the ship, all of which was earmarked for the Catholic Church. Because the Spanish were notorious smugglers, historians estimate that an additional seven troy tons of treasure were secreted aboard the vessel.

The *Margarita* was also heavily laden with riches. She carried in her hold 419 silver ingots weighing 80 pounds each; 118,000 silver coins; and 1,488 ounces of gold fashioned into 34 bars and discs, plus unknown amounts of smuggled gold, silver, and emeralds.

So the *Atocha* and the 630-ton *Margarita* were absurdly overcrowded with passengers, crew, and cargo. Aggravating the situation was the way weather was forecasted in those days. Saturday, September 3, dawned clear and sunny, with favorable winds. Because there was no visible threat of encroaching storms, and because Sunday would be the conjoining of the sun and moon—interpreted to mean that these advantageous sailing conditions would last for at least three days, more than enough time for them to skirt the treacherous Florida coast and successfully ride the Gulf Stream toward hearth and home—anchors were hoisted and the fleet set sail for Spain.

A hurricane with gale force winds out of the northeast slammed into the fleet at midafternoon on Monday, churning the surface of the Gulf Stream and turning it into a seascape of 15-feet-high waves. Next came the rain, a torrent carried on a wind that pelted the ships unmercifully. And then, just when passengers and crew thought conditions could get no worse, the sky turned black as the hurricane bore down on them. Soon all 28 ships of Spain's Tierra Firme fleet became isolated, each struggling as best it could for survival.

As the hurricane smashed through the narrow corridor separating Cuba from the Florida Keys, the tail-end galleons of the fleet—the *Santa Margarita* and the *Nuestra Señora de Atocha*—bore the brunt of the storm. For most of their combined 476 sailors, soldiers, and crew, death was less than 12 hours away.

Aboard the *Atocha*, sailors lashed themselves to anything solid, while others scrambled aloft to secure the sails of the foremast in an attempt to keep the ship's stern to the wind. Before this could be completed, both the mainmast and the foremast snapped, crashing to the deck and carrying passengers and seamen with them as they bounced across splintered timbers and over the side. The rigging had long ago been cut loose and tossed to the wind. Before nightfall, the rudder broke, leaving the *Atocha* to her fate.

Things were just as bad aboard the *Margarita*. She lost her mainmast earlier in the day; then her foresail was torn loose. And when the wind shifted to the south, pushing the ship through a seemingly endless wall of waves toward the Florida Keys' dreaded coral reefs, she lost her tiller and whipstaff. As darkness descended, passengers and crew frantically clutched the ship's railing, praying that they would not be swept overboard, sucked down into the frothing ocean. The storm raged throughout the night and continued through the early morning hours of Tuesday, pushing the fractured ship toward shallow water. Once there, the action of the waves intensified, pounding the ship without mercy. In desperation, all anchors were dropped, but they failed to hold. The *Margarita* grounded herself on a shoal.

At first light of September 6, survivors among the *Margarita*'s crew saw the *Atocha* three nautical miles to the east. In horror they saw her suddenly lifted high out of the water and hurled onto the coral reef, rupturing her keel. The *Atocha* staggered a short distance past the reef, then sank, killing all 48 of her passengers and 212 of her 217 sailors and soldiers. Within an hour, the *Margarita* began to break apart. Her demise was recorded in a contemporary English account: "The passengers when it was apparent they could not escape, saw as little mercy in the Sea, as they had endured in the Winde." When the *Margarita* sank, 143 of her passengers and crew were killed.

The *Margarita*'s 68 survivors and five from the *Atocha* were plucked from the sea by a Jamaican vessel on the very afternoon their ships perished. Once the survivors had reached Havana and told their tale, preparations for salvaging the galleons began immediately. Within days of her sinking, the *Atocha* was located because her mizzenmast still protruded above the water near the reef upon which she was impaled. Other than recovering two of her cannons, slave divers were unable to salvage any of her cargo because of the depth—she lay upright and intact in 55 feet of water—and because her submerged hatches were too tightly battened. When salvagers returned in early October with the proper equipment, however, the *Atocha* had vanished. A second hurricane had swept the area, ripping her gun deck and sterncastle from her lower structure and scattering her precious contents along a path that, centuries later, would appear to be 12 miles long and 60 feet wide.

"And now you know why I call her a Ghost Galleon," Mel said. One day she was there, her mizzenmast serving as a big X on an ancient treasure map, and then she simply vanished.

But not the *Margarita*. The Spaniards, using Caribbean pearl divers and other slaves from their various colonies, discovered her grave on June 6, 1626, at a place called Cabeza de los Martires, head of the martyrs. Spanish navigators referred to the area that way because the numerous palm trees swaying in the wind reminded them of the waving hands of those unfortunate sailors consumed by the sea, the lost souls of purgatory. Spain subsequently recovered 350 silver bars and 64,000 coins in three diving seasons before finally being driven off the spot by Dutch warships in 1628. Ongoing wars and economic ruination prevented Spain from combing the area further, Mathewson said, and from that point on, the *Margarita* and the *Atocha* passed into nautical lore.

I looked up at Mel, glanced at the large chart before me, and asked him why he still hadn't been able to find the *Atocha*.

Since 1969, he said, his crews had recorded at least 6,000 magnetometer hits each year. He had scores of charts such as the one he was showing me now, each scoured by these red-inked marks, which represented ancient bomb fragments, discarded lobster traps, or remnants of the *Atocha*. The only way to determine whether they had struck pay dirt or metallic garbage was to position the salvage boats over the anomaly, blow a hole in the deep sand, and then send divers into the water to check it out. More often than not what they had found was junk. Nonetheless, the only way to find that ultimate prize was to dig, dig, dig.

"There's one other thing that's important to keep in mind," he said, chuckling. "That's a mighty big ocean out there."

❦

Mel Fisher spoke for almost an hour and a half that day. I was later told this was almost 80 minutes longer than normal: he was noted for his short attention span, even when the subject was long-lost treasure. He spoke of his troubles with big govern-ment—the Securities and Exchange Commission and the Internal Revenue Service, how he had spent $1.6 million in lawyer fees while enduring six federal court hearings that consumed 108 hours spread over the better part of 8½ years before being awarded 100 percent of the treasures from the *Margarita* and the *Atocha* by the U.S. Supreme Court. He went on about his troubles with "small-minded government"—how the state of Florida continually sought to confiscate the fruits of his lifelong labor.

Amid this conversation, I found myself daydreaming about Robert Louis Stevenson's *Treasure Island*, seeing Long John Silver pacing the room, his peg leg making the floor's timbers shiver as he extolled the incessant greed of the Crown, his eyes gleaming, his words meant to pull young Jim Hawkins into his grandiose schemes: "Aye, the short and the long of the whole story is about here: you can't go back to your own lot, for they won't have you; and, without you start a third ship's company all by yourself, which might be lonely, you'll have to jine with Cap'n Silver."

In my mind's eye I had already "jined" Mel Fisher's band of merry men and women. The man had a fantastic story to tell, and I knew I would help him tell it sooner or later. I put aside my childlike thoughts of fictitious pirates, captivated by the scallywag before me.

Mel lifted his eyes and shifted his gaze toward me. A smile, then he said that I should take out my credit card and put $1,000 on it and become one of his limited partners. The investment would surely pay off because any day now his divers would be bringing $400 million in treasure to the surface.

"I just know it's gonna happen. I just know it," he said in a soft voice, which made me believe he had said this more for his own benefit than mine. "Just think of it, kid. *Four hundred million dollars in treasure.* And you could be a part of it; you could become a limited partner and share all the goodies. Do that and you'll be talking about this and writing about this for the rest of your life. You wouldn't want to miss out on that, would you?"

No, I wouldn't. But investing in his search was out of the question, I told him. I only worked for the newspaper, I didn't own it. Writing a story about the *Atocha* search was a different matter, though. That was a done deal.

2

Dreaming of the
Hurricane

Raging waves of the sea, foaming out their own shame; wandering stars, to whom is reserved the blackness of darkness for ever.

—Epistle of Jude

Death came for them swiftly, carried on a stiff wind that shrieked across the Straits of Florida in excess of 75 miles per hour. It lay couched among the waves, an endless seascape of 15-foot rollers that lifted high and paused before they slammed against the porous planking of the fragile wooden ship. It was hidden within the ominous clouds that smothered the sun with its blinding blackness, turning day to night.

A bloodcurdling scream from starboard as a sailor was swept off his feet, ricocheting off the stump of the mainmast before being crushed headfirst against the port rail. Muffled cries nearby as two other sailors—their hands turned to pulp, the skin having been torn away hours earlier, exposing tendons and bone—clung in desperation to the splintered remnants of the starboard railing. A woman of obvious nobility clutched a small child to her breast, kneeling frozen in terror, as she was galvanized against the fore-castle's bulkhead. In front of her, the lifeless body of a Franciscan friar rolled from one side rail to another in the grip of the ship's frantic gyrations.

It was early Tuesday morning, September 6, 1622, and the once-resplendent treasure galleon *Nuestra Señora de Atocha*, the pride of the Spanish navy, was as helpless as she was doomed. Gale-force winds had struck at noon the day before, first tearing away her sails and rigging, then shattering her rudder. Now at the mercy of the sea, her 217 sailors and soldiers and 48 passengers held on for dear life, praying for deliverance in one breath and cursing their fate in another. It wasn't supposed to have been like this. The fleet had departed Havana, Cuba, on Sunday amid pomp and pageantry, setting sail in serene conditions, under a clear sky with favorable winds.

But now, fewer than 36 hours later, the *Atocha* had gone from being a grand ship to a death ship.

Panic had hold of everyone, including the captain and his first mate. From their terror-filled eyes it was obvious that the ship was doomed, that all souls aboard were about to be sucked down into the roiling sea that swept over them. Nearby, three seamen fought for secure handholds on the ship's splintered mainmast and foremasts, whimpering all the while at the prospect of what was to come. Panic and horror did not discriminate, clasping aristocrat and commoner alike, royalty and servant, and rendering seasoned seamen and hardened soldier no more useful than their most foppish fellow victims.

Conditions on the gun deck were no better. Children, soldiers, and sailors huddled there in terror, crammed together belly to backside. They had been so since the day before, forced into great discomfort as they struggled to stay alive, resorting to urinating and defecating in wooden buckets, and eating sour salt-pork with filthy fingers. Now they were turning rancid themselves with the stench of fear.

On the port side, a bulkhead beam splintered and the sea rolled in. Some of the crew attempted to scramble for safety. There was nowhere to run. Their nakedness before the sea was an answer, although a negative one, to the litany arising from near the stern, where the friars loudly chanted their prayers, trying to make them heard over the howling of the storm. Then, as if the tempest was pronouncing its own amen, there came a horrific sound—the ghostly wailing of wind whistling through roiling sea—as the grand ship was lifted high into the air and then dumped onto the impaling fingers of Florida's outer reef.

Within seconds, timbers gave way—snapping one by one, explosions muffled by the onrushing sea—as the ship broke apart, its bow thrust upward like an accusing finger condemning a merciless God.

Moments later, new sounds could be heard as those cast into the sea—conquistadors who had never tasted defeat on any battlefield, squires and royal court accountants, uncommon men and women and children—screamed as they fought to keep their heads above water.

Soon the storm and the sea were the only sounds, and I snapped out of my daydream.

3

A Mother's Story

And then . . . when you find treasure, that's when your problems really begin.

—*Deo Fisher*

D id he tell you about the carpet of gold?"
The mention of gold snapped me out of my reverie, and I stumbled over Dolores "Deo" Fisher's question. Mel's wife had caught me daydreaming. Truth is, I kept looking at Deo and seeing my mother. Same red hair, hypnotic eyes, and soothing countenance. And when she spoke, no matter whether she was recalling the tragedies that plagued her husband's search for the *Atocha* or reliving the joys of various discoveries of long-lost gold or silver, her words were uttered with absolute sincerity.

This was a little melodramatic, sure. But nothing that had happened to me in the previous few hours seemed realistic. It was a twilight zone experience. I had been introduced to treasure; I had met a real-life Indiana Jones, albeit an aging version, and had been captivated. And now I was in the company of the treasure hunter's wife, transfixed by her wholesome, down-to-earth quality. She wore a simple cotton dress, no makeup, no jewelry other than her wedding ring. She looked me directly in the eye, even when the subject matter was not to her liking.

From left to right, Deo Fisher, Mel Fisher, and historian Dr. Eugene Lyon examining gold bars for royal stamps and seals.

I met Deo as I was leaving her husband's chart room. Mel had made the introduction hastily, then apologized to Deo, telling her that he had to check on the museum's customers. Then he disappeared around a corner, leaving his wife holding the bag. She handled the situation, and everything else, with dignity and grace. While Mel might very well be considered the world's greatest treasure hunter, Deo was the backbone of the operation. She ushered me into another room and offered me a chair and her undivided attention, sliding into conversation as if we were long-lost relatives.

She met Mel when she was 16, in 1952. He was a 29-year-old chicken farmer in Torrance, California. It was love at first sight, Deo said with a smile so genuine it was impossible to question the point. Mel was gregarious, even-tempered, and highly likable. Even then, she said, it was obvious that he was born to be a sea gypsy, although he was dabbling in the underwater realm only on

a part-time basis. He had his own air compressor and was filling
scuba tanks out of a shed at the farm. On weekends Mel would hit
the water with a homemade underwater 16mm camera in tow,
filming encounters with sharks and other creatures of the deep
for a Los Angeles television station. It didn't take him long to
realize that there was more money to be made on and in the
ocean than on shore.

He arrived at that destiny in a roundabout way because, until
the early 1960s, he had no idea what he wanted to do with his life.
Maybe music, so he formed his own swing band while still in high
school in Gary, Indiana, and he continued to play the saxophone
in bands while studying engineering at Purdue. When the Japanese attacked Pearl Harbor, Mel promptly joined the army and
was sent to Europe, landing after the Normandy invasion and following the U.S. forces all the way into Germany.

When I asked Deo what exactly attracted her to Fisher, she
blushed. Her smile was overpowering as she relived the early
years of their 32-year love affair, describing the man she not only
called the world's greatest treasure hunter, but also the world's
greatest husband and father and dreamer. There was no doubt in
her mind that someday the entire world would think of him as
she did.

Deo was uncertain when Mel first locked onto the idea of
going after the *Atocha* and its fabled horde of treasure. The idea
probably took hold in 1967, just about the time they got bored
scouring the shallows of Sebastian Inlet north of Vero Beach,
Florida, while excavating the remnants of Spain's 1715 fleet. As
Deo pointed out, Mel was never content working on just one salvage project at a time. As with most treasure hunters, the real
thrill is always the anticipation of finding treasure, believing that
the next dive will be the answer to all their prayers. Once the
treasure is located, bringing it to the surface becomes work,
oftentimes tedious and boring drudgery. Instead of being treasure
hunters, suddenly they are merely salvors, cargo haulers, transporting riches from the ocean's bottom to the surface.

In this instance, the riches were an estimated $14 million in gold coins, silver bullion, and exquisite jewelry carried aboard 10 Spanish galleons that had been gutted along Vero's reefs on July 31, 1715. When treasure hunter Kip Wagner first began combing the area for riches in 1960, Mel was dabbling in several undersea adventures from the family home in Redondo Beach, California. Besides operating his own dive shop, Fisher tried his hand at salvage, searching for wrecks without success in Haiti and the Silver Banks area near the Dominican Republic. As Deo pointed out, they brought no expertise to the enterprise. It was a learn-as-you-go process, hit and miss with more misses than hits.

But they did become quite knowledgeable about working on or near the reefs, gaining invaluable hands-on experience about how the hidden obstacles impaled ships, scattering and burying whatever riches they were carrying. Along the way they acquired an odd assortment of friends, all of whom would eventually become famous in the annals of salvage: Fay Feild, an electronics genius who invented a portable magnetometer that made it easier to detect ferrous metals at the bottom of the sea; Rupert Gates, an able cartographer and veteran gold diver; and Demosthenes "Mo" Molinar, a Panamanian mechanic.

I interrupted and asked Deo to elaborate about a magnetometer. Obviously, I said, a magnetometer can detect iron on the ocean bottom. But what does that have to do with finding non-ferrous items such as gold and silver?

She explained, in a patient manner that did not make me feel at all stupid, that iron was used quite extensively in Spanish ships for spikes, braces, hinges, and weaponry. So iron remnants would be scattered along whatever path a ship traveled when it was breaking apart. Wherever the ship finally came to rest, iron would surely be there in abundance. And where there was iron, hopefully there was gold.

Mel, Deo said, had developed an insatiable appetite for books as well as newspaper and magazine articles that dealt with treasure. As a teenager in Indiana, he had read and reread Robert

Louis Stevenson's *Treasure Island*, devouring the legacy of Long John Silver's voracious quest for those legendary pieces of eight, the Spanish eight reales, an ounce of coined silver. By chance, Fisher would also stumble across an old copy of Ferris Coffman's *Treasure Atlas*, which highlighted the world's greatest treasure wrecks. What caught Fisher's eye was the vast number of unsalvaged wrecks off the coast of Florida, mainly the doomed 1715 fleet and a hereto unknown vessel, the *Nuestra Señora de Atocha*. And then he discovered a book—*The Treasure Diver's Guide*, by John S. Potter Jr.—that would alter not only his life but also the scope of 21st-century treasure salvage. Potter described in detail the *Atocha* and the *Margarita*'s demises near the Florida Keys during the 1622 hurricane, pointing out that their combined cargoes of gold and silver were at least a million and a half pesos. And although the Spanish had somewhat successfully salvaged the *Margarita*, the *Atocha*'s treasure had been, at that juncture, untouched for 338 years.

"From that moment on," said Deo, "Mel was obsessed with the *Atocha*."

Deo said that it was impossible to be in Mel's presence and not be captivated by his dreams. "He'd start talking about adventure, about a long-lost treasure here or there, and the next thing you knew you were throwing all caution to the wind and diving in with him."

In the spring of 1963 Deo urged Mel to pursue his lust for the treasure of long-lost Spanish ships. They sold their home and dive shop, packed up the four children—Dirk, nine, Kim, seven, Kane, three, and Taffi, one—and a handful of possessions, mainly dive gear, and moved to Florida's east coast. Mel had struck a deal with Kip Wagner and his Real 8 Company, Inc., offering his services salvaging the 1715 fleet for free for one dive season, paying his own expenses. The services of Fay Feild, Mo Molinar, Rupert Gates, and financial backer Walt Holzworth were part of the deal. The payoff, if any, would be half of whatever treasure they found.

Mel and his crew spent the better part of the next year diving unsuccessfully in Sebastian Inlet. But then, on May 8, 1964, Mo Molinar found two gold disks and a gold coin in shallow water near a sandbar. Fewer than three weeks later, Fisher himself would slip beneath the surface and come face-to-face with the most awe-inspiring sight he had ever seen or imagined: the carpet of gold that Deo had mentioned.

What he found was more than 1,000 gold doubloons. In his own words: "The ocean's bottom was literally paved with gold. When you've seen something like that, everything else pales by comparison. As far as I could see, there was nothing but gold coins."

The discovery was so stunning, so unexpected, that *National Geographic* immediately showed up and reported the event in a then-unheard-of 37-page article titled "Drowned Galleons Yield Spanish Gold," which appeared in January 1965. Overnight, Kip Wagner and Mel Fisher became celebrities. They were now elite members of the "Brotherhood of the Coast"—treasure *finders*, not to be confused with the thousands of treasure *hunters* who flocked to the Florida coast once word of the great gold strike made headlines around the world.

National Geographic's dynamic photo spread would serve as a great recruiting tool for Mel Fisher later, when he went in search of the *Margarita* and the *Atocha*. The story inflamed imaginations and touched the souls of individuals, both men and women, who would become irreplaceable in Fisher's quest. Other than that, Fisher was hard pressed to find a ray of sunshine in the adventure. The treasure itself—a spellbinding array of intricate gold rings, necklaces, earrings, pendants, discs, and coins—was something that few people had ever seen before other than in museums. But because most of these items had been found close to shore, some actually having been washed up and lying loose in the sand, the concept of treasure hunting sounded ridiculously easy.

Few thought to consider the man-hours involved in recovery; the seemingly endless days of frustration; the 13-hour days, with little to show for your effort other than withered fingers from long hours in salt water; the immense cost involved in maintaining equipment, boats, and divers on a potential recovery site; or the greed that always slipped in, no matter how close-knit the divers may be.

Even Mel Fisher had no idea of what lay in store for him when he volunteered himself and his partners to help Kip Wagner. "We actually thought that the ship would be intact, lying there on the bottom, tilted a little bit on its side with its door hanging half open, just like in a Jules Verne movie," Deo said. She and Mel would dive down, ease their way through the open hatch, and there it would be—a real treasure chest—just sitting there on some rotting deck or table. Reality was quite different. Treasure hunting became one prolonged disappointment, one failure after another. "And then when you finally are blessed, when you find treasure," Deo said, "that's when your problems really begin."

These problems are fragile egos, greed, and a grasping bureaucracy. It does not matter if you are Henry Morgan, Francis Drake, or Mel Fisher; the dilemma facing 17th-century buccaneers was no different from that of modern-day treasure salvors. There was and continues to be bickering over who is the greatest of all, who is getting the most ink in the journals of the day, who is getting credit for finding one priceless item or another, who is getting the biggest percentage, and who feels as if he or she is getting screwed. And once these matters have been put to rest, if ever, there are always landlubbers to contend with. These individuals are easily recognized. Whatever power they wield has often been handed to them. Their fingernails are clean, they are well fed and well groomed, and whatever knowledge they possess has usually come through institutional study instead of hands-on experience. In the days of the Spanish Main, they were the aristocracy and the church. Today they might be well-intentioned archaeologists or historians, but more often they are politicians. Treasure hunters never see them until there is the first glint of gold.

Salvors paid the state of Florida a nominal fee for a contract that allowed them to search a specific offshore area. If they found anything of value, the state would get 25 percent of the treasure. But when Wagner and Fisher discovered gold in abundance, Florida's archaeological community immediately stepped forward, claiming that the salvors were destroying the state's cultural heritage. Leading the dispute was a state marine archaeologist who viewed all commercial treasure hunters as modern-day pirates and thieves. The archaeologist's argument was that only qualified archaeologists could properly map a wreck site, excavate, catalog, and successfully preserve the newly discovered artifacts. The obvious flaw, one as big as the ocean, was that the state had never expended its resources searching for sunken ships, either American or Spanish.

Wagner and Fisher argued that they expended their own money on research, equipment, and manpower in a search that oftentimes carried them to the brink of bankruptcy, if not to the end of their patience. If they did find treasure, they had to turn everything over to state agents, who in turn returned it only after the artifacts had been properly evaluated. By contract, the state was allowed to pick and choose what artifacts it desired before any of the treasure was returned to the salvors.

Despite intense animosity on both sides, a tenuous peace was reached. Wagner and Fisher could continue their salvage, but state agents must be present at all times, supervising the excavation of artifacts, and making sure that the salvors adhered to proper archaeological procedures. Fisher grudgingly accepted the state's edicts but privately dreamed of finding another wreck site, preferably one far greater than the 1715 fleet, one far removed from the state's grasp, well beyond Florida's three-mile jurisdictional boundary.

In between the diving and the dreaming, Mel and Deo cataloged all of their discoveries, turned everything over to the state for the eventual division, and then traveled around the state, putting on treasure-hunting seminars in an attempt to educate the public. They also had to invent ways to not only restore relics but also to preserve them, which made their vocation even more expensive. As Deo explained, everything associated with treasure hunting had a price tag, whether it was obtaining dive gear or purchasing acid by the bulk to eliminate centuries of encrustation from artifacts. The roughest part, she said, was simply trying to live from day to day. Treasure hunting was an expensive endeavor, made even tougher because even though treasure was being found, the state was in no hurry to divide the spoils.

As a consequence, while they were well off on paper, the illiquidity of their assets often left Mel and Deo cash poor.

"It was maddening," Deo said. "Even though Mel had helped find millions of dollars in treasure, we had to scramble just to feed our children."

The Fishers lived hand to mouth while their interest in the *Margarita* and the *Atocha* intensified. The only clues Mel and Deo had were those provided in Potter's book *The Treasure Diver's Guide*, that the galleons sank near the "Cabeza de los Martires in Matecumbe." The only Matecumbe that Fisher knew of were Upper and Lower Matecumbe Keys, midway between Key Largo and Marathon in the chain of Florida Keys. He obtained a state search contract for Monroe County, which encompasses most of the Keys, and he and fellow salvors Dick Williams, Walt Holzworth, Rupert Gates, Bob Moran, and Fay Feild spent the winter of 1968–1969 in a fruitless search, scouring the Gulf of Mexico and Atlantic sides of the Keys with a magnetometer.

"Funny how God just seems to put the right people in your path at the right time," Deo Fisher said. "Mel was working the 1715 fleet in the summer and magging, with no success, for the *Atocha* in the winter. But then we were introduced to Eugene Lyon, and suddenly the search for the *Atocha* took on new meaning."

Lyon was doing his doctoral research in 1970 at the Archives of the Indies in Seville. He discovered both the *Atocha*'s and the

Margarita's manifests, plus firsthand salvage accounts by Francisco Nuñez Melian "in the Keys of Matecumbe, coast of Florida." Lyon determined that the Spanish called the entire line of Florida Keys "Matecumbe." Furthermore, he discovered another Melian document, this one saying that the *Margarita*'s salvage had been undertaken at Cayos del Marques, the "Keys of the Marquis," which Lyon discovered was the Marquesas Keys. Once Lyon shared his good news with Fisher, the operation was uprooted from the Matecumbe Keys and transported to Key West.

In June 1970, Mel and Deo rented a small Key West apartment. A year later, Mel traded a gold bar from his proceeds of the 1715 fleet for the deed to a cramped four-bedroom houseboat anchored on the southern side of the island. The quarters were just temporary, Deo said. After all, now that she and Mel knew almost exactly where the *Atocha* and the *Margarita* had gone under, their dreams were about to be realized, their prayers about to be answered.

"Honest to God, we thought it would be easy," Deo said. Mel would go out there to the Marquesas in his search boat, towing the magnetometer behind it as he and the crew scoured Hawk Channel. And once they got a promising reading, they would don their dive gear, enter the water, and slowly drift down to the bottom, where all of that long-lost gold and silver would be waiting for them.

Of course, Deo said, laughing at her naïveté, the grand adventure would prove to be nothing like that. She and her family ended up living on that houseboat *temporarily* for 10 years. During that time, the *Atocha* simply teased the Fishers, surrendering her treasure one portion at a time, all the while punishing Mel and Deo for unknown transgressions.

"So many horrible things, so many tragedies," said Deo, her voice faltering as tears welled in her eyes. "Every time that it seemed as if something good were about to happen, our hearts would be broken."

4

No Warning

Hey, watch out up there!
                            —*Unknown*

O n July 19, 1975, the *Northwind*, one of Mel Fisher's salvage boats, dropped anchor near the Marquesas, approximately eight miles northeast of where six days earlier Dirk Fisher and his divers had discovered the *Atocha*'s nine cannons. The crew was in high spirits. They had found treasure and were anticipating finding all of the elusive Ghost Galleon's 47 tons of gold and silver any day. As darkness descended upon a placid sea, the crew celebrated Angel Fisher's 28th birthday with a special present, Kentucky Fried Chicken, eliminating the need for her to cook dinner. With the exception of Angel's 12-year-old brother Keith Curry, called "Sharkbait" by the crew, and Don Kincaid, the crew celebrated, then drifted off to sleep.

The ship was cramped. Although there were only enough bunks to sleep six, there were 11 aboard. Bodies were draped everywhere as the last of the night's merriment was stilled by drowsiness or stupor. Lying atop mattresses on the top deck near the wheelhouse were Bouncy John Lewis, Bob Reeves, Pete Van Westering, and little Keith Curry. Belowdeck, in the three tiny compartments slightly below and forward of the vessel's galley,

Angel Fisher, left, and her
husband, Dirk Fisher, shown
with a priceless astrolabe
(a 17th-century navigational
device) shortly after Dirk
found it.

were Dirk and Angel Fisher; Donnie Jonas and 16-year-old Kane
Fisher, Mel's youngest son; and divers Jim Solanick and Rick Gage.

Kincaid, who was aboard solely to photograph the cannons
for *National Geographic*, walked away from the celebration and
made his way to the boat's second level. He had more interest in
Bruce Lee. He positioned his mattress adjacent to the dive locker
and lay back to read a biography on the martial arts master. Kincaid could not recall precisely what time he fell asleep. The last
thing he remembered was an endless stretch of stars bobbing
high overhead in synch with the gentle rocking of the sea.

Kincaid's peers considered him a fuddy-duddy. They did not
view him as a spoilsport, for the photographer was known to have
fun with the best of them. But what grated on his fellow divers
was Kincaid's obsession with safety, which many interpreted as

weakness. Kincaid was always checking his dive tables, the tabulation of a diver's time underwater in accordance to the depth of the dive, which determined the excess level of nitrogen in the body's blood system. His oddities did not stop there. Whenever he stepped aboard ship, he always made sure the number of life jackets at least equaled the number of people on board. He also familiarized himself with every inch of the ship, making sure he had a mental picture of its entire structure, stem to stern.

Although others laughed at Kincaid behind his back, he was merely following his instinctive respect of the sea. Knowing that mistakes on the open water usually have lethal consequences, he was always working out in his mind solutions to catastrophic problems: What if he was washed overboard? What if the boat sank? What steps needed to be taken to survive?

The one scenario he could not have anticipated was how to make secure a rubber toilet fitting connected to the bilge pump, a powerful piece of equipment designed to shut itself off at a pressure of 80 pounds per square inch. The *Northwind*'s toilet fitting had ruptured that morning while the boat was docked at Key West. The failure of the fitting flooded the engine room and caused the vessel to list dangerously to starboard. One of the crew had installed a new fitting, and it was in perfect operating condition when they finally retired for the evening.

Tugboats, which push and pull other vessels, have a diesel fuel tank on both sides, and the transfer of fuel from one tank to the other keeps the vessel level during turns. The fuel transfer occurs by simply opening a loose-fitting valve. Veteran tugboat seamen always secure this valve in the off position with a piece of wire, normally a coat hanger, twisting the metal so it is impossible for the valve to open up on itself. No veteran seamen were aboard the *Northwind* that night, however.

In the dead of night, as the crew slept, the rubber hose fitting on the toilet burst once again and seawater surged into the ship's hold, causing a list to starboard. At almost the same time, the vibration of the generator forced open the transfer valve on the port fuel tank, and thousands of gallons of diesel fuel suddenly shifted to the starboard tank, increasing the starboard list. There was no bilge alarm in the engine room. There was no fire watch, either. No one was watching over the boat throughout the night in case something disastrous happened.

The stars that night were so bright that it seemed you could touch them. Another warm and gorgeous night in paradise, that was how everyone remembered it. The sea was flat, with just a slight breeze blowing inland toward the Marquesas, almost two miles away, where Mel Fisher's other salvage boat, the *Virgilona*, lay at anchor. It was deathly quiet, except for the slightest hint of water lapping up against the *Northwind's* metal hull. Perfect sleeping weather in a tranquil setting aboard a rusted, dilapidated, exceedingly top-heavy three-story diving platform with gunwales that stood a mere 18 inches above the waterline.

Kincaid did not recall the exact predawn hour when he was startled awake by the voice that echoed topside: *"Hey, watch out up there!"*

Kincaid sat up and stared into the darkness, listened and heard nothing but the sharp creaking of the boat and the soft lapping of water on the deck below him. He did, however, notice that the vessel was leaning sharply to the right. Instinct told him something was wrong. Reaching inside the dive locker, he located his glasses and put them on. He stood, peered down at the deck, and saw someone standing at the stern with his back to him. By the time Kincaid scrambled down the ladder to the deck below, the person on the stern had disappeared.

He blinked to clear his eyes, then took a step forward but was stopped by a continuous wall of water rolling over the starboard gunwale. And then the mysterious and unfamiliar voice screamed at him again: *"Hey, watch out up there!"*

Kincaid turned once again toward the stern and saw a shadow, clearly that of a man. As he started to move toward the strange figure, however, another surge of water stopped him. Although he was still half asleep, Kincaid sensed that something was tragically wrong. He said his survival instinct took control as he raced to get help.

In the tight, cramped quarters far belowdeck, Donnie Jonas was dreaming of gold, a normal occurrence for the *Atocha* divers. Ask any of the male divers who had slipped below the surface of Hawk Channel, fanned the sand, and come face-to-face with the unmistakable glint of the precious metal, and he would tell you there was nothing that compared to touching gold. Not even the greatest sex.

So, as the *Northwind* tilted precariously to starboard, Jonas was dead to the world, smiling as his subconscious mind replayed over and over his conquests at the ocean's bottom. And then being jolted from his sleep by Kincaid's rough hand on his shoulder.

Jonas jumped up and immediately checked his watch. *Five-twenty; too damn early to start work*, he thought. He rubbed the sleep from his eyes and stared groggily at Kincaid, debating whether to scream at the photographer or simply ignore him. Kincaid made the decision easy by shouting the four most dreadful words a sailor can ever hear: *"We're taking on water!"*

Jonas was on his feet immediately, screaming at and shaking Kane Fisher, who was sleeping on a nearby bunk. Convinced that his buddy was awake, Jonas told Kane that the boat was taking on water and that he was going down to check out the source of the problem. He grabbed his flashlight and headed for the engine room.

"Kane didn't go with me. Instead, he went on up to the deck and took a piss," Jonas said. "Taking that piss saved his life."

Jonas and Kincaid scrambled through the darkness, into the galley, and then down the steep stairs leading to the engine room, which already had accumulated three feet of water. To avoid disaster, Jonas had to perform two impossible feats at once: turn the transfer valve to switch the boat's fuel from one tank to another, and then shut off the flow of water from the bilge pump. Jonas's instinct dictated that he go for the transfer valve.

Jonas said: "I'm going for the valve, pushing myself through the water, like I was slogging through wet cement. I finally reach the valve and . . . Jesus! I ain't got enough time."

And then Kincaid's scream knifed through the darkness.

What happened next, said Kincaid, was like watching a slide presentation. As the images are projected hauntingly onto the screen of his mind's eye, he cannot turn away, viewing it with the calmness of an unthreatened spectator. Click: the water swirling about Jonas's knees. Click: Jonas struggling to keep his balance amid the sharp tilting of the boat. Click: Kincaid hearing the loud hammering of the generator and the water bubbling about the bilge pump. Click: Kincaid standing in the doorway of the engine room as he turned abruptly toward the stairwell leading up to the ship's galley and saw water running down the steps.

Kincaid yelled to Jonas to *get the hell out of there*.

Kincaid knew he did not have time to make sure Jonas had heeded his warning. Kincaid scrambled up the stairs and forced open the galley door. He sidestepped just in time to avoid being crushed by the galley stove as it skidded across the deck, then leaped out of the way to avoid being hit by an ice chest. He ducked out the galley doorway and made his way topside. In those frantic seconds he had already calculated what to do if he were to get dumped into the ocean in the middle of the night.

Kincaid's gear was in the dive locker, in one bag. It was his life-support system: fins, wet suit, snorkel, knife, mask, and flares. But as he scrambled to the stern, the boat went into its death twitch. Much like a bucking bronco, its bow suddenly lifted high out of the water, arching backward. Before Kincaid could react, the anchor line and a 300-pound anchor were sliding down the deck toward him. Although he had read accounts of people doing superhuman feats during an adrenaline rush, such as lifting cars, he had dismissed them as fantasy. But as the anchor line started wrapping around his legs, Kincaid actually lifted a 300-pound anchor and tossed it aside "like it weighed nothing." And then everything seemed to happen as if in slow motion.

What if you're on the ass-end of a boat that is burying itself into the ocean? How do you survive? How do you make your way to safety, toward the bow? Kincaid had already thought through the answers. So as the *Northwind* went into its death throes, he took the first fateful step.

Kincaid walked up the side of the boat—left hand on the rail, right hand on the porthole; one hand on the winch, the other on a bolt; dragging his feet after him, muscles straining. Higher and higher, and then the boat lay down on its side, throwing Kincaid into the black sea.

"Luckily, most of the crew had been sleeping outside, on the deck," Kincaid said. "All of a sudden, heads start popping up out of the water. I saw Bouncy John, Sharkbait, Pete Van Westering, Bob Reeves, and Kane. But where the hell were the others?"

When the *Northwind* flipped over, Jim Solanick was thrown from his lower bunk and landed against the starboard bulkhead. Numbed by the fall and disoriented in the dark quarters, he had no time to think about Rick Gage, who was sleeping on the top bunk. Solanick was facedown against the porthole, through which seawater now gushed, filling the cabin. To hesitate was to die. He scrambled on hands and knees through the water, down the wall toward the door. Once through it and into the corridor, he saw the night sky through the open porthole of the ship's head. Making his way to the porthole, Solanick thrust his arms through the 18-inch opening and started squirming his way to safety. The sides of the metal porthole peeled the skin off his armpits. He struggled further, lost the skin along his rib cage. With his hips wedged in the porthole, seawater pounded against Solanick's head and chest, smothering him, pushing him back down into the blackness.

"I'm counting heads," said Kincaid. "One, two, three, four, five . . . dammit. And then, all of a sudden, things started firing through the portholes, like they're being fired out of a cannon. That happens when a boat rolls over like that and the pressure builds up inside. *Whoooooooosh!* Cups and saucers, anything and everything that wasn't bolted down are flying through the air."

Including Solanick. One moment he was struggling to hold his breath as he was being sucked down, the next he was being jettisoned up through the porthole. Bleeding profusely, but safe nonetheless.

Solanick was the seventh survivor. The remaining four crew members were unaccounted for.

Twenty-one-year-old Rick Gage was thrown from the top bunk at almost the same instant as Solanick. He, too, landed against the starboard bulkhead and scrambled out of the flooding cabin toward the safety of the corridor, trying desperately to reach the same porthole that afforded Solanick his freedom. But Gage was a fraction of a second too late, and an impenetrable wall of water engulfed him and carried him away.

Angel also was thrown from her bunk. She managed to make it to the door of her cabin, but no farther. Her 21-year-old husband, Dirk Fisher, Mel and Deo's beloved oldest son, never made it out of his bunk.

5

The Curse of the *Atocha*

> The sea never changes and its works, for all the talk of men, are
> wrapped in mystery.
>
> —*Joseph Conrad*, Typhoon

I am incapable of dealing with grief, especially when it presents itself in the form of a woman crying over the loss of a loved one. When her tears start to flow, my mind shuts down, my hands lie slack at my side, and I have a deep desire to be somewhere else—anywhere, just as long as I do not have to witness her pain. It is a defense mechanism, really. It had been 17 years since the Marine Corps officer knocked on our door and told my mother and me that my brother had been killed in action in Vietnam. I held Mom for an eternity that day, her tears hot on my neck. I can still feel their heat.

When Deo Fisher's tears started that day in 1985, I placed my hand on her trembling shoulder and stammered my apologies.

What I really wanted to do was hug her and offer her a shoulder to dry her tears on. But I didn't, knowing that it was not my place. Instead, I took her hand and thanked her for her time. When I suggested that we should continue the interview later, Deo nodded as she brushed away her tears.

That's me, left, chatting with Don Kincaid.

I was still standing there when Don Kincaid came to my rescue. As he would explain later, word had circulated throughout the museum that the media were on the premises, and Kincaid, as is his nature, was merely curious. I am sure Kincaid was hoping to find one of my profession's heavyweights—maybe the *Washington Post*'s Bob Woodward or the *New York Times*'s Seymour Hirsch—but instead he encountered me, a lightweight from Atlanta, a wide-eyed and obviously confused individual who had caused Deo Fisher, the surrogate mother of all *Atocha* divers, to cry. Kincaid did not appear amused.

"You asked her about Dirk, didn't you," Kincaid said in a businesslike tone of voice when we had left the room.

I told him that I had never broached the subject. For one, I felt as if the death of Deo's son was a private matter, and if she wanted to elaborate on the subject it would be her call and not at my urging. Besides, I told Kincaid, I knew all too well how tender the loss of a family member was because I had lost my younger brother Jeff on a battlefield in Vietnam. I found it impossible to discuss Jeff's death; I was sure Deo felt the same way about Dirk's.

Kincaid smiled for the first time and offered to buy me a beer. When I declined, saying that I didn't drink, he said, "What the hell kind of newspaper reporter are you?" I told him I was a sober one, and he laughed.

Don Kincaid was one of the vice presidents of Treasure Salvors, Inc., and a database of all things *Atocha*. He also was the ultimate survivor, having joined the Fishers in their search in 1971 and having played a major role in all the tragedies that Deo found so difficult to talk about. None of this information was volunteered. I had to work at it; I had to prove to Kincaid that I was worthy of handling it with proper care and understanding.

As we walked down Greene Street toward Old Mallory Square, Kincaid played tour guide. Key West was going through tough times, he said, as we passed several boarded-up storefronts on Duval Street. The community was still feeling the financial backlash from Jimmy Carter's presidency, hard times that were compounded by the influx of tens of thousands of Cubans into Florida and the Keys courtesy of the Mariel boatlift. Jobs were at a premium, more so than normal, which made it easier for Treasure Salvors, Inc., to keep divers. I had no idea what one had to do with the other. More to the point, I told Kincaid that I was still groping around in the dark, that until hours earlier I had never heard of Mel Fisher or the Spanish galleons for which he searched.

It was obvious to me that the man was not a BS artist, so once we found a seat at the Pier House bar down by the harbor, I asked for his help. I explained that Mel and Duncan Mathewson had told me about the *Atocha*'s sinking and about Spain's subsequent salvage efforts, and that Deo had provided some background on their excavation of the 1715 fleet near Vero Beach. I asked Kincaid to pick up the story.

Kincaid is a compact, powerfully built, and deeply tanned adventurer who had recently turned 39. His short, meticulously trimmed beard gave him a nautical air. He seemed more suited on the deck of the *Calypso*, serving as Jacques Cousteau's right-hand man.

Kincaid began the conversation by emphasizing the difficulties of finding the *Atocha*, telling me to picture someone driving down Highway 1 over the Seven-Mile Bridge at 60 miles per hour and tossing handfuls of pennies into the air. No doubt about it, you know those pennies fell into the Gulf of Mexico, somewhere near the Florida Keys. "But where exactly did those pennies come to rest? That's the problem we've always faced for the past 16 years," he said. "You have no real idea of just how big the ocean really is until you get out there looking for what amounts to be a needle in the haystack."

When Mel Fisher began searching the Keys for that "needle" during the summer of 1970, he elicited the help of Fay Feild and 50-year-old Bob Holloway, with whom Mel formed a lasting friendship after meeting him soon after arriving in Key West. According to Eugene Lyon's research in Seville, Spanish divers had salvaged the *Margarita* at a depth of 5 braza (27 feet), while the *Atocha* had gone down in 10 braza (54.5 feet) of water. Using the Marquesas as his pivot point, Fisher began scouring Hawk Channel in a 40-mile-long by six-mile-wide swath, pulling the magnetometer behind Holloway's *Holly's Folly*, a sleek, 35-foot-Chris-Craft. He was paying particular attention to all areas on his chart that registered 27- and 55-foot depths, and the boat was kept on a prescribed course with the aid of a transit theodolite, a surveying instrument used to measure vertical and horizontal angles; it was mounted on one of two towers situated east to west, from New Ground Reef to Boca Grande Key, and south at Cosgrove Shoal. A diver would sit atop the tower, keeping Holloway's boat in the theodolite's crosshairs. Deviation from course was monitored by radio between boat and tower.

Throughout the 1970 dive season, despite crisscrossing what amounted to thousands of miles in a west-by-southwest arc near the Quicksands between Rebecca Shoal and the outer reef, they found nothing to indicate that the *Atocha* had gone down in this area. Then one of Lyon's researchers in Seville came across a document that said that the *Margarita* had gone down east of the Keys' last mangrove island, which prompted Fisher's crew to move its search area to Boca Grande Channel. Despite spending as much as $1,000 a day on the project, including the consumption of more than 200 gallons of fuel a day by his search boats, no sign of the *Atocha* was found.

In February 1971, Kincaid entered the picture.

That winter Kincaid found himself in a frustrating situation. New York City had been buried under a foot of snow. Because his building's superintendent was on strike, Kincaid's heat, electricity, and water had been turned off. So he said to hell with it, packed up his belongings, and headed for Key West.

"Early on," said Kincaid, who was 25 at the time he crossed over the narrow bridge connecting Stock Island to Key West, "I came to realize that you don't go to sea to be safe. Safe is sitting inside a bomb shelter and dying of hardening of the arteries."

Kincaid first met Mel Fisher at a Key West camera store and admittedly was in awe. After all, Fisher was legendary in the world of scuba diving, surpassed only by Jacques Cousteau. Kincaid could recite Fisher's exploits by heart. What he didn't know were the tales of the *Nuestra Señora de Atocha* and the *Santa Margarita*, and that Mel was in Key West searching for them. He immediately asked Fisher for a job, was put off for a few weeks, then was hired in May after he purchased 10 shares of stock at $10 a share in Fisher's corporation, Treasure Salvors, Inc. Kincaid's duties would include underwater photography, for which he would earn $60 a week, $10 more than Fisher's regular divers.

There was nothing yet to photograph, so Kincaid spent the next week acquainting himself with Fisher's dive crew: Scotty Barron, Rick Vaughn, Gary Borders, and 16-year-old Al Posada. It was a formidable salvage team, Kincaid said, especially 23-year-old Vaughn, who was a former U.S. Army paratrooper and a Vietnam veteran. In the course of this friendship, it was impossible not to notice that much of Fisher's operation was conducted on a shoestring. Kincaid's equipment, for example, was top of the line—his own fins, mask, weight belt, and scuba tanks, complete with new regulator, plus pressure and depth gauges. He took nothing for granted, especially the dangers of the deep.

His dive buddies approached the profession as if they were bulletproof. What disturbed Kincaid most was that their dive equipment was unsafe. They had no depth gauges, let alone pressure gauges. In essence, Fisher's *Atocha* divers left too much to chance: not knowing how much compressed air was in their tanks, not knowing the exact depths at which they dived. To the uninitiated, the danger is not obvious. But to those who make repeated dives at extended depths, depth gauges and pressure gauges are the difference between life and death. Breathing compressed air from a scuba tank at depths exceeding 130 feet causes nitrogen narcosis, which has a narcotic effect on the diver. Surfacing too quickly after having absorbed excessive amounts of nitrogen into your body causes decompression sickness, also known as the bends—potentially fatal formation of bubbles in blood vessels and tissue.

The start of what Kincaid and his fellow divers called "the curse of the *Atocha*" began in early May 1971 when the Ghost Galleon claimed its first victim: 22-year-old Gary Borders.

Borders and Vaughn, both theoretically on their own time, were attempting a deep-bounce dive in preparation for an unspecified Fisher deep-dive expedition on a Spanish vessel that sank in Central American waters. The depth Borders and Vaughn chose was marked on their chart at 180 feet. It was really more than 240 feet. They used their everyday tanks, minus pressure gauges, and filled them with the same air compressor they always used, which was incapable of filling the tanks past 1,600 pounds per square inch (psi). From a technical standpoint, 1,600 psi can sustain a diver for about 30 minutes at shallow depths. At 240 feet, a diver has two minutes of air at best.

"They wanted me to make the dive with them," Kincaid said, "but I had other work to do. As it turned out, they hit bottom, and then Gary's air ran out. He and Rick started up on the buddy system, but then Rick's air gave out."

Rick Vaughn suffered the bends and barely survived, but only because Al Posada got him to a hospital and into a decompression chamber in the nick of time. Gary Borders never made it to the surface, dying at an approximate depth of 120 feet. His body was never found.

Fellow divers had little time to mourn. On May 11, Kincaid's 26th birthday, Bob Holloway's magnetometer went off the scale, registering a huge anomaly in the shallows almost directly west of the Marquesas, an area known as the Quicksands. Holloway quickly killed his boat's engines, slipped on his dive gear, and dropped over the side. Soon, at a depth of 14 feet, he was staring in wonder at the corroded ring of an anchor, its massive shaft buried in the 20-foot-deep sands. The anchor's ring measured three feet across, enough room for Holloway to swim through it. This discovery was all the proof Mel Fisher needed to proclaim that he had found the *Atocha*. After all, he said, where there is an anchor, especially a galleon anchor of that size, there is a wreck of the ship nearby. Any day now, he knew his divers would be bringing up her gold and silver.

Not quite. Storms moved in, which prevented divers from exploring the area at length. Then, on Saturday, June 12, Fisher navigated his salvage boat, the *Virgilona*, to what he thought was the discovery site. But when he dived into the water, the anchor was nowhere to be found. Frustrated at having "temporarily misplaced" the massive artifact, Fisher blew a hole in the deep sands, then again entered the water and immediately struck pay dirt—in his eyes, at least. Instead of gold or silver, he found a lead musket ball. From his excitement, you would have sworn he had found jewels. Moments later, Rick Vaughn popped from the water clutching two pieces of faded pottery. Before Fisher could congratulate him, Vaughn pulled off his glove, revealing a small, blackened sphere resembling an Oreo cookie. It was a Spanish piece of eight.

Kincaid arrived on the scene Sunday afternoon, expecting to photograph the anchor. With nothing to shoot, he decided to experience firsthand what the divers encountered in descending into a freshly blown hole. Diving under these conditions is to enter a greenish-gray world of a million silver particles fluttering with the current. Sediment dances before a diver's eyes, disrupting visibility. And so it was with Kincaid as he moved cautiously through a cloud of dusted sand, able to see barely a foot in front of him as he slowly descended into the crater. The hole was about 15 feet deep, its sides jutting upward at a 45-degree angle. It was in this area, midway down the side of the berm, that he saw the shiny links of chain.

"Someone's lost some junk, some useless brass," he told himself, yet reached down and grabbed hold of the thick, long chain, frantically clutching at it as sand cascaded down the side of the steep berm, covering his hand and arm. Rick Vaughn, who was searching the middle of the hole, casually watched Kincaid's antics. After all, Kincaid was the new guy; what the hell could he be up to? Certainly not finding anything of interest. Most assuredly, nothing of value.

Because the other divers considered him a rookie, Kincaid felt as if he were the butt of Vaughn's practical joke. Not wishing to be a spoilsport, Kincaid played along and carried the brass links to the surface, figuring everyone topside would have a good laugh. Because light travels at a different speed in water than in air, it acts as a selective filter, distorting color. The closer Kincaid got to the surface, the more the chain's tint was altered. By the time he reached the surface, the chain was no longer made of brass—it was gold.

The deck of the *Virgilona* was empty, except for another diver, who was relieving himself over the port rail. When Kincaid hit the dive ladder, clutching the ball of chain in his fist, the other diver gasped and barely caught himself from falling into the sea. Within moments, Fisher and Fay Feild were pounding Kincaid on the back, congratulating him for a job well done. Kincaid's find: three pieces of ornately crafted gold chain that, combined, were 8½ feet long.

Four months later, two 6-inch gold bars were lifted from the deep sands. But then the trail petered out and the *Atocha* search came to a virtual standstill, the result of two factors, both financial. On one hand, Fisher did not have the funds to expand the search by purchasing more salvage boats and hiring new divers. On the other, in 1972 Fisher signed a contract with the National Geographic Society, which paid Fisher $20,000 for exclusive rights to a magazine article and a television special. Fisher and his divers spent the next six months fulfilling their obligation to the National Geographic Society and didn't return to the area again until May 1973.

The honor of reexcavating the spot was bestowed on Captain Mo Molinar, who positioned the *Virgilona* on the southernmost fringe of the Quicksands, slightly southeast of where the galleon anchor had been found. Holes were blown in the deep sand, and an odd assortment of artifacts was found: daggers, swords, and muskets. On May 19, divers John Brandon and brothers Steve and Spencer Wickens uncovered 36 blackened silver coins, all of which were encrusted solid to the bedrock and could be pried loose only with the aid of screwdrivers. Two days later they found 244 more pieces of eight.

"In retrospect," Kincaid said, "I truly believe we uncovered part of the *Atocha*'s stern. What other explanation could it be? After all, it would account for the large number of weapons, which were always stored in the galleon's stern, just beneath the captain's quarters."

But there was no accounting for what the divers recovered on May 25. Again, the *Virgilona*'s blowers ran at full throttle, clearing away the deep sand. This time when the divers entered the water, they were momentarily breathless—hundreds of blackened silver coins littered the hole. Before the day was over, 1,460 coins were recovered. Before the week was over, more than 6,000 coins were brought to the surface, "which is why Eugene Lyon dubbed the area 'The Bank of Spain,'" Kincaid said.

The treasure glut was far from over, however. On June 17, Dirk Fisher dove off the side of the salvage boat *Southwind* and recovered an ancient astrolabe, a priceless Spanish navigational artifact that was the precursor of the sextant. The day's discoveries also included another musket, five swords, and an additional 200 silver coins. As Kincaid described it, the *Atocha* divers were on a roll. The good times continued throughout the next two months: Kim Fisher recovered a gold bar, then two gold coins; and on July 4, Mike Schnadelbach discovered two silver bars and 14-year-old Kane Fisher found another. The bars' serial numbers matched those of three bars listed on the *Atocha* manifest.

"That discovery was the clincher," Kincaid said. "What you've got to understand is that even though we had been finding bits and pieces of treasure, we had no way of knowing for sure that what we'd found had come from the *Atocha*. Those three bars found by Schnadelbach and Kane validated everything. No doubt about it, we had the *Atocha*."

National Geographic lent its credibility by dispatching photographers to Key West to record the artifacts for an article. Fame and fortune were close at hand.

6

I Will Return

Five pieces of gold, each about the size of a quarter, and every
one of 'em had four emeralds attached.

—*Mel Fisher*

It had been quite a day, a day full of stories and emotion. I left
the museum and returned to Sugarloaf Key shortly before
sunset, brewed a pot of coffee, and reclined in a comfortable
chair on the back deck of George Lowery's seashore home. I was
transfixed by a storm moving in off the Straits of Florida. Regrettably, I would be returning to Atlanta the next morning, slipping
back into the rat race. My short stay in paradise was drawing to a
close. There would be no more fishing for bonefish, the "Gray
Ghost" of the flats. No more searching for "Big Moe," the 18-
foot hammerhead shark that dominated our fishing guide's everyday thoughts, much like Hemingway's Santiago, the old man who
went 84 days without taking a fish. No more idyllic days skimming about the nearby clumps of mangrove keys, doing nothing
more than watching nature unfold in its most profound majesty.

More than anything else, though, there most likely would be
no more moments spent with Mel Fisher and his treasure divers.
The very thought of this produced within me an emptiness that I
had never experienced before. I felt as if I were running away

from something. I didn't know exactly what that *something* was, other than it would be spectacular and that it would be happening soon. As helpless as I felt, there was nothing I could do except sip my coffee and watch the storm roll in, the effect of which only made it more difficult to leave.

In melancholy moments I recall the storm, if not my entire stay on the islands, as being eerie. One moment I could feel its gentle arms wrapped about me and hear its siren song of unseen maidens—the song of the lapping waters of the Atlantic drumming against the coral shore, of a cool west wind gently moving through the mangroves to my left and slapping against the palm fronds to my right, of clicking crickets and squawking birds of the sea. All this against a backdrop, as seen from my stilted perch, of the bright, blinking warning from American Shoal lighthouse on the horizon to my southeast. And then, as a cold chill moved up my back, the ominous black clouds moved in. Bursts of lightning streaked first horizontally and then vertically, lighting up the sea and reflecting off the clouds, resembling a neon sign silhouetting a message of bad tidings for all fishermen of the flats. Slowly the storm moved closer, eliminating the brilliance of the stars, turning them off one by one. Then came the deep-throated rumble, followed by an intense rain.

The storm rendered me small and helpless in the all-encompassing hand of nature. I could not help but envision what it must have been like 363 years earlier for the godforsaken passengers and crews of the *Nuestra Señora de Atocha* and the *Santa Margarita* as that killer hurricane bore down on them. I could not help but feel as if I had to find a way to follow Mel Fisher's treasure hunting exploits further. Try as I may, though, I saw no way of pulling it off. I would somehow find a way to keep my promise to Mel and singularly write of his exploits, but then would surely be forced to move toward more fertile journalistic ground. Regrettably, I let go of my ambition amid the clashing symphony of that storm, drifting off to sleep in the rain, my dreams filled with pirates and Spanish conquistadors, of treasure galleons overflowing with gold and silver, and of shadowy figures drifting far below the ocean's surface. I have a vague recollection of mumbling, "I will return . . . I will return."

※

I arrived in Atlanta late Monday morning, took a few days off, arrived at the newspaper Wednesday afternoon, and wrote the story of the two Ducks Unlimited hunters-turned-Florida Flats fishermen. The following day Kent Mitchell, a good friend and colleague, started ribbing me about what I had missed in the Keys. "Some guy named Fisher found treasure from an old Spanish shipwreck," Mitchell said. I told him that I knew all about it, having visited the Mel Fisher museum. In fact, I said, full of myself, Fisher's divers had been discovering treasure since 1971.

Mitchell gave me an odd look, then said, "I'm not talking about 1971. They've been bringing up treasure since Sunday. It's all over the wires."

When I had turned on my computer and consulted the Associated Press databank, I was dumbfounded. According to the AP, Mel's son Kane had discovered 13 gold bars on Memorial Day. In the days since, Kane and his crew also had recovered 450 silver coins, five pieces of gold jewelry studded with emeralds, and an 80-inch-long gold chain. According to the wire service story, archaeologists placed the value of the jewelry at $1.4 million, the gold bars and coins at $600,000, and the gold chain at $50,000.

I made a printout of the story and headed for the managing editor's office. Fortunately for me, Eddie Sears was conferring with Jim Minter, the newspaper's editor. I had always thought highly of both men. More to the point, both trusted my judgment.

I handed Sears the AP story and explained that I had just returned from Key West, having spent the past Saturday with Mel Fisher, his wife, and one of the *Atocha* divers. All I needed was a few updated quotes from Fisher and I had one hell of a story. I needed Sears's approval to proceed, which he promptly gave me.

Treasures of the *Atocha* included uncut emeralds, gold, pottery, iron spikes, and an astrolabe.

Minutes later Mel Fisher was on the telephone, chiding me for having departed the Keys too soon. "Remember that spot on the chart I pointed out, when I told you that my son Kane was getting ready to dig the area?" Fisher said, chuckling. "Well, he dug it, all right, in 45 feet of water and ended up finding 13 gold bars. Hundreds of coins, also, not to mention the jewelry. Beautiful jewelry. Five pieces of gold, each about the size of a quarter, and every one of 'em had four emeralds attached. Fantabulous, that's what it was."

Fisher said that his divers had not found the *Atocha*'s mother lode. Not yet, at least. But they were close, at the very fringe of a $400 million payday. What convinced him of this, other than the glut of treasure, was that his divers also had found a remnant of the ship's mizzenmast. "Remember when we told you how the

Spanish found the *Atocha* shortly after she sank, that her mizzen-mast protruded out of the water? Well, they figured they'd mark the spot by sawing off part of the mast and using it as a buoy," Fisher said. "We found that buoy. It was about six feet long with a hole hollowed out in the middle of it; there were spikes still imbedded in it. Tell you what—any day now we're gonna be bringing in all that treasure. I just know it."

Fisher was talking nonstop and not allowing me to get a word in edgewise. He covered old ground about his 16-year search, then described each of the recently recovered artifacts in great detail. And then he rubbed a little salt in my wounds by saying that I never should have returned to Atlanta in the first place, that I should have had a little more faith in him and said the hell with work and gone out to sea with him and the crew on Monday.

"If you'd done that," he said, "you could have been holding one of them nine-inch-long gold bars, just like I was. They're heavier than they look, know that?" He paused to chuckle at the metallic memory, then said, "You're good luck for me, that's what you are. You tell your boss that you need to get right back down here. Maybe you can do some diving. 'Course, it's pretty danger-ous because of the depth. But with a little practice you'll be okay. Don't waste any time now—get your butt down here."

I was flying high. I stopped by Sears's office and told him that I had just finished talking to Mel Fisher and that the story was golden. Literally. And then I raced to the public library and found the back issues of *National Geographic* that Don Kincaid had said heralded Mel's exploits. January 1965 detailed Kip Wagner's and Fisher's excavation of the 1715 Spanish fleet that went aground off Sebastian Inlet; June 1976, Eugene Lyon's account of Fisher's quest for the *Atocha;* and February 1982, Lyon's documentation of Fisher's discovery of the *Santa Margarita.* I would use *National Geographic* to verify all that had been told to me by Mel, Deo, Mathewson, and Kincaid.

My story, which I was quite proud of, appeared on the front page of the Saturday, June 1, 1985, edition. A page-one story is big stuff in our profession; this coup was magnified, in my eyes, at least, because the little kid in me had written it. I found myself gloating over the text the entire weekend, once again double-checking each fact to make sure I had gotten the story right, double-checking my notes and recorded tape to make sure I had quoted everyone correctly. Dates, names, and all historical incidents jelled with what *National Geographic* had written. The story was solid gold, pure and simple—a thing of sheer beauty. That's what I told myself. Mel himself confirmed this two days later when he telephoned and complimented me on a job well done. He especially liked my reference to the *Atocha* as the "Ghost Galleon bitch of the sea."

I was still basking in the glow of Mel's laudatory comments that Monday morning when I was summoned to the metro staff's conference room. Both Eddie Sears and Jim Minter were out of town, attending some obligatory high-level editors' function. For today, at least, two midlevel editors, neither of whom cared much for my reporting skills, were calling the shots. As it turned out, both thought even less of Mel Fisher.

Within moments of my entering the conference room, my *Atocha* story was systematically torn apart. Both editors said I had been sold a bill of faulty goods, that I had been far too gullible in reporting Fisher's version of the story. One editor, who had previously worked for a Florida newspaper, called Fisher a scam artist and a liar and said: "Everyone knows there's no treasure out there. That gold was probably planted." He berated me further, saying that by giving Fisher an outlet to bilk more unsuspecting investors I subsequently had made the *Atlanta Journal-Constitution* the laughingstock of the industry. If the federal and state governments, not to mention the SEC and the IRS, viewed Mel Fisher as a crook, then surely he was a crook. End of argument.

No sooner had I been chastised and told that I could forget about ever writing another word about Mel Fisher or his mythical *Atocha* than the newspaper's publisher, David Easterly, entered the room, shook my hand, and congratulated me on a job well done. He said that the phones had been ringing off the hook ever since the story appeared. In essence, the readers loved the tale. "I want you to get back down there and spend some time at sea on one of those treasure-hunting boats," Easterly said. "I want you to write an up-close-and-personal account of what it's like to find treasure."

Such was the quixotic interpretation of the thoroughly quixotic Fisher saga. But orders were orders, so I gave my detractors a whimsical smile, left the building, and went home and packed my bags. Next stop: Key West. It was time to go to sea, to get up close and personal with the *Atocha* divers, to hopefully pull on the dive gear and drop down to the ocean's bottom and experience firsthand what it was like to discover long-lost treasure.

The trip has never ended.

7

A Little Chunk of Gold

I'm on the sea! I'm on the sea! I am where I would ever be; with
the blue above and the blue below, and silence whereso'er I go.

—*Barry Cornwall*

I first met Donnie Jonas in June 1985, within days of my return to Key West in pursuit of the up-close-and-personal
story on Mel Fisher's treasure divers. It was an accidental
encounter. Don Kincaid took me on a tour of the island's bars,
and somewhere toward the end of the evening we ended up at
the Two Friends Restaurant. Clustered in the far corner of the
bar was the crew of the salvage boat *J. B. Magruder*, a deeply
tanned group of lanky, steely-eyed young men that reminded
me of a Marine Corps rifle squad—elite and bristling with con-
fidence. They were drinking and laughing among themselves,
throwing wisecracks back and forth, when Kincaid ushered me
into their presence. Just like that, the jokes were stifled, the horse-
play curtailed.

You could have cut the tension with a knife as Kincaid introduced me as a newspaperman who had proven himself trust-
worthy. There were a few friendly nods, a glass lifted here and
there in recognition. And then Donnie Jonas, the crew's captain,

smiled and politely shook my hand. He downed his drink and gave me a friendly clasp on the shoulder, then turned and walked out the door. He never said a word.

"Most of these guys will be leery of you at first," Kincaid explained, laughing off Jonas's solemn departure. "Don't take it personal. Don's good people. A good diver, a damned good captain. It might take a while, but he's got a lot of good stories to share. Don't worry, he'll talk to you sooner or later."

It wasn't until August 1999 that I finally tracked Jonas down in Key West and nervously dialed his telephone number. I'm not intrusive by nature or profession, but I needed Jonas to tie up a lot of loose ends. Kincaid had told me that Jonas had been an *Atocha* diver since 1973, and was in the water with Dirk Fisher two years later when Mel's son had discovered nine *Atocha* cannons.

My palms were sweaty and my mouth dry as the telephone rang and rang and rang. Would Jonas remember me? And even if he did, would he be willing to sit down and share with me his darkest memories? More to the point, had I dialed the wrong number?

Jonas answered on the fifth ring. I stammered an introduction, tripping over my tongue. I identified myself and told Jonas that I was writing a book on the *Atocha* search; that I had tracked down a lot of the old hands, most of whom were quite helpful. "I'm sure you don't remember me, Donnie, but—"

Jonas laughed. "Yeah, I remember you," he said. "Still remember what your eyes looked like, man. Your eyes said that you wanted to dive in the worst way; it was written all over your face. Gotta get in the water and find me some treasure, that's what your eyes told us."

We agreed to get together the next day at noon.

Jonas is exactly what Hollywood would look for to play the role of a devil-may-care treasure diver. He is 44, tall, wiry, deeply tanned, and could easily be mistaken for actor James Woods. He smiles easily and much more often than he talks. In fact, without knowing the circumstances under which he grew up, you would swear that he had spent most of his time laughing at the world.

In June 1985 Jonas was the captain of the *Magruder*, married and about as carefree as anyone that age could be. He also was leery of journalists. In 1977, Random House published an account of the *Atocha* search written by a former *New York Times* reporter. "The guy made me sound and look like an idiot," Jonas said. "Pissed me off big-time. Hell, I'm not a dummy; I've got things to say. But I got burned, man. Once was enough. That's why, whenever you guys came around looking for a story, I went into hiding. But, yeah, I'll talk to you now."

Why? Because he thought I'd done some pretty "cool" things myself. Like joining the Marine Corps; like surviving the carnage of Beirut, Lebanon, as a war correspondent in 1983. He especially liked the part where I told him I had been scared shitless during the entire Beirut misadventure, how I had volunteered to cover the war to prove to myself that I was a real man; how I had been there less than one day, narrowly escaping a sniper's bullet and then almost being crushed beneath a tank, when I began wishing I had stayed home in Georgia.

"You've got balls, man," Jonas said.

Now it was my turn to flash the leprechaun smile. Balls, yes, but a little short on brains, I told him. We shared a laugh, had a bite to eat, and then I flicked on the tape recorder, encouraging him to tell his own tales.

It was summer 1973 and Jonas was a 15-year-old bagging groceries at the Key West Winn-Dixie. When not doing this he would hang out at the docks with his buddy Kane Fisher. Although Kane was only 14, he had been diving regularly for five years. "That's all we talked about—diving and finding Spanish treasure," Jonas said.

Their treasure fever was upped a notch when, in May, the crews of the *Virgilona* and the *Southwind* made a string of discoveries of weapons, gold, thousands of silver coins, and the astrolabe. Three weeks later, on July 3, Jonas received his first taste of treasure hunting in a bizarre fashion. He was bagging groceries when Mel, Deo, and Kane wheeled several overburdened carts into his checkout line.

"Next thing you know, I'm aboard one of the new boats they had purchased, the *Southwind*, going to sea," Jonas said. "My dream was coming true."

Once the salvage boat dropped anchor at the Quicksands, the experience got better by the minute. Jonas had not come prepared for life on the high seas, so he quickly discarded his shoes and socks, then ditched his tie and white dress shirt. As soon as he borrowed "Bouncy John" Lewis's dive knife and turned his dress slacks into cutoffs, the barefoot, bare-chested Jonas almost resembled a bona fide sea gypsy, just like Bouncy John, and Kim and Kane Fisher. The transformation would be completed the following day when Jonas assisted the divers with their gear and patiently waited topside for their return. Jonas admitted that he had no idea what to expect once the divers surfaced. His anticipation was running high when Bouncy John surfaced at the dive ladder, motioned Jonas over, handed him a coiled object, then disappeared back into the water.

"Man, I'm looking at this thing, trying to figure out what it was," Jonas said. "So I go into the cabin where Deo and Bleth McHaley were sitting and said, 'Beads, look at these beads.' Of course, I knew it was a rosary—a gold rosary and crucifix with red coral beads."

Moments later, Jonas heard someone yelling for help. Racing back outside, expecting the worst, Jonas saw Kane Fisher at the dive ladder. "I need a rope, get me a rope," Kane said. Jonas tossed him a line, and then watched in bewilderment as Kane dropped back down into the water.

Minutes elapsed, then Jonas felt a tug on the line. Not knowing what else to do, he started pulling on the line, hauling up what he said felt like a couple hundred pounds of deadweight. It proved to be an 80-pound silver bar that Kane later said resembled a loaf of bread when he found it nestled on the bedrock.

Within half an hour, two more silver bars would be hauled to the surface, each of them bearing Spanish markings.

What should have been a joyous introduction to treasure hunting turned sour for Jonas shortly after Kane's discovery. In his excitement over going to sea, he had clocked out of work without informing his boss, then jumped aboard ship and took off, failing to inform his parents. But what the hell, he said; he was just a 15-year-old kid doing something that grown-ups could only dream about, diving and finding silver coins. But once the news of the silver bar discovery made the front pages of the local newspaper, his parents finally figured out where their wayward son was, raised Deo Fisher on a ship-to-shore radio, and said that if Donnie was not home immediately, they were calling the police. The *Southwind* returned to port the next day.

Jonas's troubles were not over, however. His mother insisted that he march right down to Winn-Dixie and try to get his job back. "I had a choice of either bagging groceries or being a treasure hunter," Jonas said, grinning. "The decision was a no-brainer."

Between attending school and keeping in his parents' good graces, Jonas worked part-time with the *Atocha* divers over the next two years. He said he was better off than most of his fellow divers because he still lived at home. He had no bills, a roof over his head, and a warm bed. Better yet, he didn't have to worry about where the next meal was coming from, which was more than could be said for his fellow sea gypsies. Everything considered, Jonas had the better of both worlds, despite the annoyance of the treasure trail having dried up. Nothing was being found, which equated to his buddies going months without being paid.

But then the treasure drought ended in spectacular fashion.

❋

It was Sunday, July 13, 1975, in the deep-water expanse south of the Quicksands. The *Northwind*, with 21-year-old Dirk Fisher at the helm, had been at sea for nine days. Fresh water and food were in short supply. But the boat still had enough fuel to run the blowers and return to port, so Dirk decided to give the search a few more days. The crew members—Dirk's wife, Angel; Jonas, Bouncy John Lewis, Jim Solanick, and a new diver, Rick Gage— were, as usual, in high spirits.

Dirk was up at dawn that Sunday morning, despite having put in an 11-hour workday the day before. From all appearances, this day would be no different than any other: calm sea, hot sun, and plenty of bone-weary work. Dirk glanced at the buoys, realizing they were not where they had been the day before, meaning the boat had dragged anchor during the night. No big deal; this could easily be remedied after breakfast—a long, leisurely break-fast. Despite his father having vowed to award a $2,000 bonus to whoever found a bronze cannon, there was no urgency to begin work because the vision of finding treasure was a distant memory.

Later that morning, Dirk donned his gear and entered the water. According to the ship's log, the time was 11:25.

"I was Dirk's partner and we were supposed to enter the water at the same time," Jonas said. "But there's Dirk, hurriedly putting on his tank and saying, 'You snooze, you lose. I ain't splitting the bonus money with you,' then dropping into the water. Man, I swear that he just knew that he was going to find something fantastic."

Dirk Fisher was down no longer than two minutes when he suddenly thrust his head above the water astern and started screaming. Jonas and Angel Fisher feared the worst, that Dirk had seriously injured himself, or that possibly a shark had nailed him. As they scrambled to the rear of the boat, trying to make sense of Dirk's shouting, they heard the most beautiful words they had heard in almost two years: "We're rich, we're rich. Can-nons, man. We've got cannons. Throw me a buoy." And then Mel's oldest son tucked his head and disappeared once again beneath the murky surface. Visibility was no more than four feet, and Dirk had returned to the bottom to make sure his eyes had not deceived him. Once there, at a depth of 39 feet, he ran trembling hands over the barrel of a massive gun.

Within moments, Jonas joined him, first circling the area in a daze and almost swallowing his regulator's mouthpiece when the muzzles of the huge guns slowly began to materialize out of the shadows. Jonas recovered his composure, then he, too, reached out and touched the most prized object in a treasure diver's lexicon: a bronze cannon. Until that moment, you could count on one hand the number of bronze cannons found throughout the history of treasure salvage. Dirk Fisher had found not one cannon, but five.

When Jonas and Dirk surfaced and relayed the news to the rest of the crew that they had found five cannons, pandemonium erupted on the *Northwind*. Divers first slapped each other on the back, then made a mad dash for the remaining diving equipment. Because everyone shared diving gear, there were not enough tanks, regulators, fins, and masks to go around. But that was no obstacle. Within minutes, everyone was in the water, with or without gear, scuba diving and free diving on the massive firepower of a once-proud galleon.

The discoveries continued throughout Sunday. Large ballast stones were found, then Dirk, Jim Solanick, Bouncy John, and Rick Gage uncovered gold bits—small chunks that had been sliced off gold bars to satisfy the royal tax. Some discoveries were hard to recognize and almost discarded. Jonas, again diving with Dirk, recalled one instance when his face was inches above the bedrock due to the poor visibility and he was methodically running his hands over the surface. His right hand brushed against a hard object. Jonas picked it up and was about to discard it when he felt a tap on his shoulder. Turning, he saw Dirk Fisher pull his regulator's mouthpiece out, and smile as he flashed a thumb up. Jonas's flat rock turned out to be a copper ingot.

The search was then halted as Don Kincaid and Duncan Mathewson entered the water to photograph and chart the cannons'

From left to right, Tom Ford, Captain Donnie Jonas, and archaeologist Mitch Marken holding a 17th-century water or wine vase.

location. Compass bearings were recorded, drawings rendered, and pictures taken. That completed, Dirk Fisher winched the boat to port, then a new hole was blown. A cannonball was found, but nothing more as darkness descended. For the most part, it was a restless night for the divers. Five cannons, a bit of gold, and a copper ingot surely meant only one thing: the hulk of the *Atocha* and her cargo of silver and gold had to be nearby.

The following morning, Jonas, Pat Clyne, and Solanick entered the water and broke off in different directions. Again, the visibility was poor, so poor that Jonas could barely see his hand in front of his face. Literally feeling his way across the bottom, knowing that the five cannons they had found the day before were approximately 30 feet north of him, he came to a large patch of accumulated sand.

"I'm feeling around and suddenly hit something solid," Jonas said. "Right away, my mind tells me it's a cannon. But I can't see for shit, so I start feeling around, finding the smooth barrel, then the cannon's mouth, then I break to the surface and start yelling, 'I've found a cannon.' "

Fewer than 10 feet away, Clyne also had been feeling his way through the water's gloom. Suddenly he came upon huge shadows, some of which seemed to be jutting upward out of the sand. He moved closer, timidly, fearful of what might be looming in front of him. When the shadows took shape, he was looking down the barrel of a cannon. Clyne reacted in typical fashion, wrapping his arms around the big gun and hugging it. Then he sat on the cannon, wrapping his legs around its muzzle. Once he regained his senses, he noticed the other oblong shadows nearby. Three more cannons. He immediately broke to the surface to announce his discovery.

On the deck of the *Northwind*, the rest of the dive crew saw Jonas's head pop above the surface. A fraction of a second later, Clyne's head materialized, about 10 yards from Jonas's. Both divers were screaming that they had found cannons. Unbeknownst to each other, they had approached the big guns from opposite directions. In their excitement, coupled with the poor visibility, they had not seen each other. Nonetheless, they had found four more cannons, in almost perfect condition due to the protective covering of deep sand.

Despite the boat being shifted in a wide arc, left to right, and 11 more holes subsequently being blown, nothing else was uncovered that day.

"It was as if the sea was playing games with us once again. Teasing us—letting us find nine cannons, a few gold beads and a copper ingot, but nothing else," Jonas said.

On Thursday, July 17, with various television crews filming both below and above the surface, one 3,000-pound cannon from each of the two cultural deposits was raised to the surface under the guiding hand of Mel Fisher. Because of the enormity of the task, it took up almost the entire day. But once the cannons were secured on deck, they were then meticulously examined for telltale markings that could be compared to the *Atocha*'s gun list that

Eugene Lyon had discovered in the Archives of the Indies. The first cannon that Duncan Mathewson inspected bore no markings whatsoever. The second gun was 8 feet long and bore a coat of arms, plus the notation 1607, the year it was cast. Of more importance, however, was the notation 31q (*quintale*, hundred) 10L (*librae*, pounds), Spanish for 3,110 pounds. When Mathewson excitedly scanned Lyon's gun list, his eyes riveted on the 12th cannon listed, which weighed 3,110 pounds. His next words are forever immortalized in treasure-hunting lore: "Positive identification—this cannon came from the *Atocha*."

The *Northwind* headed to port later that afternoon, hoping to reach Key West while there was still daylight because *National Geographic* also wanted film footage.

Although the crew members continued to celebrate their discoveries, they did so with a foreboding sense of uneasiness. After all, the *Atocha*'s curse was always lurking in the shadows, waiting to turn joy into tragedy. "What you've gotta understand," said Jonas, "is that whenever something good happened to us, it was followed by something bad."

As the *Northwind* approached Woman Key, a few miles west of Key West, there was a bloodcurdling scream of "Fire, fire!" from Angel Fisher in the galley, adjacent to the ship's engine room. The problem: a lifter malfunction in the engine; when it froze, oil was spewed onto the hot engine, which filled the room with smoke. Crew members Pat Clyne and Joe Spangler were able to take care of the emergency, then sighed with relief as the ship's anchors were dropped. Disaster had been averted, and in the minds of all hands, the curse had finally been broken.

On Friday, July 18, the *Northwind* made its joyous return to Key West Harbor to a throng of television cameramen, newspaper reporters, and local citizenry. Credited with the discovery of the first five cannons, each carrying a $2,000 bonus, Dirk Fisher was handed a $10,000 check from his father and then hoisted a few well-earned beers with the rest of his crew. The ship's minor maintenance problems were attended to the next day, groceries were purchased, the fuel tanks were topped off, and then everyone headed back to sea.

There was plenty of laughter and good cheer on their return to the dive site, not to mention unforgettable memories of the previous trip. To this day Jonas said he can still feel the wind and salt spray on his face, his ears still ring from the cascade of screams and shouts of joy as he and the rest of the *Northwind*'s crew hugged each other over the discovery of the nine *Atocha* cannons. In his mind's eye it was still July 13, 1975, and the sun had made its plunge into the distant horizon, dipping itself into the calmness of the vast blue-green pool. The day's diving was over for Jonas and Dirk Fisher, so now they relaxed with a cold beer, content with themselves, sharing a laugh as they watched the new guy, Rick Gage, clumsily climb up the dive ladder. Gage was giggling like the kid he was, his fist squeezing a gold bit, the first piece of treasure he had ever found. And then, in his excitement, Gage dropped the small chunk of gold and it bounced across the deck and dropped into the water.

Without hesitation, Dirk plunged into the ocean, free-diving 39 feet down and surfacing moments later with the golden artifact. Dirk was still smiling as he placed the gold in Gage's open palm.

Now Donnie Jonas opened his eyes and released a deep sigh. He fidgeted with his glass of iced tea, rotating it slowly between both hands. For the first time, his eyes averted mine. Across 24 years and after many more memories, the moment was still frozen in Jonas's mind.

"A little chunk of gold," he said in a voice barely above a whisper, and then paused a long time. "The last piece of gold Dirk Fisher would ever touch."

8

Nightmare Time

Now we've got another problem—sharks. We've got all this
blood in the water.

—Don Kincaid

Donnie Jonas said he could still feel the cold steel deck
plating beneath his bare feet as he once again plunged
into the *Northwind*'s darkness in 1975, opened the engine
room door, and reentered the abyss.

"And there's Kincaid screaming at me to get the hell out of
there," said Jonas. "I turn and see him scrambling out the door,
headed up the stairs to the galley. And then there's this gigantic
swoooooosh! The boat turns over."

Jonas had enough time to take two or three steps toward the
safety of the doorway, but then was knocked off his feet by a wall
of water before being blinded by a brilliant flash of light. His best
recollection: The rush of seawater pulled him under, shot him
across the engine room, and slammed him headfirst into the steel
deck plates, knocking him unconscious. When Jonas finally came
to, he was struggling for air.

Jonas was blind; his eyes felt as if they were on fire. Everything was pitch black. His lungs screamed for air. Diesel fuel was

everywhere, seeping into his mouth after saturating his eyes. He held his breath and floated up into a little air pocket just big enough for his head. Panic took hold. Disoriented, slowly being strangled by hysteria, Jonas heard voices on the other side of the keel's steel plating. He started screaming and pounding on the metal, ripping the skin from his knuckles, pleading for someone to open the door so he could get the hell out of this death trap.

"All I could think of was that I was gonna drown. 'Open the hatch, dammit, or I'm gonna die,'" said Jonas.

The hatch was really the keel. And it remained closed.

Topside, on the ship's keel just inches above Jonas's steel-hulled trap, Don Kincaid was struggling to get the crew to safety. There was a loud growl from the generators going full blast. The ship's lights, despite being submerged, suddenly burned intensely bright before dying.

"Now we've got no light, just blackness," Kincaid said. "No sound, except for the creaking of the boat and people in the water yelling for help. And Donnie screaming at us, trapped below."

One by one the survivors made their way to the safety of the *Northwind*'s keel, pulling themselves up the slippery, barnacle-encrusted bottom. Hands and knees were sliced open by the sharp encrustation. Buttocks were gouged. Blood was everywhere, dripping into the black ocean.

"Now we've got another problem: sharks. We've got all this blood in the water," said Kincaid. "What's worse is that people are going nuts on me; some of the survivors weren't thinking straight. Bouncy John wanted to go back into the ship and get Donnie, Dirk, Angel, and Rick Gage. I tried to talk sense to him, telling him that he'd have to go in upside down, into pitch blackness, turn corners, go up stairs. If we've got scuba gear, yes, it's no problem. Doing it without gear would be suicide. But he tried anyway."

Bouncy John, who, like Kincaid, could hold his breath underwater for three minutes, slipped off the keel, gasped, forced air into his lungs, then slipped below the surface. He popped back up within seconds. He was too excited; the adrenaline rush prevented him from staying down longer. When Bouncy John surfaced, Kincaid grabbed hold of a flashlight bobbing in the water, and despite his better judgment, he and Bouncy John tried once again.

"It was useless. My lungs felt as if they were going to burst after being down only 15 seconds. My hands were shaking like a leaf, shaking out of control like an old man with a bad case of the tremors. I was really hyped. Both of us were that way," said Kincaid of his failed attempt. But then he and Bouncy John tried again, this time making their way down to the ship's deck, groping in the dark, their fingers finding a hatchway, its door cemented shut by the pressure built up inside. Moments before making their way back to the surface, Kincaid lost his grip on the flashlight and it was sucked away.

At that moment, Donnie Jonas was convinced he was about to die. And then he felt something solid hit his chest. Frantically thrashing about, he grabbed hold of a miracle: the flashlight.

Topside on the keel, Kincaid and the other survivors heard Jonas go silent and imagined the worst. "Donnie was dead," said Kane Fisher. "I just knew he was dead."

Almost, but not quite. Jonas took hold of the flashlight, made sure everything was screwed tightly in place, then flicked it on. It worked. At that moment, his sanity returned. Now with a firm grasp on illumination, he sucked in several mouthfuls of fuel-enhanced air and pushed himself down, looking for an exit from the metal tomb. He had gone only a short distance when it dawned on him that he might not be able to find his way back to the precious air pocket. He reversed course, sucked in more air, and then secured the flashlight on a rib of the ship's bottom, positioning the light so he would clearly see it when and if he returned for more air. This task completed, he slipped through the darkened water, felt his way down along the bulkhead, his mind working in reverse: What once was on the left would now be on his right; to get out, he had to go down.

As Jonas swam through the darkness, he finally found a door. He pushed against it, but it did not budge. He tried again with the same result, then made his way back to the safety of the air pocket. He gulped air, knowing time was running out, knowing it was now or never. Making his way back to the door, he pushed again but made no headway. Every muscle in his body was screaming at him. His lungs were about to burst; they felt as if they were on fire. He strained against the door again and it opened a fraction of an inch. With the last of his energy, Jonas pushed again. The door swung open an inch, then wider and wider.

"All of a sudden I'm seeing green water, water that isn't filled with diesel fuel," he said. "But now I'm *really* freaking out. Air, man, I need air. I return to the air pocket, suck in some more air, then grabbed the flashlight and banged on the keel and screamed, 'I'm coming out, man; I'm fucking coming out!'"

Down, deeper and deeper to the now-open hatch. Through it, his mind working in reverse, going down to go up to the galley; down stairs in order to go up, swimming deeper to make his way up to the deck. And then swimming free of the doomed vessel, farther and farther before arching his back and breaking through the ocean's surface, frantically waving the flashlight in the cold, dark night.

"And then I'm finally breathing real honest-to-goodness air," said Jonas. "I'm up there bobbing on the surface, maybe 45 feet from the boat, sucking in all the air I can possibly get into my lungs. But I'm so exhausted that I can barely wave the flashlight. No way can I swim. I'm just bobbing up and down, thankful to be alive."

Bouncy John left the keel and swam toward the light bobbing in the distance. Wrapping his bleeding arms around Jonas, Bouncy John struggled as he made his way back to the boat. "Everyone says I was crying," Jonas said. "Maybe I was; I really don't remember. But if there were tears, man, they were tears of joy."

Short-lived tears, however, as Jonas started counting heads. He asked about Dirk and Angel, but received only silence from the rest of the survivors. He asked about the new guy, Rick Gage, but again was answered with silence. No one could look him in the eye. Jonas knew it was useless to attempt going back down into the boat. He had barely gotten out alive. The others, he knew, must be dead.

Kincaid was not about to allow anyone else to die if he could help it. He took Jonas's flashlight, then started gathering flotsam—a buoy ball, a small cushion, a plastic bag, and two life jackets. Kincaid placed one vest on Keith Curry, the other on Jonas, keeping an arm on him to make sure he did not drift away, realizing that Jonas was in bad shape because of the diesel fuel he had swallowed. Kincaid encouraged Jonas, telling him that the only way they were going to survive was by continuing to swim.

Although Kincaid kept encouraging his mates, he felt uneasy about their survival, for it was almost daylight, and Captain Mo Molinar would surely be going south toward the cannon site shortly after dawn. The problem was not so much exhaustion as it was the current. It was carrying the eight survivors away from the Marquesas, where the *Virgilona* was at anchor, toward the target wreck, due west of the Marquesas. Although they might live if they reached the target wreck, the problem was keeping everyone together and afloat until they reached it. Compounding their dilemma was the oozing blood from their various wounds. Sharks could be expected at any moment.

Kincaid was running these scenarios though his mind when large air bubbles started escaping from the *Northwind* and broke the surface. With the bubbles came the survivors' salvation—a small, inflatable raft, measuring two by four feet. Curry was put in the raft, and the others clung to its side.

"Bob Reeves wanted to try swimming to the Marquesas on his own, hoping to make it to the *Virgilona* in time, getting help before we all drowned," Kincaid said. "That's when I became the biggest, meanest Captain Bligh you've ever seen. No one's going to make a swim for it, I tell them. I don't want to listen to any bullshit. We're either all going to live together or we're all going to die together."

As daylight broke, the survivors fought against the current, painstakingly making their way toward the Marquesas. And then another miracle: the *Virgilona* was headed toward them. They steadied the raft as Keith Curry raised himself to his knees. Waving the flashlight back and forth, Angel Fisher's little brother was able to get Molinar's attention.

9

A Powerful Ocean

That telephone call was every mother's worst nightmare.

—*Deo Fisher*

Mo Molinar steered the *Virgilona* across the unruffled sea, his mind weighed down by a pervasive dread as he scanned the horizon. It was July 20, 1975.

Mel Fisher was like a father to Mo, caring for him and trusting in him when others had turned their backs on his smile and soft-spoken plea for work. In the years since, the 43-year-old seafarer thought of Mel's sons as his own brothers. Where the hell is the *Northwind?* he wondered. It was so unlike young Dirk Fisher to have hauled in his ship's anchors and gone off to work so early, leaving the placid Marquesas waters for the uncertainties of the open sea. No matter the activity, Dirk was a creature of habit. He preferred sleeping late; work could always wait. Even when it involved returning to the site where only a week earlier he had uncovered the *Atocha's* bronze cannons, a treasure salvor's dream.

With the sun jutting out of the flat sea to starboard, Molinar glimpsed the first hint of disaster: gently bobbing flotsam. At first it was just a speck dancing in the predawn shadow of dark sea against sunrise. Then it took shape and form, revealing a small child sitting atop a raft. As the *Virgilona* drew closer, Molinar saw others desperately clutching the raft with one hand and waving frantically with the other. He counted heads, then counted again and again, his stomach turning each time he reached the same number: eight! Only eight, not the 11 mariners he knew to have spent the night on the *Northwind*.

Molinar eased toward the survivors, drew near, and then idled the ship's engines. He scanned the harried faces, and his heart sank. Dirk and Angel were missing, plus the new guy.

Once he was hoisted out of the water, Don Kincaid, wrapped in a blanket but still shivering from his ordeal, used the boat's radio to contact the Coast Guard and give them the particulars of the tragedy. He then contacted Bob Hall, the owner of the Raw Bar Restaurant, behind which Fisher's salvage boats docked, and asked him to telephone Bleth McHaley, publicity director for Treasure Salvors, Inc. Bleth, in turn, telephoned Mel and Deo Fisher, telling them that there had been a fatal accident and to please meet her and Coast Guard officials at the harbor.

"That telephone call was every mother's worst nightmare," Deo Fisher would recall almost three decades later. "After almost six years of frustration, we truly believed that our prayers had finally been answered, that Dirk had finally found the *Atocha*. Instead ..." She paused, staring vacantly toward another part of the room, then said, "Dirk was my baby. ..."

Deo remembered sitting at the bottom of that glass tank at the Hermosa Ocean Aquarium, every inch of her body shriveled from more than 55 hours of being submerged as she shattered the women's underwater endurance record. But she forgot her discomfort when six-year-old Dirk entered the water and swam down to her, a red rose clutched in his outstretched hand. Dirk handed it to her and grinned, then kissed his mother on the cheek before resurfacing.

Deo kept her eyes tightly closed, holding tight to the memories. Dirk awkwardly plodding across the wood planking of a California dock, his fins snapping in synch with his laughter, his right hand in his father's, who was leading the way to the water. And then, still hand-in-hand, father and son plunged into the shallows, swimming along without a care in the world, breaking through the surface from time to time and spitting out the mouthpieces of their regulators and sharing their joy. It's the laughter, Deo said, that she chooses to hold on to. Dirk's triumphant grin at having mastered the intricacies of scuba at such a young age. Dirk's delight at having found his first piece of treasure, a gold coin found in 1965 from the scattered wrecks of the 1715 fleet off Sebastian Inlet. And then his most glorious moment, returning to Key West Harbor on July 18, 1975, and being surrounded by well-wishers as he stood proudly beside the *Atocha* cannons, hugging his mother as he whispered in her ear: "It's okay, Ma. Don't cry." But Deo could not help but shed those tears. Tears of joy, for Mel's and her dreams were finally being realized—the *Atocha* was at last within their grasp, thanks in large part to her firstborn son.

"Only a mother really knows how proud I was of Dirk at that moment," she said.

It was November 1999 and we were sitting at the kitchen table of Deo's daughter Taffi's Vero Beach home. My wife, June, was with me. At that time we had been married almost 33 years. As I knew had been the case with Mel and Deo's relationship, I told Deo that June had always been my strength, and oftentimes my courage.

"Your courage?" Deo asked, drying her eyes.

Indeed. Without June, I told Deo, I never would have survived the death of my younger brother, Jeff, in Vietnam. That year, 1968, had been my days of rage, when I had constantly stepped to the edge of the abyss and tottered precariously. I surely would have fallen had it not been for my wife.

Deo nodded her understanding, then said, "For the longest time I kept asking myself: *Why, Lord? Why Dirk and not me? Why did you take my baby?*" For the longest time she could never get those questions out of her mind; they remained unanswered, so she just never spoke of them—until now, which prompted her tears.

When Deo could at last find the correct words, her voice seemed distant, her eyes focused far, far away. Despite the passage of time, she said her grief had always been close to the surface, but never shared. Mel never came to terms with Dirk's death. He never spoke of it. He never allowed Deo to display pictures of Dirk in the family home.

No matter how bad things might appear, Deo said that Mel always could find a solution. If they needed money, somehow he managed to find a way to get it. If they were feeling down in the dumps, Mel would find a way to smile and make everything better. Mel had a gift from God in that regard, she said. "But he never ever found the solution to why Dirk died. He could never ever come to terms with it."

And for the longest time, neither could Deo. She lived with the guilt—tormenting herself how unfair it was that she should live a full life. Mothers should never live long enough to bury their children. Dirk was so young. His life was just beginning. He had so much to live for. And then, in an instant, everything that Dirk was and would ever be was snatched away.

Far out at sea, years before, the *Atocha* divers were coming to terms with their own grief. There had always been an unspoken bond among them. Although they came from all walks of life, had varying degrees of education and vastly different likes and dislikes, their shared passion was identical. The bond linking these diverse men and women who scoured the ocean's bottom and shared comparable risks ran thicker than blood. The covenant was stronger than life itself.

And so it would be in death, as they went about the somber task of recovering their own.

Mo Molinar started the *Virgilona*'s engines, turned the wheel, and followed the oil slick that led him to the *Northwind*'s grave. After anchors were dropped, John Brandon, Tom Ford, Spencer Wickens, and Tim March donned dive gear and slipped beneath the water. Angel's body was the first to be recovered, found near her cabin's doorway. Ford gently brought her to the surface and handed her to Molinar, who wrapped a sheet around her and placed her on the deck. Dirk Fisher's body was next. March pulled him from his bunk, Wickens bound him in a sheet, and then they carried him to the surface. With Angel and Dirk now on board, Kincaid silently slipped into his dive gear. He would help recover Rick Gage's body. Kincaid had no other option, he said. Not only was Gage a shipmate, but also Kincaid knew that if he did not go back down into the water and confront the *Northwind*'s demons, his fear of the unknown would remain with him forever.

Kincaid found Gage in the shower room, near the porthole through which Solanick had escaped. Kincaid helped carry the body through the boat's narrow corridors, then guided the body to the surface, where it was laid beside those of Dirk and Angel Fisher. And then the *Virgilona*'s anchors were raised, and the grim journey to port was made.

For the most part, captain and crew rode in silence, their ears reverberating with the steady drone of the ship's engines. Molinar went belowdeck to be alone with his grief, turning the ship's controls over to Kincaid, whose hands tightly gripped the ship's wheel. His fellow divers stared blankly into the billowing V cut into the ocean far behind the ship's stern. On the ship's bow, Jim Solanick sat in silence with his arm around Keith Curry, trying to solace Angel's little brother.

No one could bear to look at the three sheet-draped bodies positioned near the port gunwale.

A second boat dispatched from shore carried Kane Fisher and Donnie Jonas back to port. Although both survivors were wrapped in blankets, Jonas could not stop shivering. Every time he closed his eyes, he kept seeing the steel plate of the *Northwind*'s keel as it pressed down upon him, that precious bubble of air growing smaller and smaller. And just when he thought he could endure the pain no longer, he felt the reassuring hand on his shoulder and the soothing words, "Damn, brother, it's good to see you. I don't know how the hell you managed to get out of there. But I'm sure glad you did."

As Jonas recounted those words, he closed his eyes and released a deep sigh, then said, "Kane sat beside me the whole way home. I've never forgotten what he said to me that day. I'll always remember it. His brother's dead, yet there's Kane trying to cheer me up. Didn't help much, though. It was a sick trip, riding back knowing my three friends were dead."

Mel and Deo Fisher somberly greeted the survivors when the *Virgilona* finally docked that morning in Key West, embracing each of the crew and sharing their tears. Deo's recollections of that fateful morning remain somewhat blurred, although once she had learned the details of the ship's sinking, she could not take her eyes off Donnie Jonas. Her heart cried out for Donnie then; likewise today, almost three decades later, as she lamented, "I can't even imagine what Donnie went through. Surely it was divine intervention. God touched him in a very special way."

Everything else, though, was a dizzying swirl of faces and emotions, Deo said. There were so many people huddled about the dock—sheriff's deputies and Coast Guard officials, friends and coworkers. And, of course, the media, all of whom wanted answers to the unanswerable: "How does it feel to lose a son? Did you ever think something this tragic might happen? Would the search for the *Atocha* continue?" Deo could only cry as she politely excused herself, moving away from the vultures and again seeking out the *Northwind*'s survivors, wrapping her arms around them one by one and holding on for dear life.

"Looking back on it now, I have come to grips with the tragedy. Dirk is gone, and I know that God had his reasons," Deo said. "But on that sad morning, all I could do was thank God that he had spared the rest of the crew. I hugged each of those boys so much that it hurt, like they were my own, which they were. We have always been family. We always will be."

Deo Fisher hugged Kincaid and said, "I am so thankful that you are here." Deo said something similar to each of the survivors, then Mel said, "My son is dead, and I accept that. It's a powerful ocean; it takes men and ships. So if any of you guys have problems, I have broad shoulders."

Anyone other than Mel and Deo Fisher would have been a basket case, Kincaid said. "Despite their loss, they remained strong. Instead of falling apart or going off and mourning, they stayed there at the dock and comforted all of us survivors. That's all anyone *ever* needs to know about Mel and Deo."

And once the comforting was done, Kincaid and the remainder of the crew filled out the paperwork for the Coast Guard and the sheriff's department, and then were fed by Bob Hall. They ate in silence, and then went their separate ways.

A week after the *Northwind* tragedy, Bob Moran flew Deo Fisher and Angel Curry's mother in his seaplane to Vero Beach, where Dirk and Angel Fisher were to be buried in Johns Island Cemetery. All of the *Atocha* divers flew to Vero in a chartered DC-3, a trip on which a lot of alcohol was consumed. "Getting shit-faced was a self-defense mechanism. We sobered up in time to carry the caskets, then started all over again," said Kincaid, pointing out that they were vibrant pallbearers, wearing gaudily colored Hawaiian shirts throughout the ordeal, making a brash statement about their unique individuality.

With the exceptions of Solanick and Kincaid, a year would pass before the other survivors returned to the sea.

I met with Moran in April 2000. Moran is 71, retired and living comfortably aboard a spacious houseboat in Key West. Despite his age, he retains the wiry physique of a for-hell-bent soldier of fortune, which he most assuredly was in his youth. Not to mention being one hell of a treasure diver. Moran spoke with me for more than three hours, filling in the gaps of the *Atocha* search from the time he first joined Mel Fisher in 1965 until they parted company in 1983. For the most part, his memories were joyous—tales of wondrous gold baubles he'd found along the *Atocha* trail. But more often than not, each of his stories seemed to revert to one sore subject: Dirk's death.

Almost three decades later, some images still haunt Moran. Mel would be standing in his galleon office, his hands clutching a fistful of unpaid bills as he stared straight ahead, into the void of bad memories, unable to speak as well-wishers tried to console him. Across the room, Deo would be attempting to keep her mind busy, working on a grocery list for the *Southwind* so everything would be in perfect order whenever it was ready to leave port. But Deo said that she knew that day might never come. And then she would shudder and cry out for Mel, who rushed to her side and tenderly embraced her; silent, for there was nothing he could ever say to end his wife's torment.

Those who had survived the trauma of the *Northwind's* sinking were two blocks away, bellied up to the Chart Room Bar at the Pier House. They resembled dead men walking. The divers were reliving yesterday, too afraid to face the realities of today, trading tales of finding unbelievable riches extracted from the sea and sand, their discoveries of gold chains and fistfuls of silver pieces of eight. Yet they were broke, unable to pay their bar tabs, let alone their other bills.

Donnie Jonas would not have been hurting financially had it not been for his strong sense of right and wrong. Shortly after the *Northwind's* sinking, he was called to Mel's office. Jonas wasn't encouraged by the summons. Because he had been the *Northwind's* engineer, he figured Mel was about to officially lay the blame on his shoulders. Instead, Jonas was commended for his courage. As Mel explained it, corporate officials at Eveready batteries wanted

Jonas to participate in a commercial, reenacting his escape from the *Northwind,* showing the world how reliable Eveready flashlight batteries were in time of trouble. In return for Jonas signing a contract, Mel's corporation would not only receive free batteries and nautical lights, but also Jonas would receive $50,000.

Although he was broke, Jonas declined Eveready's offer. He told Mel that under no circumstances would he make money off the death of his friends.

Later, as he sat at the Chart Room Bar at arm's length from his compatriots, Jonas said, "Man, if I ever get married and have a son, I'll never let him be a treasure diver. If he wants to get rich, let him work for the government or become a lawyer."

Jonas's sentiments were well founded. Since the earliest days of the *Atocha* search, the state of Florida had battled Mel and his divers at every turn. The first shot fired by the state across Fisher's bow was the 1968 restructuring of Florida's sea boundaries in the Atlantic, the Gulf of Mexico, and Florida Keys, extending it beyond the traditional three-mile limit to include the outer reefs. Although the *Atocha* and the *Margarita* had gone down 37 miles west of Key West in the uninhabited Marquesas Keys, this legislation thus assured that all Treasure Salvors, Inc., discoveries would not be exempt from state jurisdiction and its 25 percent cut of the booty.

Although Fisher's lawyers took the matter to court, where the U.S. Supreme Court contemplated Florida's claim of ownership of the *Atocha* site, the state remained steadfast and refused to relinquish its hold on any of the treasure Fisher's divers had recovered since 1971: a gold cup, three gold bars, one gold disc, a gold rosary, a gold religious medallion, two gold rings, 10 gold chains, three silver bars, silver spoons, silver candlesticks, a silver plate, plus 24 swords and 19 arquebuses, the invaluable pilot's astrolabe, and more than 6,000 silver coins. Mel valued these artifacts at $6 million, yet by his own calculations he had spent almost that much of his and his investors' money in bringing them to the surface. Only when Fisher's suit was about to be ruled upon by the U.S. Supreme Court did state officials finally agree to a division of the spoils. This occurred four months before the *Northwind* sank. Two weeks later, the Supreme Court invalidated Florida's restructured boundaries.

But then, in June 1975, the federal government laid claim to the *Atocha* wreck site. Privately, Mel was furious over the federal intrusion. He had not begun the *Atocha* search to become rich. He had no problem sharing the galleon's wealth with his investors, divers, and staff; not even with his archenemy, big government, even though it continued to treat him as if he were a criminal. All he wanted to do was find the big pot of gold at the end of the rainbow, and then move on to another shipwreck. The federal government, however, was deaf to these sentiments. The bottom line: Mel Fisher had found gold, and Big Brother wanted it. The U.S. Department of the Interior, in case number 75-1416 filed in U.S. District Court for the Southern District of Florida, claimed complete jurisdiction over the *Atocha* and its treasure.

Fisher and his maritime lawyer, Dave Horan, went to Washington, D.C., where they acquired the services of an additional lawyer familiar with Beltway politics. They were pitted against an undetermined number of government lawyers led by Robert Bork, the U.S. solicitor general and former acting attorney general. The government's position on the first day of negotiations was a demand for one-fourth of the treasure. At the conclusion of the fourth day Fisher said, "The government wanted it all." Fisher had no choice but to file an admiralty claim for civil damages.

In the meantime, Bob Moran was doing everything he could to keep the operation afloat, scrounging a handful of divers and sending them to sea to live aboard a dilapidated vessel, the *Arbutus*, a 187-foot former Coast Guard buoy tender that was towed to the area where the *Atocha* anchors had been discovered. Moran anchored the vessel permanently at the site, then blew hole after hole after hole, digging virtually nonstop in the area for more than a year. Despite the incredible number of man-hours and effort, no treasure was found.

Nevertheless, Treasure Salvors, Inc., enjoyed moments of glory. On February 3, 1976, the U.S. Admiralty Court in Miami ruled in favor of Mel Fisher, declaring that the U.S. government had no legitimate claim to the *Atocha* or its treasure. The Department of Justice appealed the decision. Exactly one month later, Pat Clyne discovered a silver bar in the area of the Quicksands. Ten days later, a second silver bar was brought to the surface. Then nothing.

In June 1976 the National Geographic Society, which Deo Fisher describes as a godsend, provided a one-two-three punch on behalf of the Fisher family. *National Geographic* magazine ran a 24-page story outlining the *Atocha* search, followed six months later with the airing of its 54-minute documentary, "Treasure," which set a Public Broadcasting System ratings record. Then the society presented "The Treasures of the Atocha," a breathtaking display at Explorers' Hall in Washington, D.C. For Mel and Deo, this was a small measure of gratification for all the sweat and blood they had poured into the exploration. Making the occasion even more special was the appearance of Spain's Queen Sophia.

Only *National Geographic* could have pulled off something of this magnitude, Deo said. All of Mel Fisher's divers were invited— and everyone dressed properly for the occasion. There were no cutoffs and ratty T-shirts. In short, Explorers' Hall awed the divers. They sat in ornate oak chairs of the sort normally reserved for royalty, and they walked from room to room and viewed pictures of themselves that Don Kincaid had shot over the previous five years, plus pictures taken by Bates Littlehales and the rest of the *National Geographic* photography staff.

It was a moment of individual triumph for the divers. Although relatively unknown to the rest of the world, on this evening they were treated as heroes, their bigger-than-life likenesses hanging directly above various displays of treasure they had discovered. And wherever they looked, said Deo, there was Mel—seemingly in sort of a daze and with that ever-present drink in his hand—smiling and chuckling to himself, knowing his dream had almost been fulfilled. It was truly an amazing sight because despite his personal trauma, Fisher was shaking hands with various dignitaries and reliving the various moments of discovery, and these gentlemen were hanging on his every word, in apparent awe of a real-life adventurer.

Toward the end of the festivities, Mel approached Queen Sophia, a trained land archaeologist, and formally presented her with the finest of the recovered *Atocha* cannons. Queen Sophia provided the perfect summation of the evening when she described the treasure display as "proof of the most fascinating endeavors of our time." Mel was actually embarrassed; for one of the few times in his life, he was at a loss for words. Then, finally recovering his composure, he reached into his pocket and extracted a small jewelry box. By the time he had done so, Queen Sophia, surrounded by her bodyguards, was leaving the grand room.

Earlier, while they had been viewing the gold artifacts, Fisher had gotten the queen's attention by shouting "Sophie," an obvious breach in protocol that she had politely overlooked. Not wishing to repeat the error, he now rushed to her side, his hand out, the jewelry box in his open palm, his words well chosen. "Excuse me, Queen Sophia, but I've got something for you," Mel said, stepping closer and opening the box. "Before Dirk died, this was the last piece of gold he found. I'd like you to have it."

Queen Sophia was visibly touched as Mel handed her the necklace.

It was a small moment of triumph, said Deo, within a tragedy-plagued saga that seemed to have no end.

Bad luck at sea continued. Despite constant searching within the corridor bordered by the discoveries of the *Atocha* anchor and her nine cannons, little trace of the galleon was found during the next three years.

10

Aboard the Rock

If you like your coffee with sand for dregs, a decided hint of salt in your tea, and a fishy taste in the very eggs—by all means choose the sea.

—Lewis Carroll

It was June 16, 1985, midmorning. Sun glaring off the ocean, slight wind playing with my hair, salt spray flicking my face. Of this I was certain. At that time, though, I couldn't remember the day and didn't know if we were plowing through the Atlantic or the Gulf of Mexico. Not that it mattered, for this was the beginning of a dream come true.

I was en route to the *Atocha* trail, at sea and destined to stay there for a week or so aboard one of Mel Fisher's salvage boats, the *Saba Rock*. Life was good, with the promise of it getting even better, even though I was chattering away like a maniac, my spoken thoughts bouncing from one end of the fast boat to another.

Ted Miguel, Mel's chief of operations, was an Easter Island statue, an old salt who had retired from the U.S. Navy with the rank of captain. His gnarled hands were braced against the boat's wheel, his eyes shifting in my direction from time to time and seemingly burning holes through me. We'd bonded as only people from competing branches of the military service can bond. He was navy through and through; no-nonsense, humorless, and all spit and polish—every hair in its place, every thought gleaned from the manual compiled by brilliant sea dogs of long ago. Men like Jones and Dewey, Farragut and Halsey and Nimitz. Men who could determine fathom at the blink of an eye, who could judge the wind and set a proper course in their sleep, which I was sure Miguel still could do. Miguel was unsmiling and uncommunicative. In brief spasms of conversation, much like short bursts from a .50-caliber machine gun, he told me that he'd joined Fisher's operations seven years ago after spending a lifetime in the navy. He had become interested in undersea exploration in the course of locating several German World War II submarines that had been sunk by American warships in Florida's coastal waters.

Then Miguel asked, "So why'd you join the Marines?"

"Neat uniforms," I said, the words rolling out with no thought.

Miguel smiled. "Never known a jarhead who wasn't a smart-ass."

I took a deep breath and tried honesty. "I liked the idea of someone putting a rifle in my hands and letting me break things, paying me to do it instead of putting me in jail."

Miguel laughed for the first time and said, "Oh, yeah, you're going to fit in perfectly with this mob. You'll be right at home."

I allowed the comment to slide, concentrating instead on what Mel Fisher had told me about the *Saba Rock*, the largest of his salvage fleet. The ship had a crew of nine. It was a unique crew at that, because among the divers was a husband-and-wife team plus another engaged couple. Maybe that's why I had pictured a Keys version of *The Love Boat*, complete with pristine accommodations and a happy-go-lucky crew. But as we neared the vessel, I could not help but feel deflated. The crew, as I would soon discover, was sullen, mainly because it was finding no treasure. There was no love lost for their vessel, either. The *Rock*, as everyone called it, was a 156-ton cargo vessel that appeared to be on the verge of sinking. Its most noticeable features, aside from its 185-foot length, were lots of disused equipment and rust.

As we got within several hundred meters of it, the *Rock* seemed to glare at me defiantly. It was as if some obscene reddish-brown creature had sullenly lifted its head from beneath the gently sloping waves and double-dared me to come closer. Miguel noticed my disappointment. "She's a sore sight for sore eyes, isn't she?" he said as he maneuvered his boat alongside the *Rock's* port gunwale, dropped me off, and laughed as he gave me a mock salute and headed back to Key West.

To this day I can close my eyes and recall what my first high sea adventure was like aboard the *Rock*. Had I lived a normal life up to that point, my recollections might be interpreted as colored by unfulfilled fantasy. But normality was notably absent from my life even before the treasure-hunting bug bit me.

I had survived Marine Corps boot camp, moving up life's food chain from the lowest of the low, a Marine maggot, to a prize-fighting ring and a three-round boxing exhibition with light-heavyweight contender Mike Quarry, emerging battered and shattered—this under the guise of journalism, my *Requiem for a Paperweight* that I wrote as a firsthand account of the horror boxers endured. In another privilege of journalism, I had ventured into the Middle East's killing fields, where I was the beneficiary of the bad marksmanship of Shiite Muslim snipers and later of Hezbollah gunmen as I helped carry wounded civilians from a burning building in West Beirut. I confess to being scared witless every time weapons were jabbed into my throat and chest by various warring factions on both sides of Beirut's Green Line, the street without joy that separated the various warring factions, much like Vietnam's demilitarized zone. If that was not enough, I am a recovering alcoholic, having remained sober one agonizing day at a time since November 5, 1982. God only knows how many near-death experiences I had walked away from drunk.

So when I say that I have never experienced anything as exhilarating as being aboard a treasure salvaging boat, it is not a testosterone-induced statement. Granted, it was not exactly a cruise on *The Love Boat*. But on second glace, the *Saba Rock* proved to be more homey than homely. While it truly was a rust bucket, it also was a sanctuary from the everyday insanity of normal existence. We were 37 miles from Key West with no land in sight, anchored on a fairly gentle sea that at all times seemed to cleanse my mind of worry and frustration. The sun and humidity were punishing, yet relief could be found in the huge shadow cast by the wheelhouse or by simply standing in the ever-present breeze on the ship's bow. Having neither telephone nor television as diversion meant that when not diving you expanded your mind by talking with someone or by reading. Because the sea is a constant peril, a few days on the water brings a cleansing realization that life is too short to waste on bickering and argument; so you take what fate hands you and press on.

Without knowing exactly why, I found myself drawn to Syd Jones and his wife, K. T. Unlike divers Paul Busch and Jeff Ahern, both young and pursuing career goals based solely on whim, Syd and K. T. seemed grossly out of place. When they spoke, their words were carefully calculated and well intentioned. No matter how mundane my questions might have been, they were willing teachers, eager to make sure I fully comprehended their answers. Equally as refreshing was their honesty. Their explanations about how they arrived at this point in time were never flip or self-serving.

Syd Jones is a towering presence, in height and intelligence. No matter the subject, no matter whether he agreed with me or was adamantly opposed to the stance I took, not once did he utter a mean word—even when it was obvious that he was angry. When he spoke, he looked me straight in the eye, even when the words were a long time in coming, being thought out and then re-thought before he spoke.

Syd arrived "at the party" in 1979 at a time when Ted Miguel was attempting to beef up the accepted image of an *Atocha* diver. Having convinced Mel that the operation could prosper only by cleaning up its act, Miguel sought to hire college-educated divers,

A weary Syd Jones and his wife, K. T. Budde-Jones, aboard the *Saba Rock* in June 1985. Times were tight and no treasure was being found.

young men without a shot-and-a-beer mentality whom he could consider professionals. Miguel would tell me weeks later that Jones fit the bill. Yes, Syd was as starry-eyed as any other would-be treasure diver who had been captivated by Mel Fisher's exploits as depicted in *National Geographic*'s 1965 retelling of the discovery of Spain's 1715 fleet off Vero Beach and most recently by *National Geographic*'s television documentary on the *Atocha*. And yes, Syd had immediately afterward turned his attention toward diving and the study of archaeology, consuming every-thing he could find about the romantic lore of the high seas. But could a 27-year-old college boy from Menomonee Falls, Wisconsin, cope with the realities of what would soon become a truly professional treasure hunt?

The bottom line was that Syd Jones did not want to face another brutal winter. Granted, he had graduated from college, had a good job as an internal problem solver for a large company, and had all the trappings of success. He also was bored to death, which prompted him to telephone Treasure Salvors and speak with Deo Fisher. When he offered his services, Deo said the company was hiring. Jones quit his job that day, figuring the Fishers had hired him for $50 a week and a small percentage of whatever treasures the company would find. Then he received a letter from Treasure Salvors stating that Ted Miguel would determine whether Jones would be hired. Syd immediately traveled to Key West and experienced what he will always remember as the worst interview of his life, being quizzed by an unsmiling Miguel, who asked endless questions and did not acknowledge that he was pleased with the answers.

Jones told Miguel that he was a certified diver who was familiar with boats and the mechanics of them, that he was capable of rebuilding engines, that he'd spent a lot of his time around racecars, that he was teachable and trainable. "And every time I would answer a question," Jones said, "Ted would ask: 'What else?'" While Jones struggled for another piece of his life story, Miguel had already been convinced of this young man's worth. Besides being a qualified diver, Jones was a college graduate. End of discussion; he was hired on the spot.

From that moment on, Jones said that his life changed drastically. His initial on-the-job lesson was learning "how to do a lot with little." The dive equipment the *Atocha* divers used was obsolete; the boats they dived from were even worse. He was immediately put to work refitting Fisher's salvage boats, chipping away rust and repainting. When he went to sea, it was at Miguel's side, scouring Hawk Channel with the magnetometer, learning the intricacies of proper charting. To most, this type of work would have been mindless at best. To Syd Jones, it was a breath of fresh air, especially after his first few weeks on the job in which he became immersed in the old way of doing business. Although Mel's way of doing things was fun at first, Jones admits to being a pretty straitlaced guy.

"I quickly got bored with the dysfunctional way the company was run—no up-to-date equipment, no compressors to pump the tanks, no metal detectors to use on the bottom to help us find treasure," he said. "While we had none of what I call the essentials, we always had plenty of beer."

※

K. T. Budde is pretty and blond. She not only has a mind of her own, she also is willing to fight for her right to use it. During my brief stay on the *Rock,* no one outworked K. T. All she demanded was a fair shot, an equal opportunity to show off her skills. Given that, she repaid her superiors by carrying her own weight and then some.

K. T. had known Syd since childhood, and had even double-dated with him in high school. It was at his insistence that she visited Key West in December 1980, entranced by Jones's exploits on the high seas, diving and finding long-lost treasure. Soon, K. T. took diving lessons back home in Wisconsin, revisited the Keys the next April, and took her first open-water dive on the *Margarita* site. Smitten by the experience, she was determined to become a treasure hunter. She was 28, college-educated, and a special-education teacher in the Milwaukee school system. Because she had taught juvenile delinquents during her first year of teaching, she felt more than qualified to work with the divers whom Syd had described to her.

In June 1981, K. T. took a leave of absence and began working for Treasure Salvors, Inc., without pay. Animosity was instantaneous. Her male diving cohorts were a tad old-fashioned: To them, a woman's place was in the kitchen or the bedroom. Until K. T.'s arrival there had been only one other female diver, Damien Lin, who worked the treasure trail in 1979. The rest of the women who served aboard the salvage boats did so as cooks or pleasure for the crew. K. T. wanted to be a treasure diver, not the object of someone's sexual gratification. Naturally, there was a lot of friction.

"To succeed I had to show everyone that although I couldn't stand up to pee, I was more than willing to do everything else that the men did," she said. "And I did."

K. T. swabbed decks, filled diving tanks, cooked, cleaned quarters, and emptied bilge tanks without complaint, working the 16-hour days just like her male counterparts, but without the usual $120 weekly salary. While fellow divers mocked her efforts, Mel Fisher was quietly assessing K. T.'s performance. Two months into the job, Mel watched K. T.'s strength and determination as she hauled two massive 12-volt batteries from the salvage boat to the dock. Mel pulled Ted Miguel aside and told him to hire K. T., at regular wages, with no reservations. It proved to be a typical Key West story: K. T. went to visit one summer and never left. And in the process, the stingrays and barracudas became her friends. Finding gold was not all that bad, either.

Syd, who was preparing to make another dive with K. T., interrupted our conversation. We could continue the interviews later that evening, he said. After all, there was work to do. He gave me a thumb's up, hobbled over to the side of the ship, his fins making flip-floppy sounds as they struck the deck, and said, "Most people think that all we have to do is jump in the water and there, right before our eyes, we find the ship and its chests full of silver and gold. But what we really do, for little money, is have long periods of boredom broken up by short moments of excitement. This isn't all about gold and silver."

Life at sea is many things, most of which are mundane and mind-numbing. The ship's crew had been anchored at or near this spot for almost three months. Because it was a $3,000 round trip to take the boat back to Key West, the *Rock* seldom returned to port. When freshwater ran out (as it did on my second day at sea), when groceries ran short (as they did on day 4), or when the ship's diesel tanks ran dry (as they would on day 6), Fisher dispatched a resupply boat from shore. Everything else centered on blowing holes, diving on those holes, and, when nothing of importance was discovered, dreaming of treasure that some-day would be found or reminiscing about treasures found in the past.

Syd, in typical low-key fashion, reminisced with the crew about his greatest day at sea, August 23, 1980, when, as captain of the *Swordfish*, he dived on an anomaly that was some distance from where his compatriots were bringing up the *Margarita* treasure. What Syd discovered was a clump of melded cannonballs and what he said resembled a "hive of golden bees"—nine gold bars and eight gold chains twisted together in a mound. Admittedly, my eyes were every bit as large as Busch's and Ahern's.

Not to be outdone, K. T. turned to me and asked, "Have you noticed that pile of junk at the stern, most of which are old, rusted sardine cans? Did you see Paul and Jeff taking time to open the sardine cans that they brought up earlier this morning? Well, there's a darned good reason why."

It was July 1982, and K. T. was working aboard the contract boat *Golden Venture*, captained by Grady Sullivan, as they were diving in the Quicksands. K. T. was in the water with Rico Ingerson, who was running his handheld metal detector up and down the blownhole's berm. It was almost 6:00 P.M., and the divers were completing the final moments of searching their last hole of the day, their air supply almost exhausted, when Ingerson recorded a hit on his detector. K. T. explained for my benefit that the most grueling part of any dive is trying to recover an item from within a berm because its steep slope causes an avalanche of sand when a diver digs into it. If the artifact lies within a depth of six inches or less, recovery is fairly easy. Whatever Ingerson had found was far deeper, and he and K. T. dug with no result, resurfaced for fresh tanks, and had the ship's captain lightly blow the hole again. Back in the water, they continued digging, again running low on both air and daylight.

At almost 7:30 P.M. Ingerson finally stuck his hand deep into the cascading sand and extracted a badly oxidized box that appeared to be a sardine can—discarded junk from a lobster fisherman.

"Rico was going to discard it when something about it struck my eye," K. T. said. "He handed it to me and I shook it. Something inside it rattled."

Once they had made their way to the surface and onto ship, Ingerson joined the rest of the crew to make the ship secure because of an impending storm. K. T., however, was still fascinated by the small metal box, and she crouched by the starboard gunwale, which afforded the best light and protection from the increasing wind and threat of rain. She shook the box again, listened to the tinny rattle and immediately thought: *Emeralds?* Beckoning crew member Dick Klaudt to join her, K. T. sprayed phosphoric acid, a mild chemical that dissolves calcareous encrustations without damaging the object, onto the lid of the box. She gently lifted its lid and saw green.

"I closed the lid and thought, *Holy shit*," said K. T.

They screamed in celebration when she opened the box again and showed Klaudt its contents—seven iridescent green stones, each the size of a child's thumb, seemingly floating in milky seawater. When K. T. took hold of what she thought was one emerald, she found herself holding an enormous gold cross. The rest of the crew quickly joined them, and Ingerson reached into the box and extracted an ornately crafted gold ring, likewise adorned with a huge emerald, from what would prove to be a silver box. The reverse of the cross was engraved with the image of a saint holding the Christ child.

To this day, that artifact remains the showpiece of Mel Fisher's museum, a priceless heirloom that archaeologists have dubbed "The Bishop's Cross."

All of us allowed those sobering words to sink in; then we retired for the evening. I cannot speak for the others, but my dreams that night were of gold and emeralds.

Although my bed was a sleeping blanket on deck, it provided me with the most spectacular moments at sea. It was there, curled up under a wide blanket of stars, that I tried to digest all I had seen and heard—all of the images of the divers' frustration after

Diver K. T. Budde-Jones shows off the heavily encrusted silver bars she recovered south of the *Atocha* mother lode site.

scouring the ocean's floor without success; all of the conversations brimming with equal parts hope and hopelessness, of tales of treasure both lost and found. There is little sound on the emptiness of a black ocean, only that of waves lapping against a steel hull. The air is brisk and clean. Without a doubt, this adventure was the most pleasant week I had ever spent. The waves rocked me to sleep.

The true beauty of a treasure hunt is that everyone works equally. Yes, the ship's captain called the shots and everyone obeyed without question. Living aboard ship is to function outside of a democracy. Yet even Ed Stevens, the ship's 24-year-old captain, dived. When he was not in the water, he was moving the ship's anchor lines to position it to blow another hole. And while he was doing this, everyone else kept busy filling diving tanks with the ship's compressor or cleaning diving gear or preparing gear for the next dive.

Spend enough time at sea and it's easy to comprehend why the federal and state of Florida governments failed to grasp the pure essence of Mel Fisher's treasure salvaging operation. There is no middle management on a diving boat, no nonessential personnel whose job is to make sure you breathe properly through your regulator or who stand idly by to make sure you pull on your fins in accordance with company regulations. Everything is said up front, without hesitation. There is a brutal honesty about all things at sea. It is not a place for wimps, for complainers, for the weak of heart.

Spend a little time at sea and you can actually feel the water reaching out for you, sinking its claws into your soul. The sea is at all times beautiful and ugly, gentle and angry, compassionate and mean-spirited. While it is nothing that you should ever take for granted or turn your back on, the sea also becomes a part of you, a lifeblood of sorts, its salt water running through your every thought. As it does, you while away the hours doing everything within your power to keep the boat afloat, for even though your soul is at one with the sea, you certainly don't want the connection to be permanent. So you toil, mindlessly yet with purpose. No one looks over your shoulder, for everyone knows better than to slack off. Mistakes at sea oftentimes have lethal consequences. Every crew member has specific tasks, and every task is carried out in accordance with self-preservation. Do the job right, and you might not die. Do the job right every second of every day, and even then dying is out of your control. The sea may have a mind of its own, but it has no conscience.

Spend enough time at sea and you finally understand why farmers refuse to leave the soil, even when they go broke. The sea is as addictive as any drug. Willingly, I had sampled it and was hooked. All it took was a week aboard the *Rock* and I wanted to become a treasure hunter. Knowing that the divers made little money; knowing there were no guarantees that the *Atocha* would ever be found; knowing that the work was equal parts frustration and despair, with a minuscule moment of jubilation; knowing that these guys and gals were nothing more than dreamers who had walked away from normal society. Knowing all this yet still wondering, Where do I sign up?

For seven days I watched, listened, and learned. I saw the terror on 19-year-old Jeff Ahern's face after he surfaced after having come face-to-face with a torpedo that he said was still "sizzling." I watched at night as Ruben, Gato, and Sterling Rivers, the Caribbean deckhands, conducted Spanish lessons for the diving crew. In return, our Spanish brothers learned English from us—how to order a beer and how much to pay for it; how to ask tourists if they could buy their daughters, and that $50 was too much.

The days melded together. The crew found nothing on the first day, bomb fragments on the second, nothing on the third, and twisted iron spikes on the fourth. Silver coins materialized from the mud early on the fifth day, but then the treasure petered out.

There is danger, too, aboard the ship, for huge mechanical wheels are grinding away all over the deck. The crane, which will be used should the crew be fortunate enough to find the *Atocha*'s 47 tons of treasure, was a relic from the 1920s. The winch, which is used to position the boat's three big anchors, was stripped from a World War II vessel. At the moment it was broken; one of its gears had shattered.

Danger is not just on the sea but swims in it as well. On my third day, Busch, 26, a graduate of Wisconsin's Stevens Point College, was diving in a hole when a sand shark dropped in on him. He screwed up and nudged the shark with his metal detector. Irritated, the shark—a little critter, only a five-footer—moved closer. Busch quickly retreated. "No way am I going back into the water. Not today, anyway," he said.

11

Death in the Water

Sometimes, through no fault of your own, accidents happen. . . .
—*Don Kincaid*

I t wasn't until the fall of 1999 that Don Kincaid supplied the details surrounding the *Atocha* search's second death. Kincaid had given up treasure hunting a decade before and spoke from the comfort of his Key West apartment. He was 54, still trim and shipshape, and sailed for a living now, taking paying customers aboard his huge catamaran *Stars & Stripes* for sunset excursions far from the treacherous body of water under which he once toiled for the *Atocha's* elusive riches. Nonetheless, Kincaid's thoughts of those adventurous and often tragic days were never far away.

"What you have to understand," said Kincaid, clenching his fists at his side, "is that treasure diving was something we learned as the search progressed. For the most part, it was trial and error. And some of the errors were very tragic."

He looked away, focused on something beyond my comprehension. The silence grew. Then he said, "Sometimes, through no fault of your own, accidents happen. . . . "

It was Monday, August 6, 1973, and danger was the last thought on anyone's mind on that extraordinary afternoon, a perfect day for diving. The weather was exceptional: a powder-blue sky pressed against the bottle-green water; a soft wind tempered the heat, which hovered at 86 degrees. And the sea, while always possessing the potential to inflict disaster, had lain down for the occasion. The only disturbance, other than the muffled conversation of a diverse mix of crew, divers, and guests, was an intermittent swell that gently rocked the *Southwind*.

The salvage boat was anchored in the Quicksands, atop the Bank of Spain. Any day now Mel Fisher expected his divers to uncover the *Atocha*'s mother lode, his favorite phrase to describe the galleon's vast treasure of 47 tons of silver and gold. Joining Fisher's 17-year-old son Kim, who was the *Southwind*'s captain, were veteran diver–crew members Bleth McHaley, Mark Hansen, and Patty Strahan, plus Kincaid, who was under contract to *National Geographic* to record stills of all treasure finds. Accompanying Kincaid was renowned *National Geographic* underwater photographer Bates Littlehales and his 11-year-old son Nicholas, whom everyone called Nikko. Rounding out the crew were stockholders Mr. and Mrs. Jud Chalmers.

It was almost 3:00 P.M. when the *Southwind* dropped its anchors and the crew readied the vessel for salvage operations. The deflector, twin sections of a 12-foot-long fuel tank that had been cut in half and welded side-by-side with metal braces, was lowered over the stern and secured by a diver at the rear of the ship's props. Another diver signaled with a thumbs-up to Kim Fisher at the helm, and within seconds the serenity was shattered by the metal-grating growl of the twin diesels, which unleashed the combined 1,200 horses that powered the vessel's three-bladed, 43-inch bronze propellers. Situated five feet below the waterline, these corkscrewing buzz saws churned the ocean, pushing tons of seawater against the deflector, which in turn sent it cascading against the ocean floor. This process is called "blowing a hole."

It's how treasure salvors are able to actually touch the past, by blowing away the accumulation of centuries of sand.

One hole was blown in the 20-foot-deep sands a mere 23 feet below the keel. The ship was repositioned a few feet to starboard and then another hole was blown. Amid the demonic noise and treasure-induced anticipation, Kincaid checked his camera gear and, as always, listened in awe to the advice shouted to him by Bates Littlehales, a legend when it came to underwater photography. Bleth McHaley and the rest of the diving crew fussed over Nikko Littlehales, who stood four-feet-six and weighed 85 pounds. It was obvious to all that Nikko thoroughly enjoyed his role as mascot.

Although only 11, Nikko was a certified diver and, with almost two years of scuba experience, had almost as much diving time as any crew member because he accompanied his father on underwater assignments whenever possible. He doubted if he would ever get used to the noise of a salvage operation, bellowing these sentiments to McHaley, who nodded her agreement as she helped Nikko with his diving gear.

All eyes darted to fellow divers, who were likewise trying to be heard over the engines and generators. Because of this din, the ritual of checking gear was an exercise in sign language, a thumbs up to indicate full compressed air pressure in the diving tanks, another thumbs up to guarantee a diver that his pressure valve was turned on.

Kincaid's eyes and mind recorded the moment as Nikko adjusted his miniature diving tank and rinsed his mask. Kincaid noted the time of day and the gentle sea conditions, which he knew would be of no concern. The only thing that bothered Kincaid was the way the *Southwind* was anchored, facing east with the current flowing toward the starboard side as it moved under the boat. He voiced his concern. His fellow divers agreed and immediately added extra lead to their weight belts. The added poundage ensured that they would descend rapidly, negating the pull of the current.

Still not satisfied, Kincaid reminded everyone that there was no such thing as being safe at sea. That was just an illusion.

"Believe me," he said, "every time you board a boat or enter the water and return home safe and sound, you've cheated death."

It was 4:02 P.M. when Bates Littlehales, camera gear in hand, entered the water off the side of the boat. He dropped straight through the current to the bottom.

Nikko was next, balancing awkwardly atop the ship's starboard rail because of the rubber fins on his feet. Kincaid helped support the lad, who gave a thumbs up and then, with his left foot, stepped out and into the sea. Nikko slowly drifted down, but then appeared to pause as if to adjust his mask. In that instant the invisible hands of the current took hold of him.

Kincaid was about to enter the water, his right foot on the railing, when he heard the unmistakable noise—*clunk, clunk, clunk*—of something striking the three-bladed props. Kim Fisher was in the wheelhouse, and despite the earsplitting roar of diesels and generators, he also heard the ominous noise and immediately killed the engines. Within seconds, Bates Littlehales broke the surface 15 meters astern and screamed, "Where's my son? *Where's my son?*"

Another diver, who had been standing at the stern when Nikko left the boat, had already dived into the water to inspect the props, which had steel cables strung around them. The gaps between cables were small enough to protect an adult from possible injury, but not a child. Within seconds the diver burst through the surface and confirmed everyone's worst fears: "Nikko's been sucked into the props."

It took the combined efforts of three divers to extract the lad from the massive propellers. They carried Nikko's body to the surface and gently eased him onto the boat's deck. Mrs. Chalmers and Bleth McHaley, both registered nurses, frantically treated the boy's injuries as best they could. There were small, deep gashes on Nikko's left arm, legs, buttocks, and upper body. His left arm was grossly distorted; shattered bones had punctured the skin. There was little blood.

Kim Fisher's call to the Coast Guard for emergency medical assistance was sent at 4:22 P.M. That done, McHaley gently stroked

Nikko's uninjured right shoulder as Kim knelt at the boy's side and administered mouth-to-mouth resuscitation.

"It was obvious that Kim's efforts were of no use," Kincaid said. "The boy was mangled."

Both Coast Guard helicopters in Key West were down for repairs. The only seaplane available had just had its gas tanks pulled. Help finally arrived from the Coast Guard station at Fort Meyers. As the helicopter hovered overhead, a rescue diver dropped into the water and a rescue basket was lowered. Moments later, the chopper lifted off, transporting Nikko and Bates to the Naval Air Station at Boca Chica Key.

More than an hour and a half had elapsed from the time of the accident until the arrival of the rescue chopper. By the time it landed at Boca Chica Key, Nikko Littlehales was pronounced dead on arrival.

The sheriff drove Bates home that evening to his rented home on Dey Street in Key West, where Don Kincaid, Bleth McHaley, and marine biologist Nada Yolen stayed up all night, to no avail, attempting to ease Bates's grief.

"To this very day, I avoid Dey Street," Kincaid said. "I try never to go near there because I can still hear Bates's screaming and crying. To him, understandably, the tragedy made no sense. Nikko was just an 11-year-old kid out there on the water looking to have a good time."

In the wake of Nikko's death, Mel Fisher had the *Southwind* pulled into dry dock, where steel cages were welded around the ship's propellers to prevent a repetition of the calamity. Bates Littlehales worked only one more underwater assignment for *National Geographic*, a dive on the Yorktown shipwrecks that he made years later shortly before his retirement. Kim Fisher was so shaken that he retreated as far inland as he could, walking away from his father's treasure salvage operation to join his girlfriend in Michigan, where he also attended college. His last act before leaving was a curt yet chilling notation in his ship's log: "Today was clouded with tragedy."

12

Margarita and Myths

The difference between fiction and reality? Fiction has to make sense.

—Tom Clancy

As I would discover in the years that followed, much of what I would be told about Fisher's recovery work when I came on the scene in 1985 had been couched not to offend Mel, who because he was so impatient was either in the habit of supplying only half the pertinent details or leaving them out altogether. Some of this skewing of the facts had to do with a treasure salvor's penchant for secrecy—understandable, for too many people were desperate to confiscate what Fisher and his divers had found. Some of the misrepresentation had to do with Mel's love of family, his habit of bestowing glory on his sons at the expense of others.

Whatever the case, the numerous myths of the *Atocha* search had been repeated so often that they came to be regarded as fact.

Only after Mel's death in 1998 was I able to piece together the unembellished story of the *Atocha-Margarita* quest. In the instance of the discovery of the *Margarita*, truth itself proved to have a historical element.

It began with an innocent distortion, that on May 12, 1980, then-20-year-old Kane Fisher, who was captain of the *Virgilona* at the time, dived through the bottle-green waters of Hawk Channel and came face-to-face with six silver ingots resting beside a galleon's rotting wooden timbers. That is how the discovery was reported by every major magazine and newspaper. All were in error because they were misled in details large and small.

According to the log of the *Swordfish*, which was on site that day, the discovery occurred on May 10, 1980, and the diver who made the find was Don Durant. But what is even more startling is that Mel Fisher had dived on that precise location nine years earlier, the day he *really* discovered the *Margarita*.

In the fall of 1999, Don Kincaid told me that he was stunned in the mid-1980s when his eyes traveled down the page of one of the logbooks that the Fishers had to keep in accordance with state salvage regulations and came to rest on the notation, in Deo Fisher's hand, "We've found a wreck 3 miles east of our present wreck site, and we feel it's the *Margarita*. There are great quantities of ballast all around." Although Kincaid did not recall the exact date when Deo made the entry, he did remember that the notation was made during the spring of 1971. He also remembered thinking, *Now it all makes sense.*

Kincaid had been on Bobby Jordan's boat in 1980 when they had found the *Margarita* exactly where Mel Fisher said it would be. From that moment on, he had wondered whether Mel was clairvoyant.

"We had known where she was since 1971," Deo Fisher told me in November 1999. "Mel was out there magging near the Quicksands with Faye Feild and Bob Holloway. When they moved east, closer to the Marquesas, they got this very big anomaly and dove on it."

No doubt about it, Mel told his wife, the ballast and other materials were the remains of the *Margarita*. Everything that Eugene Lyon had discovered about the wreck seemed to fall in place that day—the depth, 27 feet; the location, as stated in official Spanish reports by one of the survivors: approximately three miles northwest of where the *Atocha* went under. Yes, this was a treasure hunter's dream come true, a 600-ton galleon once brimming with treasure.

Normally this would have been cause for celebration. But what Mel and Deo also knew from Lyon's research in the Archives of the Indies in Seville was that the galleon had been salvaged by Spain during four consecutive dive seasons, beginning in 1626. According to Spanish documentation, Francisco Nuñez Melian had thoroughly excavated the wreck site, salvaging 380 silver ingots and more than 67,000 silver pieces of eight. Everything considered, Mel chose to put off salvaging the *Margarita* until later. Deo said her husband's reasoning was rational. Mel had a tunnel-vision work ethic; although he was a world-class dreamer, he was incapable of pursuing two dreams at once. Of greater importance, he had already invested a vast amount of time and money in the *Atocha* search, and to abandon it now to salvage a wreck that offered little promise of treasure would be too great a gamble. To Mel's way of thinking, the *Margarita* was a negative and the *Atocha* was a positive.

"Of course," said Deo, "what neither of us knew was the tremendous amount of contraband that had been smuggled aboard the *Margarita*; we had no idea that she was filled with so much gold."

According to her manifest, the *Margarita* was carrying 419 silver ingots, 118,000 silver coins, and 1,488 ounces of gold in 34 bars and disks. Simple math would dictate that despite what Spain had recovered, there was still a king's ransom left among her rotting timbers. In retrospect, the divers said that their minds were locked onto the *Atocha*.

No one gave the other ship a second thought until rival salvors Olan Frick and John Gasque began encroaching into the Quicksands area during the winter of 1979, despite Mel Fisher's having a state salvage permit for the locale. Fisher immediately got an injunction preventing Frick and Gasque from further searching the area, and Don Kincaid delivered the subpoenas aboard a Coast Guard cutter with the aid of two federal marshals.

Fearful that Frick and Gasque or other competing salvors would disregard the injunction and chance upon the *Margarita*, Fisher gathered his crews together in February 1980 and fashioned an ad hoc game plan. Ted Miguel, captain of the *Swordfish*, would search to the west of the *Atocha* discoveries, and Bobby Jordan, a subcontractor who captained the *Castilian*, would search to the east.

Although everyone thought Mel was sending them off on a wild-goose chase, he simply smiled and said that the *Margarita* most definitely was within their grasp.

Jordan's deal with Mel was the envy of the other crews. He would be getting $100 a day plus provisions and fuel for his boat. He would also receive a percentage of treasure found; 2 percent if it was from the *Atocha*, 5 percent from the *Margarita*. If Jordan were to discover an altogether different wreck, he would receive half of whatever riches were uncovered. In light of these generous arrangements, Fisher's lieutenants were stunned by Jordan's openly hostile attitude. Whenever Mel mentioned the *Atocha* and the *Margarita*, Jordan ridiculed him, saying the galleons were nowhere to be found in Hawk Channel; and if they were, he would damn well search wherever he wanted.

On February 18, 1980, with Don Kincaid aboard the *Castilian*, Jordan dropped anchor at the exact location Fisher had told him to mag and immediately discovered ballast, a grapnel anchor, pottery shards, a huge copper cooking cauldron, and a cluster of silver coins. Divers working north and northwest of this location discovered three gold bars, the largest of these weighing more than four pounds. On April 12, two more gold bars were found, then thousands of silver pieces of eight and a concentration of swords and arquebuses were brought to the surface. Amid the ensuing celebration, Jordan stayed to himself, refusing to echo the sentiments that Fisher's crew had, indeed, found the *Margarita*. When Jordan did speak, it was with Ted Miguel, arguing that he had found a new wreck and deserved a 50-50 split of the treasure. Jordan was still complaining about his share of the riches when he took the *Castilian* into port on May 9.

At noon on the day after Jordan's return to port the *Swordfish* had completed a side-scan survey and also was about to head to Key West to refill its scuba tanks. Company finances being what they were, none of the salvage boats had air compressors, which meant that when the supply of compressed air was exhausted in the boat's 15 tanks, they had to be refilled at a local Key West diving shop. Before the *Swordfish* left the site, however, Miguel received a radio message from the nearby *Virgilona* that it needed another diver. The *Swordfish* complied by dropping off Don Durant. Approximately half an hour later, another message was sent from the *Virgilona:* "We need help with our whaler," treasure salvors' code indicating that something spectacular had happened.

"We could hear a lot of laughing and celebrating in the background," said Syd Jones, who was first mate of the *Swordfish* at the time, "so we knew something big was up."

What had happened was that Don Durant went for a swim. After he was dropped off in response to the *Virgilona*'s request for help, he had been told that all of the ship's scuba tanks were nearly exhausted. Bored at not being able to participate in the crews' efforts, which were focused on a site near where Bobby Jordan found the gold bars three months earlier, Durant entered the water. He had gone no more than 50 yards east of the boat when he paused and dipped his head below the surface. As easily as that, he discovered the *Margarita*'s main pile—timbers, silver bars, and a coin chest lying fully exposed on the bedrock. When Durant screamed the news of his discovery, pandemonium broke out on the *Virgilona*. The vessel was quickly repositioned and anchored over the site; then the crew scrambled for diving gear. Within minutes, six silver bars, one gold bar, and the chest of silver coins were resting on the ship's deck. Shortly thereafter, the *Swordfish* anchored stern-to-stern with its sister ship, and another treasure frenzy got under way as the crew scrambled around the diving locker, hoping to find a tank with even the barest amount of air left in it.

Before the divers could hit the water, however, Ted Miguel halted further recovery. Fearing inadvertent damage to the galleon's exposed timbers, Miguel said the area would need to be properly mapped before anything else was brought to the surface. Following a brief but volatile yelling session from his divers, Miguel finally relented, telling his crew that he would lightly dust the southernmost tip of the area and that they could slip below the blowers and pick up whatever loose coins they could find. Everything else, though, must remain undisturbed. While the other divers were grabbing handfuls of pieces of eight, Jones made a quick sketch of the area, making detailed measurements and recording compass bearings of the various artifacts.

"And once that was done, all of us had to return to port," Jones said. "We've discovered the *Margarita*'s main pile with all its silver and gold, and there's nothing we can do about it because we're out of air; we can't dive. Such was life as a treasure salvor."

Once the boats were refitted and resupplied, the crews returned to the site and began scouring the area. Quickly, another gold bar and three more silver ingots were discovered, then an entire chest of 3,000 silver coins. Two days later, a silver spur was brought to the surface, then six more gold bars. Meanwhile, at port, Eugene Lyon examined the initial discoveries, comparing the markings on the six silver bars to those listed on the *Margarita*'s manifest. Five of the bars were identical matches.

At this point, though, some of the bitterest conflict in the history of Mel Fisher treasure hunting broke out. Bobby Jordan was not convinced of the ship's provenance, and on May 21 he filed a claim for the wreck site in federal court. Two days later, he steered the *Castilian* to the salvage area with Treasure Salvors, Inc., representatives R. D. LeClair and Frank Moody aboard. As soon as the *Castilian* anchored, LeClair, 29, made his first dive in more than four months and discovered 55 pounds of gold in the form of 15 bars and one disk. Within minutes of this discovery, other divers uncovered five gold coins, four small silver bars, and 600 silver coins. And then everything got out of hand.

Frank Moody's version of what happened next was summarized in a few words: "We went for a little boat ride, had a few beers, and then returned to Key West." LeClair's version, as told to me in June 1985, sounded as if it had been lifted from a James Bond novel. He said that Mel Fisher's instructions to him before he went aboard the *Castilian* were "to play secret agent" while helping Jordan with salvaging operations. Because Mel did not trust Jordan, LeClair was to monitor his movements but not be obvious about it.

After LeClair's gold discoveries, Jordan took his boat to the nearby Marquesas and anchored for the night. When LeClair tried to radio Fisher headquarters and inform Mel of the vast amounts of gold they had uncovered, Jordan stepped in and took the hand microphone away from LeClair, saying it was too dangerous to use the radio, that would-be pirates might intercept the message and immediately rush to the scene. LeClair told Jordan that he would "talk in code to Mel," but Jordan again refused to allow LeClair to contact Fisher.

Later that evening, LeClair overheard Jordan on the ship's radio relaying a cryptic message to his wife about "finding fish and should he turn them over to the fish farm." At two o'clock that morning, when it was LeClair's turn to stand watch, he discovered that the ship's M-1 carbine was missing. As LeClair would discover later, Jordan had taken not only the M-1 to bed with him but also all of the boat's weapons.

At daybreak, according to court documents, Jordan was later charged with false imprisonment. Jordan took the *Castilian* back to Key West, where he made a brief stop and then left the harbor— but not without having been seen by Don Kincaid, who immediately got in touch with Bob Moran, who hopped in his seaplane and eventually spotted Jordan's boat docked 20 miles up the Keys at Finley Riccard's house on Summerland Key. Moran immediately called Mel Fisher, who in turn contacted federal authorities.

Riccard, who was Bobby Jordan's financial backer, had a federal marshal on hand, who immediately confiscated the treasure that Jordan had brought from the wreck site.

LeClair and Moody left the ship the next day; then Kincaid once again had the opportunity to serve a subpoena on the high seas, this time in the company of a Coast Guard crew wielding M-16s and a 20mm deck gun, all of which were aimed directly at Bobby Jordan and his *Castilian* crew. Jordan appeared before Judge William Mehrtens on June 2. Mehrtens listened to opposing statements and then removed Jordan from further work on the *Margarita*, stating that Jordan had embarked "upon a course to unjustly enrich himself." The gold that Jordan had taken was returned to Treasure Salvors, Inc.

Back at sea, the *Margarita* continued to be a gold rush of artifacts. Two bronze cannons were discovered, but neither could be identified as having come from the *Margarita*. Then, on July 8, diver Pat Clyne entered the water with photographer Don Kincaid, who was again under contract with *National Geographic*. They descended 18 feet to the bottom and were about to begin fanning for treasure when Clyne spotted a blackened silver bar lying in the sand. Finding treasure was not a new experience for Clyne. So even though he said he was mildly excited, his first response was to make sure that Kincaid captured the moment on film. For the first time, Clyne said, the *National Geographic* would be able to record the discovery of treasure in real time instead of the typical fare, shooting a reenactment.

As they hovered over the bar, Clyne fanned the sand away as Kincaid snapped picture after picture, pausing only when he saw the first glint of gold. Kincaid reached down and took hold of the stub of an intricately crafted ornamental chain that, when fully uncovered, was eight feet long. Kincaid handed the gold chain to Clyne, then continued to snap away as Clyne pulled what seemed like an endless golden thread from beneath the sand. Attached to the first gold chain was another. And another and another. Watching Clyne that day was like watching the Energizer Bunny.

He kept pulling and pulling until he had extracted 15 chains attached end to end—176 feet of thick, ornate gold.

The *Margarita* yielded other spectacular finds, including a diamond set into a gold ring that was found by Donnie Jonas and a gold ring adorned with seven emeralds, discovered by Frank Moody. From a purely personal point of view, however, the most stunning of the recovered artifacts was that discovered by Dick Klaudt. Diving directly under the blowers while they were running at full blast, he was smacked in the head by a heavy object. When the shower of sand cleared, Klaudt found an eight-inch ornately etched gold plate at his feet—the plate upon which Mel served me cake during our first meeting on that memorable 1985 Memorial Day weekend. That little footnote aside, before the summer of 1980 was over, the *Margarita*'s yield was staggering: 106 pounds of gold fashioned into 54 bars, bits, disks, and nuggets, plus handfuls of gold flakes; 43 gold chains, 53 gold coins, and 12,000 silver coins. Treasure was recovered in such abundance that Fisher and his divers became media darlings, their exploits glorified on the front pages of every major newspaper from coast to coast.

The crowning coup on the public relations front came from the *National Geographic*, which once again immortalized Mel in February 1982 with a 14-page magazine story written by Eugene Lyon and illustrated by Don Kincaid's stunning photographs.

The fact that Mel had found the *Margarita* in 1971 instead of 1980 was never mentioned. It was a secret that would not be revealed until years after Mel was dead.

13

Raising Kane

The pang, the curse, with which they died, had never passed
away; I could not draw my eyes from theirs, nor turn them up
to pray.

—*Samuel Taylor Coleridge,*
"The Rime of the Ancient Mariner"

The figure and his vessel materialized from out of the
sun's glare, from out of the twilight of the gods, as if riding on the musical wave of Wagner's *The Valkyries*. The
ship was much abused, more derelict than industrious, painted
navy gray, the color of which was now sadly faded. Yet the craft
moved with admirable speed, slugging its way through the rolling
seascape off our starboard bow, at times both majestic and fear-
some.

It was June 1985, and I stood in awe at the bow of the *Saba
Rock*, mesmerized more by the man at the helm of the onrushing
ship than by the ship itself. The helmsman looked like what I
imagined a Viking warrior must have looked like: tall and defiant,
his tanned chest insolently thrust forward, his shoulder-length
red hair splayed back by the wind, hands locked fast upon his
ship's helm, with his chin up and his eyes on the lookout for new
lands.

Kane Fisher, right, captain of the *Dauntless*, examines some of the gold bars he and his crew recovered from the *Atocha*.

One of my crewmates approached and quipped, "Well, look who's here. It's Mel's Golden Child."

I had to stop and think for a moment, trying to remember the names of Fisher's sons, then asked if the creature on the approaching boat was Kim. My crewmate laughed. No, he said, Kim was over on the East Coast recovering treasure from the 1715 fleet; he would really be pissed if he knew I had confused him with his younger brother. I was told that Kim was Joe College; Kane was quite the opposite.

My mate said that Kim had endearing qualities, like being civil in the company of strangers and having the capacity to take orders. Kane, on the other hand, was rude, insolent, and quarrelsome.

Hoping that Kane would ease his boat up to ours so I could have the opportunity to talk to him, I was disappointed when the rusty gray vessel turned southeast toward deep water. Nonetheless, I would soon get an earful about Fisher's younger son.

Depending on the source, Kane Fisher was a glory hound, a spoiled brat, a hell raiser, or the world's second-greatest treasure hunter.

The majority who condemned Kane refused to go on the record, either out of fear of Kane's retaliating physically or a desire not to embarrass Mel.

Kane was 26 at the time, old beyond his years. He was very much his father's son—stubborn and hardheaded and prone to hard living, adventure, and lusting after treasure. Kane's credo: If it's good enough for Dad, then it's good enough for me. This, understandably, did not endear him to most people. It also did not help matters that in Mel's eyes Kane could do no wrong. Mel carried this to extremes, always pushing his son into the spotlight, oftentimes creating tension among the crews of competing salvage boats.

When I finally had the opportunity to talk with Kane and asked him to explain this animosity, he looked at me as if I were from another planet. He did not have time for this crap, he said. He was in the business of finding treasure for his dad, not playing Dr. Ruth to a wanna-be treasure hunter, a nosy damned newspaperman at that. Or words to that effect.

At that time during the *Atocha* search, Kane was a bundle of raw nerves, scouring the ocean like a man possessed. In the summer of 1985, Kane was on a mission, the particulars of which he shared with no one, not even his mother and father. He was driven as only those who have experienced death and destruction and heartbreak can be driven. People observing him could only conclude, given his self-destructive behavior, that he saw himself as bulletproof. If he did not care for your looks or the way you carried yourself, he looked through you. If he saw you as a threat, he glared at you with eyes that seemed on fire.

Because his father tolerated me, Kane reluctantly reciprocated. I was an unavoidable nuisance, a tiny shell in his dive fin. So he grudgingly gave me a few moments of his time between trips to sea. His responses to most of my questions were curt and usually one-syllable. But the words that have always left an indelible impression on me were those at the conclusion of a fractured interview. Until that moment, his eyes had been focused at something over my left shoulder. But then they suddenly locked onto mine—eyes that offered no mercy, that reached deep into your soul. Yet, in a soft voice, totally void of anger, he said: "You know what? I'm just tired of all this shit. All you guys want to talk about is treasure. What was it like finding the *Margarita*? When will we find the *Atocha*? And when we do find it, what's all that damned treasure gonna be worth?"

Then he paused, as if to take measure of my fighting qualities, then said: "Let me tell you something—ain't nothing that can replace family. Ain't nothing worth more than family."

Kane is six-feet-six, and when he is peering down at you, unsmiling, his eyes glistening and his hands clenched at his side, you tend to grow a little weak in the knees. That's exactly how I felt that day, weak and intimidated. And foolish, too. He had every right to be angry with me, for I was far too captivated by gold and silver to remember the raw nerve that still twitched over the loss of my younger brother in Vietnam. In hot pursuit of a story no one else was following, I had failed to give Kane's personal demons any thought—or even to wonder if he had any.

To understand Kane Fisher circa mid-1980s it is necessary to view the Treasure Salvors, Inc., operation during that tumultuous time. Money was tight, tempers short, patience threadbare, and everyone had a theory about where the *Atocha*'s mother lode would be found. In 1973, retired U.S. Navy commander John Cryer compiled information on the 1622 Tierra Firme fleet and tracked its course during the hurricane that caused the *Atocha*'s sinking. He pinpointed the reef that tore out her bottom and the approximate location at which she went under—in 55 feet of water, on a line southeast of the Quicksands. Archaeologist Duncan Mathewson agreed with Cryer's finding, as did cartographer Ed Little, who had charted every discovery over the years and viewed a virtual straight line of artifacts leading away from the Quicksands toward deep water.

Mel was paranoid about deep water, however. He feared it to such a degree that by the spring of 1983 the mere mention of it would send shivers up his spine. Four hundred years earlier it was not uncommon to gaze upon a mariner's chart and see the notation, *Beyond this point there be monsters.* Mel would stare at his own salvage chart and run his finger in a southeasterly direction past the Quicksands, then suddenly freeze, for in his mind's eye he saw the mariner's warning of old.

Despite an abundance of evidence to the contrary, Mel had convinced himself that the *Atocha* rested somewhere within the shallow depths of the Quicksands. He liked the area's deep sands for several reasons, mainly because of its shallow water and because it continued to produce treasure. His unspoken reason was personal. Although his son Dirk had been insistent that he would find the bulk of the *Atocha*'s treasure in deep water, he had died in the attempt. Mel was not about to sacrifice anyone else just for the sake of finding treasure. Whenever I asked his assessment of deep water he said, "It's a spooky place to work."

Deep water was not only spooky but also cursed, at least in Mel's mind. Rather than go there, he relied on his own theories, one of which his salvage boat captains jokingly called the "pinball search." Although Fisher would huddle with lieutenants and formulate a comprehensive search plan, it usually would be discarded within hours of the salvage boat's arrival at the predetermined site. If the respective captain reported that nothing had been found diving on the first blown hole, Fisher would revert to the search tactics that prevailed in the late 1970s—bouncing from one anomaly to another, blowing a hole, making unsuccessful dives, then motoring to another anomaly. In the course of an eight-day trip, if the captain had used a crayon to record all of Mel's dictated changes in course, the result would have resembled a child's scribbling.

As winter embraced the Keys in 1983, bringing its stout winds and rough seas, the more knowledgeable members of Treasure Salvors, Inc., wished for only one thing: if only someone or some thing could divert Mel Fisher's attention to the deepwater area.

Their expectations would be answered by the most unlikely of salvors: Kane Fisher.

On paper, the chain of command of Treasure Salvors, Inc., was unequivocal: Mel Fisher was the supreme commander and Ted Miguel called the shots at sea. If something significant was discovered at any predetermined diving site, control of the ensuing excavation reverted to Duncan Mathewson; artifacts would be appropriately tagged and cataloged, and their location recorded on the ship's chart. If treasure was found in abundance or if timbers were located, as had been the case with the *Margarita*, PVC grids would be laid out at the site and everything properly photographed. Office staff, captains, and crews carried out their orders accordingly.

This organizational chart did not apply to Kane, captain of the *Dauntless*, who listened only to his own counsel. On the plus side, Kane possessed his father's uncanny instinct for finding treasure despite the absence of charts on the *Dauntless*. Kane navigated between the Marquesas and the Quicksands by motoring from buoy to buoy, each one representing a key point on the *Atocha* trail: the Bank of Spain, the *Atocha* cannons, or the *Atocha* anchor. Although Andy Matroci, who was the boat's first mate at the time, told me that Kane was quite adept at navigating in this manner, Matroci and the rest of the crew had no idea what location they would be working on any given day until the boat's anchors dropped. They were merely means to an end, props for a stage on which Kane Fisher was viewed as a one-man show.

The learning curve under Kane's command was fuzzy at best. Matroci noticed that some of the crew had no diving experience whatsoever and that R. D. LeClair, Kane's first mate, had little patience with rookies. "I kept asking him questions and he kept getting pissed off. I wasn't trying to be a pain in the ass; I just wanted to know what it was, exactly, that I was supposed to be doing," said Matroci. "Finally R. D. says, 'No more questions. If you want to know something about this operation, go get some books.' I ask him what books I should get, and he says, 'Dammit, I said no more questions.' That was one strange first experience with those guys."

It wasn't until midsummer 1981 that Kane and his crew finally accepted Matroci. Scouring the hardpan bottom, Matroci fanned away the sand from a solution hole and discovered a gold bar. He immediately surfaced, deposited the bar into the hands of Kim Fisher, then returned to the bottom and discovered a second bar.

"Just like that," Matroci said, "I became one of the guys. I was finally accepted because I'd found gold."

In an effort to make himself feel as if he were contributing more to the operation than simply finding treasure, plus growing weary of not knowing where he was at sea, Matroci enlisted the aid of Syd Jones, asking the *Swordfish*'s captain to teach him the basics of underwater archaeology and the finer points of keeping charts and plotting the areas he worked with the Del Norte navigation system. Kane also recorded his ship's Del Norte information, albeit reluctantly. Kane, like his father, had an inherent mistrust of anyone who might steal what he viewed as rightfully his. There were too many people out there who would love to pilfer the *Atocha*'s treasure, so why make it easy for them by providing a damn map?

It was late 1983 when Matroci, after 20 months of recording data on the ship's charts, reached the same conclusion that Commander Cryer, Eugene Lyon, and Duncan Mathewson had reached 10 years earlier: the *Atocha* had traveled northwest when she lost her cannons. When Matroci started to explain his theory, Kane smiled and said, "Yeah, I know. She came from the southeast." Knowing he had an ally, Matroci said they could find the main pile before anyone else by plotting a line from where the nine *Atocha* cannons were discovered toward the southeast, varying

Andy Matroci examines several of the gold coins he recovered from the *Atocha*.

their search pattern by one degree in either direction if nothing was found. Kane had already reached that conclusion.

Throughout the next 18 months the *Dauntless* slowly worked down the "Line" in 15-meter increments, making meticulous circle searches. More often than not, the crew's efforts achieved nothing—no treasure, no ballast, no artifacts whatsoever. But gradually the Line extended, much to the amusement of fellow divers, who, while experiencing the rush of finding an occasional gold bar or coin in the Quicksands, would point toward the distant horizon and say that the *Dauntless* was "somewhere out there stuck in the mud." Rival captains believed there was no money to be found in the deep water, echoing the sentiments of Mel Fisher, who in the summer of 1984 found himself strapped for cash. Once again, regular paychecks were a thing of the past, and some of the divers were able to sustain themselves only by using food stamps.

There seemed to be a correlation between finding treasure and being laid off. In 1981 and again in 1983, despite the glut of treasure being excavated from the *Margarita*, Fisher had exhausted his corporate funds and had no recourse but to lay off most of his diving crews. Investors had grown wary of his on-again, off-again salvage exploits, and the only sure way Mel knew of keeping an infusion of cash flowing was to continue bringing up more gold.

"You can't run a salvage operation of this size without investors, and the only way you continue to get investors and keep them happy is by bringing up treasure. No more wild-goose chases," Mel would tell Kane, admonishing him for searching anywhere but in the treasure-laden Quicksands. To appease his father, Kane reluctantly would abandon his deepwater search for a few weeks, then tire of the drudgery of scouring the deep sands, raise anchor, and head back southeast to the Line, which, depending on the exact compass bearing, was an area between 5 and 7½ miles in length. It would prove to be a continual game of cat and mouse between father and son, for until proof to the contrary was ascertained, Mel Fisher would not move from the shallower water.

It wasn't until the fall of 1984 that Mel finally became a believer in his son's efforts. It began innocently enough, said Matroci, when divers Ed Hinkle and "Cocktail Bill" Reighard came up with the most telling of artifacts, a square spike. In the days that followed, the Line was extended by the discovery of other remnants of the doomed vessel—a single musket ball, then a cannon ball, another twisted 12-inch spike, and then barrel hoops. Finally Mel Fisher was convinced that the hull of the *Atocha* and its 47 tons of silver and gold most definitely lay southeast of where the *Atocha* cannons and anchor had been found. All of the company's assets and energy would now be concentrated on "Kane's Trail."

"Just like that," Matroci said, "our Line became 'Kane's Trail.' Not our trail, but Kane's. But at least everyone was now on the same page."

✸

Seventeen years later, when this book was under way, Kane Fisher's demeanor had softened with age. No longer the company's loose cannon, no longer the hell-raiser of old—no longer challenging authority while being able to get away with it because he was Mel Fisher's son—he could reminisce about the seemingly unending search for his father's Ghost Galleon without the rage building up inside.

In 2001, Kane was 41 and lived in Vero Beach with his wife, Karen, and their five children. His oldest son is named Dirk. Vero, Kane said, is more family-oriented than Key West. It also keeps him close to his mother. He continues to carry on his father's legacy, diving regularly on the remnants of the 1715 fleet. But not with the passion of yesterday.

Kane does not know why he held on to his grief for so many years. Kane told me that there is no explaining why, even though Dirk had everything going for him, had every reason to live a long and prosperous life, that God chose to end it so abruptly. There also is no way of Kane's explaining his outrageous behavior. He said that maybe it was his belief that he should have died that night in the water instead of Dirk. Maybe that is what compelled him to burn one bridge after another, distancing himself from friends and family.

"What you have to understand is that Dirk was my hero. I idolized him," Kane told me, sharing publicly for the first time his most private thoughts. "All I wanted to do was be like him; find treasure for Dad like Dirk did. And when he drowned that night, when there was nothing I could do to save him, something inside me died with him."

He remembers the overwhelming emptiness he felt on July 20, 1975, when he embraced his mother and father at the Key West dock, having to find the courage to explain how the *Northwind* had flipped over, trapping his brother belowdeck. Having to explain that Dirk was dead and that he had survived. Kane remembers the conversation verbatim. He remembers the incessant interviews with the sheriff's deputies and the Coast Guard personnel. He even remembers what he ate that day—Kentucky Fried Chicken.

But most of all he remembers the guilt, the rage, the unremitting screams from deep inside him that had no outlet other than rebellion.

So he became the ultimate dissenter, pure and simple. Maintaining his boat was someone else's responsibility. Taking orders were for the other captains and crews. Kane would do as he damned well pleased. There were no recriminations, no reprimands from his father. Only silence, the unspoken grief that father and son shared.

"Dad never spoke to me about Dirk's death. It was just too much for him," says Kane. "From that day forward, all we talked about was finding the *Atocha*. He had his own ideas where she was. Everyone had a different theory where she went down. Of course, they were all wrong. Me? I knew where we'd find her all along because I was following Dirk's plan. He knew she'd gone down in the deeper water. And he would have found her except . . ."

Kane lowered his head and looked away. Understandably, this is a subject that still eats away at him, so he politely flipped the figurative calendar and forged ahead, reminiscing about helping find the *Margarita* and how comical it was to be returning to port on that day in 1981, with the *Virgilona* struggling to make headway with only one engine. She sat low in the water because of the preponderance of silver bars and thousands of silver coins, treasure that was estimated to be worth at least $4 million. And trailing behind in his ship's wake was a flotilla of Cuban boats, part of the Mariel boatlift, refugees who had asked Kane and his crew to lead the way to freedom, to the shores of Key West. Kane laughed at these memories. And then he grew serious once again as he recounted the frustration in the three years that followed, searching Hawk Channel without success.

"Everyone had their theory where the *Atocha* was, and I had mine—Dirk's theory," Kane said. "I knew those cannon he'd found just didn't drop there from out of the sky. I knew they'd come from the gun deck, once the second hurricane had struck and ripped loose the ship's upper structure. And I knew there was no way in hell that second hurricane had disturbed 47 tons of treasure. The *Atocha* was somewhere between the outer reef and where Dirk had found the nine cannon. Dirk knew it; I knew it. So I just followed his lead."

This pursuit was not a one-man show. Andy Matroci shared Kane's belief, as did the rest of the *Dauntless* crew, that the prized galleon lay in deeper water. And, yes, the Line they searched was a team effort, and it was the *Dauntless*'s trail.

"Dad is the one who dubbed it Kane's Trail. I had nothing to do with that," Kane said. "No one is stupid enough to believe that one person was responsible for finding that ship. If someone believes that it was all my doing, then I apologize. Nothing out there on the *Atocha* trail got done without teamwork. And even though some folks thought that I didn't know what the hell I was doing, I ignored them and stuck with what my gut told me to do—follow Dirk's lead. In that regard only, I made it happen.

"To be honest with you, though, the treasure didn't mean shit to me. If I could dump all of it back into the ocean and get my brother back, I'd do it in a heartbeat."

But that was impossible, so he continued to search for the *Atocha*. He was driven to find the galleon, and only then would he be able to get on with his life.

"What you've gotta understand is that when I returned home the day after Dirk died, I wrote in my mother's Bible that I wouldn't give up the search until I died. I'd lost my brother

Dirk Fisher holding the
astrolabe.

searching for that ship and no way was I going to give up looking
for her. I had to find the *Atocha*, no matter what. I had to do it for
Dirk."

Ten years to the day after his brother's drowning, Kane kept
his promise.

14

Mother Lode

There was chest on chest full of Spanish gold, with a ton of plate in the middle hold, and the cabins riot of stuff untold.

—Young E. Allison

E ven sea gypsies have their limits. The crew of the *Dauntless* was tired of diving day after day with little to show for its efforts. Tired of being ridiculed back in port: "Oh, you're one of *them*—one of ol' man Fisher's treasure divers, huh," which was always followed by laughter. They were tired of missed paychecks, the grueling work and spartan living conditions at sea. They were even getting tired of each other.

It was Thursday, July 18, 1985, and the crew was running out of light and patience. Nothing new about that. Kane Fisher had run out of tolerance months ago, thinking that any day his divers would find the *Atocha* and her 47 tons of treasure. But all he and his divers had found were pottery shards and twisted iron spikes, stuff only an archaeologist would find appealing. In the past four weeks his divers had explored almost 100 magnetometer hits, to no avail. Today had been more of the same, and now, because of the 54-foot depth, all but two divers had reached their limit of bottom time.

Kane paced the deck, keeping one eye on the bubbles off the starboard gunwale that popped to the surface from his divers, the other on the horizon. Storm clouds were moving in, a sign that Hurricane Bob was about ready to strike. Kane shook his head in exasperation, then moved to the wheelhouse, to be alone with his frustration.

"You wouldn't believe the aggravation we'd gone through," Mel's youngest son would recall years later. "It was driving all of us nuts; everyone was on edge. We knew she was near, maybe in the next hole or the next. Sixteen years of this shit, that's what we'd lived with. Sixteen years of being teased, being frustrated, coming up empty."

Three boats were working "Kane's Trail," the southeastern line running from the Quicksands to the outer reef. The *Bookmaker*, under the command of Kim Fisher, had magged the area the day before and recorded seven promising hits; the *Swordfish* dropped buoys on these, and Kane and his *Dauntless* divers investigated five of the anomalies and came up empty. Divers on the *Swordfish* had better luck at their site, bringing an encrusted heavy iron mass to the surface and discovering that they had found a 17th-century swivel gun. The tension on both boats was unbearable. The crew on each boat wanted nothing more than to be the one who finally found the *Atocha*'s mother lode.

It was 6:30 P.M. Daylight was rapidly fading as Kane Fisher entered the water with Steve Swindell. It was Kane's first dive of the day. He had no more than reached the flat, heavily silted bottom when his metal detector started buzzing. No matter where he placed it, it buzzed. "The entire bottom was alive," he would recall. The first thing he noticed was a 60-pound chunk of ballast. Nearby, protruding from the mud and silt, was the neck from a large olive jar. A barrel hoop lay exposed, surrounded by pottery shards. Kane grabbed the hoop and surfaced. He had been in the water fewer than three minutes.

Andy Matroci and Greg Wareham were killing time on deck when they heard Kane yelling at the dive ladder. Kane tossed the remnants of the barrel hoop onto the deck, then returned to the bottom. As Matroci bent down to retrieve the hoop, he saw a blackened silver coin at his feet. He turned to Wareham and asked if Kane had said anything about silver coins. Before Wareham could respond, Matroci held up the barrel hoop and said, "You ain't gonna believe this shit." Four more silver coins were attached to the encrusted remnants of the hoop.

Back at the bottom, Kane tapped Swindell on the shoulder to get his attention, then with forked fingers pointed to his eyes and then to the lumpy shadows directly in front of him. Because of the poor visibility, Swindell was at first baffled by Kane's emphatic gestures. When his eyes finally adjusted to the murky surroundings, he saw why Kane was excited—a chest of silver coins half buried in the mud, surrounded by copper ingots. Swindell grabbed one of the ingots while Kane scooped up handfuls of coins, and then they surfaced.

Too many times in the preceding 18 months Kane had thought he was on the verge of finding the *Atocha*'s mother lode. Too often he had been burned, getting on the radio and excitedly relaying the news to his father back in port. And then nothing would be found on the next dive or those that followed, and he would have to radio Mel again and give him the disheartening news.

"You can only eat crow so much," Kane would say as darkness descended on the site. "Let's keep this to ourselves until we know for sure."

He and Swindell returned to the bottom and retrieved six more copper ingots and approximately 100 silver coins; then dive operations were suspended for the night as the crew waited out the approaching storm. Conversation over dinner was forced. Sleep was fitful, despite gentle seas rocking the boat.

The next day was more of the same. The divers recovered a few thousand more coins and scores of copper ingots, several unidentifiable iron pieces, and silver plates and spoons. Normally when a salvage boat captain blows a new hole, he shifts the boat's anchor lines 30 feet in either direction of the last hole. In this instance, Kane Fisher shifted the boat only five feet at a time, knowing he might be sitting on the *Atocha*'s mother lode. New holes were blown and the divers continued to find treasure throughout the day. Soon five-gallon buckets filled with coins were stacked all over the deck. But when Kane finally radioed Treasure Salvors headquarters that afternoon, Mel questioned the significance of their discovery because no silver bars had been found.

Archaeologist Duncan Mathewson visited the site that day and was not impressed. He told Kane and his crew that the coins and barrel hoops had not come from the *Atocha*. Instead, the artifacts obviously had been dumped by the *Margarita* when she was breaking apart.

The crew sat on the deck in dejection that night, each questioning Mathewson's verdict that the *Atocha* had not been found. The archaeologist must be wrong, Bill Barron said. No way could anyone make such an asinine assumption, not after having seen the array of copper ingots and pieces of eight; coins by the handful, by the bucketful.

Saturday, July 20. For the past nine years, this day had been one of mourning and remembrance for the Fisher family. Ten years ago, just when everyone thought the *Atocha* was within their grasp, Dirk and Angel Fisher and Rick Gage had died when the *Northwind* capsized. Now Kane and his crew had narrowed a 363-year-old nautical mystery to a small stretch of sand and silt resting 54 feet below the surface.

At 8:15 A.M. Kane lowered the blowers over the ship's props and began blowing the day's first hole. The first set of divers entered the water 45 minutes later and found coins, pottery, and barrel hoops. The second diving pair surfaced at 11:00 A.M. with handfuls of blackened pieces of eight. The boat was shifted five feet to starboard, and the day's third hole was blown. It was now Andy Matroci's and Greg Wareham's turn to dive.

Matroci said it was a gut feeling that prompted him to suggest to Wareham that they disregard diving on the hole and instead do a bit of exploring by swimming to the southeast. Who knows?

Maybe they just might find something spectacular. Wareham thought it was worth a try. They entered the water at approximately 11:30 A.M. and, with the aid of Matroci's compass, moved to the southeast, parallel to each other.

To this day Wareham and Matroci disagree as to how far they swam away from the hole. Matroci claimed it was only 50 feet, Wareham said 100 feet.

All Matroci saw was pristine rippling sand. No treasure, no timbers.

What greeted Wareham's eyes froze him in his fins and sent his heart racing.

"Everything's so cloudy, so dark," Wareham said. "Then I see this huge clump materialize up ahead from out of the shadows, and the closer I got all I could think was *Holy shit.*"

Silver bars were sticking up out of the mud everywhere, jutting up and out at odd angles. Wareham's hands started trembling. He moved closer, then spotted the rotted remnants of a ship's timbers and "an honest-to-goodness treasure chest—just like you read about in those pirate books."

Wareham's first instinct was to rush to the treasure chest. He paused, then rubbed his shaking fingers over the ship's timbers. Silver was silver, he said; the timbers were history, something few people are ever blessed enough to touch. That completed, he turned and went in search of Matroci, who, frustrated that his hunch had not paid dividends, was about to return to the blown hole.

"Just as I started to go back, I felt this hard rap on my shoulder. Scared the shit out of me. When I turned, there was Greg— his face was literally exploding, his eyes were bulging, and he was frantically waving his arms up and down and pointing somewhere off in the distance," said Matroci, who shot past Wareham in the direction his diving partner pointed.

Visibility was murky, eight feet at best. Matroci had traveled no more than 30 feet when he hit the brakes, dumbfounded by what he saw. Rising out of the blue-gray shadows were straight lines that looked like blackened loaves of bread—silver bars stacked atop each other. The bars were stacked four feet high, 20 feet wide, and 75 feet long. His first thought: It's a lobster condominium. The antennae of lobsters seemed to protrude from every crevice of the stack of silver. Thousands of silver coins covered the sand at the base of the silver bars.

Matroci and Wareham hugged each other, shook hands, and then paused to catch their breath. Knowing nothing in their lives would ever again be the same, they circled the mound of silver in a daze, pausing from time to time to reach with trembling fingers to stroke the bars. And then Matroci picked up one of the 80-pound bars, hoisting it as far as his kneecaps, then carefully replaced it. This was his way of pinching himself to make sure he wasn't dreaming. And then the divers decided it was time to share the discovery with their captain and crewmates.

Matroci's and Wareham's heads burst through the rolling surface shortly after noon, their words reverberating from one salvage boat to the other: "It's here, it's all here. The mother lode! It's right down here."

Kane Fisher immediately scrambled to the wheelhouse, grabbed his radio's microphone, and called Treasure Salvors headquarters. His words resonated throughout the renovated warehouse: "Put the charts away. We've got it, we've got it—silver bars!"

Captain Tom Ford had pulled the *Swordfish* alongside the *Dauntless* minutes earlier. Knowing that Kane was on to something spectacular and sensing that today would indeed be the day that Mel Fisher's dreams would come true, Ford had asked for and received permission to join them. He no sooner had positioned his boat than he saw Matroci and Wareham pop out of the water and heard them shouting that they had found a pile of silver bars.

As divers from both boats entered the water—everyone shouting and screaming, stricken by treasure dementia—the storm moved in, pelting the crews with a stiff, hard rain. Then the wind intensified, churning up five-foot seas, which enhanced the insanity of the moment.

Andy Matroci wanted nothing more than to reenter the water and glimpse the silver bars once again, but he was called to the radio. Mel was on the line. Matroci recalled the ensuing conversation as the highlight of his life. Not only had he and Wareham put the big X on Mel's treasure map, but also he got to tell Mel what his dream looked like—an immense reef of silver bars with lobsters living in it.

"To this very day I can still hear Mel's laughter," said Matroci. "After everything that had happened to him over the past 16 years, it was good to hear him laugh. I could hear everyone back in the office yelling and shouting. I guess it was just as insane back there."

Once Matroci broke the connection, he joined the massed confusion at the main pile, where 15 other divers hovered over the treasure horde. Syd Jones was the first of the *Swordfish* divers to examine the mother lode, then his wife, K. T., and J. J. Bettencourt dived on the site. K. T. had come prepared, wearing a brand-new BC (buoyancy control device), knowing she would be unable to bring a silver bar to the surface without it. Even though she said she had prepared herself mentally for what she might someday see, the wreck site stunned her. "Silver bars and lobsters everywhere," she said. "And right in the middle of all these silver bars, standing like a sentinel, was a World War II practice bomb."

Once K. T. and her colleagues determined that the 500-pound bomb posed no threat, she decided to bring a silver bar to the surface. Every diver had a mental checklist of items he or she most desired to extract from the sea. K. T. had already found more than most: gold jewelry, gold coins, and gold chains. But at the top of her list was a silver bar, so she went for it.

"I know I shouldn't have done it, that I should have waited until we'd properly mapped the site and carried out the proper archaeology," she said. "But I just couldn't help myself."

She enlisted the aid of Bettencourt, but despite their efforts they could not hoist the 80-pound bar more than a few feet off the bottom. Greg Wareham joined them and released their weight belts, which allowed K. T. and Bettencourt to drift slowly to the surface. With the massive coral-encrusted bar in hand, which sliced into their fingers as if it were coated with razor blades, they surfaced downcurrent from the boat. They could not drop the bar because divers were below them; they might crush someone's head. Nor could they swim the bar back down to the bottom because they had exhausted their tanks' air supply. In desperation, they waddled their way to the boat, and then struggled to grab hold of the dive ladder. Finally the treasure was hoisted onto the *Swordfish*'s deck.

As to who gets the credit or the blame for recovering the first silver bar, Tom Ford had no doubts whatsoever—it most definitely was a team effort. Because of the intense competition between boats, the crews of both raced to the bottom, intent on being the first to recover treasure from the mother lode. Ford could not recall who brought the basket to the bottom, but that he and his crew loaded it with silver bars, surfaced, and then began hoisting the basket and bars onto the boat. While Paul Busch filmed the event with his 8mm camera, Ford and the rest of his crew pulled on the ropes like wild men, straining to get those bars to the surface.

"Basically, we all lost our minds at the same time; we all went nuts at the same moment," Ford said. "That's what treasure fever does to you, and each person who was out there has to come to terms with their own guilt. It wasn't just one person screwing up out there—it was all of us."

The guilt was only an issue because archaeologist Duncan Mathewson made it one. Mathewson found himself in an impossible situation that Saturday, attempting to monitor the recovery site from shore via ship-to-shore radio. When he pleaded for the divers not to disturb the archaeological integrity of the wreck, to quit bringing silver bars to the service, the divers ignored him.

After all, for years they had been searching in vain for the *Atocha*'s mother lode. Now that they had found it, everyone wanted to personally excavate a small portion of her riches. And they did so unabated for at least two hours. Mathewson's response was to fall back on his academic principles, castigating the crews of the *Dauntless* and the *Swordfish* two days later for raping and pillaging the wreck site.

This did not set well with the divers, who thought of Mathewson as Mel Fisher's deskbound marionette. While Mathewson pontificated in comfort on shore, the divers did all the grunt work. Who the hell was Mathewson to tell *them* what they should or should not do? The divers thought of themselves as seagoing warriors; they appreciated only those officers who led from the front, not the rear. You earn respect; you cannot command it. As such, the divers responded to Mathewson's condemnation by saying, "What we get paid to do is find treasure and bring it up; that's why we're called treasure salvors."

Mel Fisher eventually was able to get both sides to meet in the middle, and respect for the archaeology of the site became the rule of thumb after the first day's treasure gluttony. But 17 years after the incident, which everyone calls "The Great Silver Bar Orgy," Mathewson's accusations remain an exposed nerve.

The *Dauntless* crew members collectively washed their hands of guilt by picking on the easiest target, the only woman diver, K. T. Budde-Jones. Sure, Kane Fisher had often vowed that when they found the mother lode, they would bring up all the treasure in one day. "But it wasn't us that started the feeding frenzy," said Andy Matroci years after the fact. "When Kane saw K. T. bring up that first bar, he said, 'All right, let's bring some stuff up.' There was no stopping Kane now."

The *Dauntless* crew—Thomas Barham, Frank Lutz, Bill Moore, Bill Barron, Del Scruggs, Chuck Sotzin, Steve Swindell, Matroci, and Wareham—started an ad hoc bucket brigade, attaching rope to milk crates and buckets to hoist the silver bars from the bottom to the surface. With the steady rain and heavy seas,

Diver K. T. Budde-Jones uses
an airlift to remove sediment
around the *Atocha* mother
lode site.

the deck of the *Dauntless* soon was awash and slick with silver
oxide. Divers lost their footing and slammed elbows and knees
against unyielding steel, shouted expletives, and then resumed the
madness as they dove back into the turbulent ocean.

Tom Ford's memories of the silver orgy remain vivid—watching helplessly as bar after bar was brought up from the bottom
and dropped onto the *Dauntless*'s deck. Ford could not complain
too loudly because silver bars were stacked on his deck, too. But
after the first frenzied hour, he finally came to his senses. Fearing
that all of the *Atocha*'s archaeological data would be destroyed,
Ford sent Syd Jones and Michael More down to the silver bar
reef to establish a benchmark, a stake driven into the bedrock
from which measurements could be made. Quickly they estab-
lished a north–south line that extended 300 feet from the main

pile. A few days later, Jerry Cash would arrive from port and begin taking precise measurements, dividing the entire area into precise grids. And while Cash was doing this, Ford said that he, Syd, and K. T. began recording where every item had been found.

Kane wanted to blow holes at the main pile.

"I was able to stop Kane from doing that, but he knew that he was *really* in charge of the operation because he was a Fisher," said Ford. "Kane's outlook was 'Fuck art, let's dance.'"

Kane did lightly dust the site at about 2:00 P.M., knocking off the centuries of built-up silt from the treasure, plus exposing the expanse of *Atocha* timbers. "And that's when the mad dash really began, to make sure we got all of the archaeological data correct," Ford said. "It was a horrible experience. I had arguments with everyone, even those divers who should have known better than to destroy the recovery site."

The silver bar orgy went unabated for another hour. As the afternoon wore on, Mel Fisher was on the radio, telling Andy Matroci that all treasure recovery must stop immediately. Jim Sinclair, one of the company's conservators, heard Mel's explicit orders, then accompanied Matroci to the boat's dive ladder, where Kane Fisher was winching silver bars from the bottom, using a basket. When Matroci told Kane that his father wanted all salvage to cease, Kane said, "The hell with that," then slid beneath the waves.

The combination of exhaustion and the ongoing storm finally brought a halt to the treasure frenzy at about 4:00 P.M. But the damage had been done. Stacked on the deck of the *Dauntless* were 175 silver bars, almost eight tons of treasure. The boat was listing badly and riding low in the water, in danger of sinking. That evening the crews transferred half of the booty to the *Swordfish* and stacked the bars belowdeck, making sure the weight was evenly dispersed.

The excitement back at Treasure Salvors headquarters was almost as feverish as that at the recovery site. Bleth McHaley had been on the telephone since 1:00 P.M., first calling *National*

Geographic headquarters, then contacting every major newspaper from coast to coast. Although no one was certain exactly how much treasure had been found, Bleth placed the dollar amount at $400 million. Mel, who stood at Bleth's side throughout the day to supply a firsthand touch to reporters' inquiries, said the treasure might be valued as high as $600 million. Mathewson lent his expertise, telling reporters that undoubtedly this was the greatest of all maritime discoveries, one that ranked alongside the unearthing of the city of Pompeii or the discovery of King Tut's tomb.

By Sunday afternoon, amid a lull in the storm, more than 400 newspaper reporters and newscasters from every major television network had descended on the Key West headquarters, each trying to corner Mel Fisher. They failed to connect, however, because Mel; his wife, Deo; daughter, Taffi; son, Kim; Mathewson; and Don Kincaid had motored to the wreck site Sunday morning, bringing with them 32 bottles of champagne. Once there, Mel and Deo donned diving gear and slowly descended far below.

"I just couldn't stop crying, even with the regulator in my mouth," Deo Fisher recalled years later. "After all those years of doubting our own sanity, our dreams had finally come true. And there was Mel, as always, leading the way, my hand in his as we slowly descended toward our dream. And then the main pile came into our view. . . . My God, I just could not stop the tears."

Kincaid journeyed to the bottom with Mel and Deo to photograph the moment. It took every ounce of composure he could muster not to be overwhelmed. Kincaid managed to steady his camera as Mel reached out to lay his hand on the mound of treasure.

"Mel's hand was trembling so bad that all he could do was brush the back of it over the silver bars," said Kincaid, who, at that instant, pressed the camera's trigger and recorded Fisher beaming proudly as he touched his lifelong dream.

Once everyone was back aboard ship, the celebration began in earnest aboard the *Dauntless* and her sister salvage vessels, the *Swordfish, J. B. Magruder, Bookmaker,* and *Virgilona,* which were

The aging, rusty *Dauntless*, from which divers and airlifts were sent to the bottom to help recover 30 tons of silver bars.

anchored stern-to-stern directly over the recovery site. Champagne corks popped, plastic glasses were raised in salute, and everyone toasted the *Atocha* and the man who had found her: Mel Fisher, the greatest treasure hunter the world had ever known. "Now, I wasn't crying, mind you," Mel would say, laughing off the moment. "But there were a lot of tears because I finally came to the end of the rainbow and saw the pot of gold."

But by no means was the glory all his, Fisher insisted. A lot of hard work by a lot of fantabulous people had gone into the search. Everyone deserved credit, especially his "Golden Crew," the kids who not only had believed in him but also had stayed with him through all those years of frustration.

The champagne had no more than been poured when Jimmy Buffett pulled alongside the *Dauntless*. Buffett had been fewer than two miles away, engaged in a photo shoot for his latest album, using Mel's salvage relic *Arbutus* as a backdrop, when he heard about the discovery on his boat's radio. Soon he was sitting on a

Jimmy Buffett, right, sitting next to Mel Fisher on July 21, 1985. The silver bars had been recovered from the *Atocha* the previous day.

pile of silver bars, Mel Fisher at his side, singing the chords of "A Pirate Looks at Forty":

> Mother, mother ocean, I have heard your call
> Wanted to sail your waters since I was three feet tall . . .
> And in your belly you hold the treasures few have ever seen
> Most of 'em dreams, most of 'em dreams.

"It was a pretty cool moment, this being a dream no more," said Donnie Jonas, who was there for the free concert that Sunday but did not participate in the initial discovery because his boat, the *Magruder*, had been tied up at shore because of a contractual dispute with Treasure Salvors, Inc. For the past seven months, Jonas had been trying to renegotiate a new contract with Mel Fisher for a higher percentage of the *Atocha* treasure. When Mel balked, Jonas said he was going to sell the boat for $150,000 and that the boat would remain at dock until the right buyer came along. When the mother lode was discovered, Fisher immediately purchased the *Magruder*, named Jonas captain, and sent him and his crew to sea. Said Jonas: "It's the only battle I ever won with Mel."

Mel Fisher partied with his crews until late Sunday afternoon, then left for Key West because the storm was again intensifying. Hurricane Bob, downgraded now to a tropical storm, blew through the Marquesas early Monday morning just as I arrived at the recovery site.

I missed Buffett's concert because I had been attending my wife's 20th high school class reunion in Belvidere, Illinois. I was a reluctant attendee, knowing the *Atocha* might be found any day. Then again, I had already spent the better part of the summer at sea, away from my wife and daughters. My options were limited— keeping my marriage or losing the mother lode. As it turned out, I got the best of both worlds. My wife and I were on the dance floor that Saturday night when the music was interrupted by the announcement that I had an urgent telephone call. The caller was Bleth McHaley, who said, "We found her—a reef of silver bars. Mel says for you to get your butt back down here."

Which I did, catching a red-eye flight to Miami, then renting a car and making the three-hour drive to Key West. Captain Tom Ford escorted me to the site on the *Swordfish* just in time to experience the storm's full wrath. I was terrified by the combination of howling wind, stinging rain, and the six-foot waves that lifted the salvage boat, suspending us momentarily in midair before dropping us back down with a heart-stopping jolt. All I could do was hold on for dear life as I rode on a nautical roller coaster. Casting leery eyes to starboard, I saw nothing but a wall of darkness, an angry sky stabbing into a skewed horizon from which endless waves marched toward us, onward and onward, slicing through a near-blinding sheet of rain. In that moment of breathless anxiety, it appeared to me as if we had been singled out by Mother Nature herself, vindictively caught within her crosshairs.

A sudden cry of pain came from my left, where Bill Barron knelt near the dive ladder, hovering over a clump of blackened silver coins. He had slipped on the deck, almost losing his grip on the treasure. He quickly recovered his balance, however, scraping his knee first against the railing and then on the rusted deck. But not to worry, he yelled. The bloody knee would heal soon enough. Of greater importance, he had managed to hold on to the 150-pound slab of silver and not drop it into the water.

Barron smiled, yelled for me to quit fretting and enjoy the moment, then merrily went about his work hoisting more treasure from the *Atocha*'s 363-year-old watery tomb. I nodded and forced a grin, then tried to swallow, but found it difficult because it seemed as if my stomach were lodged in my throat. My fear was all too obvious. My knuckles were white from my death grip on the ship's railing, my right arm numb from the tightly wrapped rope snaking up my biceps, the lifeline that secured me to the ship's deck. It was impossible to take notes, so I took in the chaotic panorama with my eyes, which I knew were as big as saucers, my mind trying to record all about me. It was no easy task, for nothing anyone could have said could have forewarned me about the actuality of surviving at sea in a storm.

Mel Fisher had tried his best to dissuade me earlier that morning, reminding me that the sea, even during the best of times, was no place for the faint or weak-hearted. Surviving a storm was another matter altogether. But I had told him not to fear, that I was up to the task. Bravado had overridden better judgment, which was stupid of me. But no way was I going to miss the opportunity of a lifetime, not when Mel had rewarded me with the best seat in the house. While journalists from all over the world and television crews from every major network were back at port waiting for the story to come to them, I was being allowed to participate in it firsthand.

It was midafternoon and all around me the crews of the four salvage boats went about their business, hoisting treasure from the trembling hands of the 28 divers in the water. Confusion does not begin to describe the scene. It was a mad scramble of men and women battling the elements, divers entering and exiting the water, shouting instructions and encouragement to one another, trying to hear and to be heard over the roar of the wind.

There was a shout to my right. The boat lifted, then settled back into the water. Only then did I see the bobbing head of diver K. T. Budde-Jones, who had spit out her regulator and bellowed her discovery to those of us on deck. Clasped tightly in her left hand was a worm-eaten, encrusted board. She eased her way to the side of the ship, riding the crest of a wave, then braced herself against the steel hull and carefully handed the slab of wood to crew member Mike More. To all outward appearances, the board did not seem like much. To an archaeologist, though, the artifact was priceless—a section of a Spanish treasure chest. Before now, none had been found. But far below the waves were a score of such chests, most of which were still intact, having been buried under five feet of sand and silt for more than three centuries.

Treasure chests, pocket sundials, ancient sewing needles, the sole of a leather boot, the scabbard of a dagger, animal bones, and the ship's timbers. Artifacts by the hundreds were being lifted from the *Atocha's* tomb, the most spectacular of which was the silver—hundreds of massive encrusted bars and tens of thousands of silver coins, those legendary pieces of eight that the fictional pirate Long John Silver had sold his soul for.

As I watched in amazement, the mounds of coins and blackened silver bars stacked on the ship's deck grew larger and larger, the residue of silver oxide rendering the bounding deck even more treacherous. But I did not have to worry about slipping on the residue and being cast into the sea. Although my knees were shaking out of control, no way could I possibly move; I was immobilized by fear as the story and the storm unfolded all around me.

As the day wore on, it became impossible to continue salvage operations. And that's when I joined Mike More, who stood at the railing of the *Swordfish*, oblivious to the rain and howling wind, his mind 54 feet below the towering seas, where he had touched mounds of treasure only moments before. The 30-year-old native of Seattle, Washington, said he should have been excited. Instead, he felt an overpowering sadness.

"For all these years it has always been the *elusive Atocha*. Where is she? Will we find her today or maybe tomorrow? But now the mystery is gone," he said.

Soon, anchors were weighed and we painstakingly returned to port.

15

A Tale of Two Kings

The most precious treasure is never fully known . . . The jewel
on the forehead of the Golden Buddha is only half-visible to
common men.

—Lu Yu

The media had him boxed in. It was Tuesday, July 23,
three days after the discovery of the *Atocha*'s mother
lode, and Mel Fisher suffered the ills of a serious hang-
over as he sat on the front steps of his Greene Street museum.
His head throbbed, his throat was parched, and he badly needed
a drink. But he fought the urge to get up and walk away, as was
his habit when he tired of any confrontation.

"Tell you what, kid," Mel said, pulling me to his side as, with
bloodshot eyes, he squinted into the maze of television and newspaper cameramen pressing in on us as they jockeyed for position.
"You know almost as much about this thing as me. So you sit here
and tell 'em a few stories while I go get me some rum."

When Mel saw my panic, he laughed and added, "Just kid-
ding." And then he forced a smile, lit another cigarette, and
patiently answered questions. To his left were reporters from
the *New York Times* and the *Washington Post*, to his right were

magazine writers from *Life* and *Time*, and in front of him were reporters from the rest of the Americas, not to mention Germany,
Italy, England, and Japan.

Mel tried his best to accommodate everyone, wading through
the repetitious questions: Yes, he said for the hundredth time,
finding all that silver certainly was fantabulous. And then he
posed for the cameramen, sitting atop a stack of silver bars just
inside the museum's entrance. That task completed, Bleth McHaley whispered in Mel's ear that it was now time for the *Today* show
interview. Mel nodded, then turned to the media and said, "You'll
have to excuse me, I've gotta pee." And then he took me by the
arm, ushered me into the museum and out the back entrance,
offering his apologies to McHaley and the television crew, telling
them he would return in a few minutes.

We paused at the old navy docks west of the museum to
watch Mel's divers unload tons of silver bars from the *Swordfish*
and the *Dauntless*. The divers paused in their million-dollar manual labor, ignoring the rain and joking with Mel about their job
security, wondering what the hell they were going to do now that
they made his dreams come true. Mel merely chuckled and said
there was enough treasure out there to keep them all busy for at
least the next two years. That seemed to satisfy everyone, and
they continued hoisting 80-pound silver ingots off the salvage
boats and loading them onto the flatbeds of a Jeep, a Land Rover,
and a dilapidated pickup truck.

Mel then bummed a cigarette and said, "C'mon, I need something to drink and something to eat, in that order." And then he
started walking, taking the back streets that led to the Two Friends
Restaurant. He broke the silence only once, wondering aloud
where all those television and newspaper folks had been when he
really needed the publicity. And then he laughed at himself, shuf-
fling along in a slow, loping gait until we reached the restaurant.
There he waved to the bartender and gave the hostess a fatherly
hug, then grabbed a corner table on the patio and ordered a
Bloody Mary. He sat in silence for a few minutes, content now to

be away from the circuslike atmosphere of the museum. Silence as he watched the first drops of rain splatter on the sidewalk outside, then another chuckle at some thought he would not share.

"Never imagined it could get this crazy," Mel said, downing his drink and promptly ordering another.

For the next hour, between bites of ham and eggs, he talked in haphazard fashion, reminiscing about his son Dirk and how ironic it was that his divers should come across his multimillion-dollar payday on the anniversary of Dirk's death, and then jumped around the calendar of his 16-year *Atocha* quest—from his initial days diving with wife, Deo, to the fallings-out he had with various company personnel—and then darted back to the present with a startling statement: "Bleth's gonna let you guys know later this afternoon, but my divers at Sebastian brought up even more treasure the other day."

His son Kim was in charge of the Sebastian Inlet operation, which continued salvaging the 1715 fleet, and on the same day that Greg Wareham and Andy Matroci found the reef of silver bars, diver John Brandon's crew discovered an intricately crafted gold cup, an emerald-studded bracelet shaped like a snake biting its tail, and 61 gold coins from the northern section of the *Corrigan*'s wreck. That treasure had already been valued at $300,000.

I could not help but shake my head in amazement. Months earlier, Mel had to scrounge money for diesel fuel to enable his salvage fleet to continue searching for the *Atocha*'s elusive prize. Now the sea was surrendering its treasure to him quicker than he could possibly count it. This wasn't all that surprising, considering the man's history. Being in Mel's presence was to be in the company of a walking, talking contradiction.

It was high noon in the twilight of this $400 million man's life, and he was laughing as he stared toward the darkened sky, knowing that storms always have been a major part of his life, that squalls have seemingly followed him everywhere. The wind was blowing and rain splattered his drink, but he paid these no mind. He joked about having shared the cover of *Newsweek* with

John Wayne, his all-time personal hero, three years earlier when the magazine did a story about people who seemed to be larger than life. Ever since Saturday's discovery of the *Atocha*'s mother lode, Fisher's stature had been greatly magnified in almost everyone's eyes.

Fisher laughed and said, "Yep, me and John Wayne. Imagine that. 'Course, there is a little bit of a resemblance, right?"

I laughed with him, not at him, for Mel always had been the last person you would imagine to be cast in the role of an adventurer. Even today, at 62, three years after a successful battle against cancer, he appeared to be a midlevel executive on his way out instead of being the king of treasure hunting, a multimillionaire on his way up. He smiled when I told him that and fingered a gold pendant, a llama, dangling from a gold chain around his neck. When I asked about the llama's significance, he said he had found it in Peru, then quickly changed the subject. Treasure hunters, he said, are a rather secretive lot. They keep their thoughts, not to mention their future adventures, to themselves.

"After all," he said with a wink, running a weathered right hand through the wisps of thinning hair, "it ain't easy being a treasure hunter."

"It's not easy being Indiana Jones, right?" I asked.

"Yeah, I like that—Indiana Jones," Mel said. "Sorta fits, doesn't it? I'm always off chasing after something; always have been, going on 40 years now. Loved that movie, by the way—*Raiders of the Lost Ark*. I've seen it at least a dozen times. And the beginning of it is just like a lot of the treasure hunts I've been on."

Without waiting for a response, Mel forgot all about his secretiveness and spun a tale that had me hanging on his every word. It all began two years ago, when the search for the *Atocha* had stagnated and boredom crept in, when he and wife, Deo, vacationed in Peru. There was no civil war going on at the time, so being the adventurous man that he was, he decided to sort fact from fiction concerning a legend spoken of by the great Spanish conquistador Francisco Pizarro. As was his habit, refusing to elaborate on the *how* and the *when*, Mel said that he had stumbled across some documentation, a copy of the diary of Pizarro's barber, who was one of only 17 survivors of the invading army of 1,200.

"The diary is very accurate, so much so that it almost cost me my life," Mel said. "I was looking for this stash of gold, but I got trapped in a cave. Barely got out alive. A slab of stone fell from the ceiling, blocking the cave's entrance. You know, just like in the Indiana Jones movie, when the guy grabs the relic and arrows start flying out of the wall, then the big stone—"

When he noticed my obvious disbelief, Mel smiled that disarming smile of his and said: "Really. It did happen."

So I played along with him, two little kids refusing to grow up, thinking, So what's next, Indy? Where's the next great adventure?

Mel hesitated, again fingering the golden llama. His eyes took on that faraway look—the same look I'd seen months earlier when he had told me another seemingly far-fetched story, that of the *Atocha*—and I could almost see him flipping back the pages of history, mentally traveling to far-off lands of intrigue, pillage, and conquest until he came to the jungles of the Amazon Basin. Once there, he spoke of the high grasslands of the Andes and of Machu Picchu and of a people the world knows little about, except through legend.

And then he asked: "Have you ever heard about the legend of the lost gold and silver of the Incas?" Within moments, a strange transformation took place. It was obvious, in Mel Fisher's mind at least, that the search had already begun.

"Atahualpa was the kid's name. He was the emperor of the Incas, the boy king." Fisher recounted Pizarro's 1532 invasion of Peru; his battle with the Inca army and subsequent capture of Atahualpa; and the legend of "the tears of the sun," the treasures intended to ransom the Inca king. According to the legend, this Inca gold was hidden in 67 locations after the Spanish killed Atahualpa before all the intended ransom had arrived.

"Of course, that's legend and it's easy to laugh it all off," Mel said. "Besides, a man would have to be crazy to venture into the jungles of Peru now, what with those Shining Path guys cutting off heads and shooting each other, waging war and all that stuff. Then again, once the revolution's over and things quiet down a bit, I'm gonna go back. Like to go back right now, in fact, because the treasure is there, just like the Inca hill people say it is. I know this because I've seen it with my own eyes."

Ordinarily, this is the point in the conversation when normal people roll their eyes and laugh, or simply stand up and walk away. Then again, when Mel Fisher's doing the talking, painting wondrous word pictures about long-lost treasure, it pays to listen. Mel said that if anyone doubted what he was saying, all they had to do was look it up at the local library.

"You see, two years ago this Indian said that if I treated him and his people right, he'd show me where four stashes of the Inca treasure were hidden," Mel said. "Now remember, there's supposed to be 67 of these stashes. And this Indian said that him and his nephews already cleaned out one of the stashes, getting about 200 kilos [approximately 440 pounds] of gold nuggets—big ones, about the size of apples. 'Course, that got my attention, so I agreed to the Indian's terms and we went in search of a treasure cave, which turned into a trap with the big stone almost crushing us. We did escape, though, or I wouldn't be telling you this story, right?"

Fisher said that once they had escaped from the cave, the old Indian took him to a hidden volcano lake, where Mel stripped and free-dived into the milky green water.

"And that's where I found this here little piece of gold," said Mel, again fingering the llama pendant. "This is nothing, though, compared to what else is in that lake—life-size golden llamas. Seen 'em with my own eyes, no foolin'. Fantabulous, huh?"

With that, he downed the last of yet another drink and reached for his billfold. "Whoops," he said sheepishly, "I must have left it back at the museum." Once I had paid the tab, Mel said, "Now don't forget. Check out what I've said in the library. I ain't making this stuff up."

A month later I visited the Atlanta Public Library. Sure enough, Pizarro's encounter with Atahualpa was well documented in numerous historical texts, told almost word for word as Mel had related the tale. Among the many books, there were color photographs of the few treasures that had survived the Spanish conquest: drinking beakers, ceremonial knives, and beautiful hand-crafted plates, all fashioned from gold.

But the most striking artifact was that of a solid gold llama, identical to the one Mel Fisher wore around his neck.

16

Catching Green Fever

One does not discover new lands without consenting to lose
sight of the shore for a very long time.

—Andre Gide, The Counterfeiters

It was with deep regret that I said farewell to Key West in
August 1985 and returned to Atlanta. As far as the newspaper
was concerned, the *Atocha* saga had run its course: Mel Fisher
had found his wrecked galleon and its $400 million in treasure,
meaning he and his divers would live happily ever after, which
meant that my grand adventure on the high seas had ended.

As one of my newsroom bosses quipped, "Now you can start
working for a living again."

The transition was difficult. There would be no more idyllic
hours rubbing elbows with sea gypsies, men and women whose
eyes were riveted to the ocean's bottom, not locked on the next
rung of the corporate ladder. There would be no more days spent
in the company of modern-day pirates as they ambled from one
island bar to another, showing off their tans and the silver coins
that dangled from the rawhide strings wound around their necks.
No more awesome vistas of bright stars high overhead, providing
the perfect blanket for a night spent sleeping on the deck of a

salvage boat. No more wind and rain and rolling seas; no more treasure, either.

My life returned to normal. I resumed writing about the great outdoors, extolling the virtues of sharp-eyed marksmen who drew down on deer and quail, capturing the tranquillity of local fishermen who practiced their craft on Georgia's bountiful lakes. Mel Fisher and his family and dive crews were never far away—not in my mind's eye, at least. Their lifestyle had become an itch that I found impossible to scratch. As such, boredom soon proved to be a constant companion. No story I pursued in the months that followed compared to the one I experienced in Key West. No characters I would interview came close to being as carefree and dream-driven as Don Kincaid, Donnie Jonas, K. T. Budde-Jones, or any of the other deep-sea divers I had come to think of as kindred brothers and sisters.

Combat veterans know that once you have experienced the hell of a free-fire zone, been shot at and somehow survived, nothing again is ever the same. It is the ultimate high, and every remaining life experience is mundane. Your view of the world is forever altered; things that used to seem important suddenly become irrelevant. All that matters is that you are alive. God has blessed you infinitely, misdirecting that bullet past your ear instead of into your chest or sending those blistering mortar or rocket fragments into some less fortunate soul. You are either fully intact, or merely wounded and mentally seared for the rest of your life. But you are still breathing. For reasons that you will never be able to comprehend, you have received a free pass. It is the wise man or woman who takes advantage of this, living each remaining moment of life to the fullest.

Anyone who has spent any time at all on the high seas, breathing in the salt air while steadying himself or herself on a pitching steel deck, also has experienced the great escape. Compound this emotional breaking of life's restrictive chains by donning diving gear and slipping beneath the waves and free-falling through milky green waters to a far-below destination, then skimming the sands and sediment and actually discovering the metallic riches of a long-dead civilization—do this and you might be ruined for life. It matters not whether you are 19 or 59, for in no time at all you realize that you have experienced what only a handful of people have experienced. More often than not, it is a once-in-a-lifetime adventure. Sadly enough, that is just the way life works. For one reason or another, most people stop pursuing their dreams. They bury their imaginations under a mound of debris that has no true value—new jobs, new relationships, new cars, new homes, and new toys, none of which enables them to leave a lasting mark on life. It appears to be a universal curse.

In February 1986 my malaise was somewhat cured when the newspaper sent me to East Africa to cover a war waged by Ethiopia against Eritrea. I know it sounds bizarre, but before this grand adventure I had slipped into a black funk. I had turned 40 the month before and suddenly found myself feeling as if I were over the hill. My wife, June, had given me a surprise party complete with black balloons and gag gifts, all of which bore a message of doom: "Lordy, lordy, I'm 40." I became depressed. Overnight— to me, at least—it seemed as if I had become a card-carrying member of life's Establishment. Without my consent.

Peering down a frustratingly narrow road that evening, all I saw was unspeakable boredom. Scary, for I feared what surely would come next: a suit and tie, shiny shoes, manicured nails, driving a BMW. Good grief.

But then the familiar sounds of warfare rode to my rescue: the gratifying *thunk* of a mortar shell leaving its tube, the high-pitched scream of incoming artillery, the always recognizable din of AK-47s chattering away. Life was good. Even better, I hooked up with a battalion of Eritrea People's Liberation Front (EPLF) fighters atop a mountain fortress, taking a front-row seat in the trenches as they battled the Ethiopian army to a standstill. As an added bonus, combat units of the Soviet Union, which called the shots for Colonel Mengistu Haile Mariam, the Ethiopian dictator-butcher of the moment, had joined the attacking Ethiopians.

Working alongside the EPLF was good sport. For the past 12 years they had been doing their best to contain the world's population, at least when it came to the Evil Empire and Mengistu's henchmen. Outnumbered and outgunned on the battlefield, the EPLF had more than held its own. When I joined up with the Eritrean battalion in March 1986, they were in a fierce fight to hold on to a mountaintop called Denden, a 4,600-foot maze of jagged peaks and intricate trenches. A mere 600 feet below us, in the trenches of Wanja Mountain, was the Ethiopian Third Army, plus a contingent of Soviet military advisers. The fighting was continuous yet one-sided. Despite Ethiopia's 120mm artillery, attack helicopters, and MiG-23s, the valley separating us was littered with enemy dead. Denden held out day after torturous day. And at night, when the guns had grown silent, we would stumble back to our caves and drink tea and talk about better days.

It's funny what you talk about when you are really scared. The fighters spoke of long-ago friendships, before they had tasted war; none had seen their families in more than six years. And when pressed to explain what I did for a living when not being so stupid as to walk into the middle of a firefight, I talked about Mel Fisher and his 16-year quest to find the lost treasure galleon *Nuestra Señora de Atocha*. The fighters got a kick out of those stories. Because most of them had known nothing but war, it was difficult for them to imagine men and women pursuing such sport. Yes, they called it sport, for the concept of earning a living searching for something lost simply did not equate. They kept laughing at my stories, thinking it silly to seek treasure, especially when the only thing they had been searching for during years of constant warfare was freedom.

We went back and forth in this vein, them laughing and me trying to find a correlation, when I groped at straws, saying that seeking treasure was no different from fighting for freedom. For example, I said, picking over the bones of a lost treasure galleon was no different from what they had done the day before in the valley they called Keleb Amora, roughly translated from their native Amharic to English to mean "food of the vultures." It was there, in a figurative sense, that the bones of dead Ethiopians who had unsuccessfully attacked our position were picked clean, stripped of weapons and ammunition. In either case, whether it was long-dead Spaniards or equally dead Ethiopians, the vanquished had no use for their worldly goods. Those Ethiopian treasures were much like the Castilian treasure—one person's gold and silver was another's AK-47 or rocket-propelled grenade launcher. It's all in the eye of the beholder.

Even though that half-assed explanation elicited knowing nods, I sure did miss Key West. I fantasized about fried shrimp dinners and water—lots and lots of water, for here it was as scarce as the reality of democracy. We subsisted on greenish-black water, long contaminated by diesel fuel and decomposing corpses. Drought, famine, and worldwide indifference were the rules of thumb.

A month later, while walking through the desert at night with Sebhat Ephrem, a member of Eritrea's politburo, the 13-man elected cabinet of Eritrea's de facto government, Mel Fisher's plight once again came to mind. Sebhat, while explaining why his people refused to give up in the face of tyranny, quoted Thomas Paine at length. He spoke about freedom of choice, how no one should hassle you if your motives are pure, how government needs to be predicated on a cornerstone of "We the people."

Admittedly, I was weakened in mind and spirit, having endured without much success Africa's inhospitality; I suffered from malaria, yellow fever, and black-water fever. Maybe that was why Mel's plight popped into my muddled mind, how the U.S. government had battled him at every turn, yet failed miserably to understand that nothing's gained by taxing or confiscating people's ambitions, desires, dreams, and fantasies.

❈

And then, shortly thereafter, I was out of Africa. But Africa was not out of me. Despite the fevers, I compiled my war stories, which appeared in a special section, "Eritrea: A Lonely War." Much to its credit, the newspaper rewarded my wife and me with an all-expense-paid vacation to a destination of our choice. Which was how I ended up back in Key West in May 1986.

Indeed, my itch sorely needed scratching. Not to mention catching up on a story after an absence of almost 10 months.

Having survived another war zone, plus a few more near-death experiences, I honestly did not know how much more time I would be allotted in life. Not that I had a death wish or was being morbidly fatalistic. I just felt as if I were nearing the end of a long race, and there were so many things I hadn't experienced. Like scuba diving. What bothered me about the entire *Atocha* saga was that I had been forced to rely almost exclusively on other people to describe the underwater world, our last frontier. No big deal to most people, but I did not like being a part-time player on anyone's team. I needed to taste it and touch it as well as see it.

Despite well-intentioned denials from archaeologists and their brethren in academia, treasure hunting is not something one learns from a book. Yes, by turning the pages of history texts we can share the tingle that Hiram Bingham felt in 1911 when he took that first step upon the great stone stairway that led to the clifftop citadel of Machu Picchu. And we can gasp, as did Howard Carter in 1922, when he first broke the great seal that unveiled the splendors of Tutankhamen. Nonetheless, we are only voyeurs, incapable of experiencing the visual impact of history in the making. In this same vein, the intimacy of being a treasure diver eludes those who confine themselves to interviewing those who have spent their lives combing the ocean's bottom. No stockpile of adverbs can replace firsthand experience, the actual exposure of one's senses to the wind and the water during the crossing of a slippery deck on trembling knees as a ship rises and falls with the very heartbeat of a summer storm.

And when it came to Mel Fisher's quest for the *Nuestra Señora de Atocha*, no words could adequately describe the sensation of drifting along with the current at 52 feet, anticipating the uncovering of silver coins only inches ahead. Or better yet, fanning away the sand and clutching a gold coin.

When the *Atocha*'s hull structure was finally uncovered, gold coins were found by the handfuls, and blackened silver coins adorned the sands like dandelions in a meadow. I wrote of the discoveries in such fashion because that was how the divers described it to me; they were always my point of reference. Over several months, the one question I continually asked was: "What is it like to find treasure?" The response was always the same: "Man, there's nothing like it in the world. It's better than sex."

Because I had never dived—celibate, from a treasure salvor's viewpoint—I had only their words to describe the experience. In essence, I had covered the story of a lifetime secondhand. So far.

In May 1986 the *Atocha* presented yet another surprise: emeralds.

The first of these were discovered in November 1985 with the onslaught of a winter front that produced 45-knot winds and turbulent seas. Once the bad weather struck, Mel Fisher ordered the mother lode site sealed. The *Atocha*'s exposed timbers were covered with plastic tarps and weighted down with ballast. When Kane Fisher complained to his father, asking what he and his crew were to do now, Mel responded in typical fashion: go for the emeralds.

"Of course," Fisher told me, "Kane didn't know what I was talking about. Maybe even *he* didn't believe me when I told him there were emeralds out there."

"Mel liked to say that he remembered someone, he didn't say *who*, reading to him from a document, he didn't say *where* the document came from, about a court-martial that occurred in Havana right after the *Atocha* and the *Margarita* survivors were brought back to port," said Don Kincaid, smiling at the absurdity of the story. According to Mel, one of the surviving sailors was reprimanded for smuggling emeralds aboard the *Atocha*. The sailor, knowing he would be hanged if found guilty, defended himself by saying: "Why are you bothering me about a little smuggling, when I helped the fleet's admiral smuggle a 70-pound box of emeralds onto the *Atocha?*"

Kincaid said that the story sounded credible enough, especially in light of the fact that Spain's admirals were every bit as corrupt as their passengers and crew. Then again, Eugene Lyon, who had transcribed every known document pertaining to the *Atocha* in the Archives of the Indies in Seville, was forced to plead ignorance when asked to verify Mel's emerald story.

Nonetheless, Mel kept insisting that the story was true.

Kane told Mel that it was seven miles from the mother lode to where the cannons were found, and another three miles from there to the Quicksands. So where, exactly, should he begin looking for those emeralds? Mel responded as only he could, telling his son: "If I were the admiral, I'd be keeping those emeralds under my bed."

Because the *Atocha* probably capsized when it broke apart and the trail of recovered artifacts pointed toward the northwest, Mel told Kane that he should start looking about 100 yards or so northwest of the mother lode.

Mel told me that Kane humored him by moving the *Dauntless* 100 yards to the northwest of the main pile, diving down, and promptly finding a thumb-size emerald worth $800,000. Later that day he found a 70-carat stone valued at $1.2 million. Soon the crew recovered 315 of the brilliant stones, ranging from 0.5 to 77 carats each, the total value of which was placed at almost $30 million. Given that Mel claimed there were at least 70 pounds of emeralds smuggled onto the *Atocha*, they would be worth several billion dollars.

In the next five months, an additional 167 emeralds were discovered. But then, on May 14, 1986, Fisher's divers struck a second mother lode. Kim Fisher made the first discovery, uncovering a 40-foot gold chain. Moments later, Bill Barron fanned away the sand and found a watermelon-size clump of gold coins and gold nuggets. And then almost an hour later, 32-year-old Pedro Estrada was working the airlift in a berm of sand when a green flash suddenly blinded him. When he peered up toward the end of the airlift, Estrada could not believe his eyes. It was raining emeralds. Estrada had inadvertently hit a pocket of emeralds, and now the luminescent green stones, jettisoned from out of the end of the airlift, were slowly falling back down on him. Estrada said the emerald shower transfixed him, his eyes darting from one brilliant stone to another as they lazily cut through the current and dropped at his feet. Suddenly snapped from his reverie, he scrambled to pick up the treasure, hyperventilating as he did so, consuming almost half a tank of air in minutes. When he finally surfaced, shouting the news of his discovery, his crewmates made a mad dash to the recovery site.

Finding an emerald and then actually holding one in your hand is an experience that is not easy to describe. Bill Barron, 31, a transplanted Californian who ventured to the Keys three years earlier to work for the Florida Keys Marine Institute for Delinquent Children, had been diving for Mel Fisher for the past two years. He told me that touching gold and silver does tend to take your breath away.

"But when you hold an emerald in your hand, I swear to God you can almost feel its heat," he said. Equally disturbing was that once you had found an emerald, your mind suddenly played tricks on you. He called it a variation of gold fever. "Find emeralds and all of a sudden you've got green fever, your eyesight is screwed up. Just like that, every damn pebble down there is an emerald. You've got to experience it to believe it."

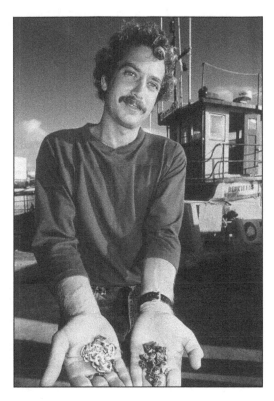

Andy Matroci shows off the emeralds and a gold chain he found near the *Atocha*'s exposed timbers.

It was these stories that greeted me upon my arrival in Key West. Just like that, the fevers I had contracted in Africa were replaced by another. So excited was I that I paid no attention to Mel's divers huddling with my wife. Their conspiracy went undetected until the evening of May 18 as I stood upon the rolling deck of the *J. B. Magruder* alongside its intrepid captain, Donnie Jonas. We had just arrived at the *Atocha* diving site and I was expecting nothing out of the ordinary, just another movable feast of watching divers break through the surface with these fantastic green treasures.

It was only as the sun gracefully dipped into the distant horizon that it dawned on me that it was too late to return to shore. Cool. I would be spending another night at sea.

Before I had time to celebrate, however, my reverie was shattered when Jonas turned to me and said, "Know something? We're all getting sick and tired of your stupid questions: 'Gee whiz, what's it like to find treasure? What's it like down there at the bottom?' Well, we've had enough of those dumb questions, and by God we're going to do something about it."

I'll be the first to admit the mental shortcomings of journalists, especially mine. So when Jonas chewed on me, I immediately imagined that he and his crew of modern-day pirates were going to keelhaul me or even worse, make me walk the plank. But then I noticed his crew—Pat Clyne, Ralph Budd, Pedro Estrada, Bill Barron, Vince Trotta, Julie Fisher, Don Deeks, Paul Busch, Christian Swanson, and Mitch Marken—laughing at my discomfort. And then my thoughts went spinning out of control when Jonas said, "Get a good night's sleep, because tomorrow you're going diving with me."

I honestly don't think I slept a wink. Caught between nightmares and fantasy of actually discovering something that had not been touched by human hands in 364 years, I lay there in my bunk drenched by a cold sweat. Dawn arrived too soon. Breakfast was a cup of coffee and a cigarette. My stomach was a bagful of butterflies and hornets. And just about the time I had decided that discretion was the better part of valor, a smiling Jonas thrust a diving mask into my hands and said, "Okay, it's time for us to go find some treasure."

My training was brief. Jonas showed me how to clear the mask of water and told me to keep breathing through the regulator's mouthpiece, no matter what. He also cautioned me that I would have to clear the pressure from my ears every 10 feet or so.

I immediately gazed out at the vastness of this mysterious ocean and fought back the urge to back down, cursing myself for being a dreamer. Then again, this was another opportunity of a lifetime. Quitting was a disease. Quit once and it was all too easy to quit the next time.

I prayed: *Lord, please take care of me.* I prayed again: *Jesus, don't fail me now,* then glanced once again at the sea, imagining all sorts of demons and monsters, not to mention hungry sharks. I paused, trying my damnedest to think of a good excuse, when I had a vision. Standing before me was my Marine Corps drill instructor, Sergeant Martin. He was foaming at the mouth, screaming at me the very words he had screamed so long ago: "C'mon, Smith! Show me some balls!"

And just like that, I scrambled into Don Deeks's gear and jumped into the water. I'm a good swimmer, but I had no experience of *the deep.* So I dived, and I almost died because I used up all my air way too quickly, and I found emeralds, and Jonas helped me back up to the surface.

Safely aboard ship, Jonas was far more impressed that I had not panicked than he was about the eight peanut-size emeralds I had discovered—a fair-size fortune in uncut stones that would make its way into the ship's safe to lie side by side with the 2,189 gems, later appraised at approximately $70 million, that would be brought to the surface in the next 15 days. These riches paled, however, in comparison to the cheers and congratulations and hugs I received that day from the crew. Nor can a price tag be placed on the "You did good, kid" I would receive from Mel Fisher a few days later.

For the moment, however, I was gratified to be accepted into the world of dreamers. I would make two more dives that day, each more exhilarating than the previous one because I finally felt at home. I took time to notice my surroundings, noticed that I was not alone down there, swimming in sync with jacks and the other plentiful species of the deep. I returned to the *Atocha's* timbers and was humbled once again by the full scope of history as I brushed my hands across the Ghost Galleon's scoured remnants.

That's me clutching the dive ladder after finding emeralds on my second dive in May 1986.

And just as before, I was overcome with tears of joy. There is no shame at crying in the face of newfound adventure.

In retrospect, I had not only become one with the ocean but also with the men and women who toyed with and toiled against its wrath day in and day out, months and years on end. I felt unique, even bulletproof after having not only survived one deadly experience but also two others of a far less threatening nature. And later that evening, sitting inside the ship's cabin with the rest of the crew as they huddled around a well-worn table cluttered with gold chains, gold coins, and several plastic sandwich bags filled with emeralds—more than $3 million worth of treasure—we shared life experiences on a placid ocean, cooled now by a pleasant breeze.

Bill Barron and I stepped outside the cabin and leaned over the railing to watch the fish that darted in and out of the reflection of the ship's navigational lights. Every once in a while, if you were lucky, you could spot a shark. I told Barron that apparently all the predators had taken the night off, which prompted his deep laughter. Barron stood in silence for the longest time, his eyes cast upward as if studying the stars, and then he reminisced about the past two years searching for the *Atocha*. He said that people used to laugh at him and his crewmates, saying they were nothing more than dirt bags with a diving skill who were simply thrown into the water. Treasure divers were the outcasts of society, Barron said, and in all honesty that's exactly what they were; they did not fit in anywhere except working on a salvage boat. After all, their world was that of fantasy, if not sheer lunacy. And what better place to play this insane game than at sea, far removed from normal society.

"When you get right down to it, ours is a world of dreams—Mel Fisher's dream," said Barron. "I know this might sound silly, but all of us divers truly believed we could fulfill Mel's quest. In essence, we thought of ourselves as the knights who helped out King Arthur."

I fell asleep that night to the rhythm of the sea, my mind far below the surface, my hands trembling as I plucked emeralds from out of the sand. Instead of wearing the standard apparel—the diving mask, regulator, and a compressed-air tank on my back—I was adorned in gleaming armor. Silly, yes. Nonetheless, it was the deep sleep of gratification, for I had made my first dive as a treasure hunter and exited the water as a treasure finder. Life does not get any better.

When I finally did return to that hotel room where, without doubt, the most patient wife in the whole wide world awaited me with open arms, I was quickly brought back to reality.

June said that she saw it first in my eyes, an unmistakable yearning to conquer more frontiers. She also saw a strange glow about me, one that surely was about to compel me to do something rash, something foolish, which I most certainly was about to do. But before I could speak, June said, "Absolutely not. You've got a good job already. You're not going to become a treasure diver."

I blushed, then told her that she had it all wrong, that I was just going to suggest that we go out for a shrimp dinner.

"You're lying," she said, wrapping her arms around me. "But I still love you."

So it was that I put my dreams away. Not burying them, mind you. Just putting them aside temporarily, knowing there were better days ahead. And most certainly at sea.

17

The Trouble
with Treasure

There are only two tragedies in life: one is not getting what one
wants, the other is getting it.

—Oscar Wilde

They came, they saw, they conquered. And then, much like
their buccaneer predecessors, they disappeared shortly
after the *Atocha*'s booty was divvied up.

Unlike what the newspaper reports of the day would have liked
you to believe, none of Mel Fisher's divers became millionaires. A
handful prospered. But for the most part, the divers hauled away
their fair share of silver bars, silver coins, emeralds, and assorted
17th-century trinkets, then struggled to sell the treasure because
of the sudden glut of antiquities on the market. Once this task was
finally completed, the majority of them walked away from Treasure Salvors, joining the real world they had once viewed with
such disdain.

"We all grew up and moved on," said Donnie Jonas.

By no means was Jonas trying to make light of the moment when, on Thursday, October 16, 1986, the computer on the third floor of Fisher's Greene Street headquarters finally completed 60 hours of calculations and flashed a message that 600 investors and employees had anxiously awaited: *Division Complete. Congratulations Treasure Salvors.* Instead, Jonas viewed the occasion as a reality check. Sure, there was plenty of excitement. In fact, hundreds of voices bellowed in unison, its echo reverberating throughout the old converted navy warehouse. Then 25 champagne corks popped, the corks ricocheting off the high ceiling and bouncing to the floor like spent bullets. And then the treasure was dispersed, first to Fisher's long-suffering investors, then to his divers. The division was based on a point system that took into account the individual's job description, performance, and length of service. As such, the least that any diver would receive was 0.1 percent of the *Atocha*'s vast treasure horde. A long-term diver would receive 0.4 percent, and a salvage boat captain would receive 0.6 percent.

"As for what the average diver received? First of all, we were paid in treasure, and treasure ain't real money," said Jonas.

Jonas knew he would be carting off more treasure than he could possibly carry, so he showed up at the division with a brand-new wheelbarrow and immediately started packing his loot into it—150 silver coins, two silver bars, and a fistful of emeralds for being a long-term diver; then his share from owning the *Magruder* and being its captain over the years, another 300 coins and eight silver bars. By Jonas's calculations, he carted off almost one ton of silver, which he promptly wheeled out of the building and across the street to the Barnett Bank. When he returned to Treasure Salvors headquarters, Mel handed Jonas his W-2 form. According to the Internal Revenue Service, Jonas had earned $300,000 in 1985. Even when he petitioned the IRS, asking for and receiving permission to have the treasure reappraised, which decreased his taxes by more than half, he still owed the IRS $42,000. Jonas's reaction was as predictable as it was understandable: he felt as if he had been robbed.

"Anyone who thinks all of us got rich is mistaken," said Jonas. "I had to scramble my ass off just to pay taxes. Couldn't buy groceries or pay the bills because a silver coin wouldn't buy shit."

Other than the immediate Fisher family, no one was spared the anguish. The government threatened to place a lien on Pat Clyne's house unless he came up with $12,000 within two weeks. He averted this disaster only because Deo Fisher wrote him a personal check. Months would pass before Clyne was able to sell a portion of his treasure and use the proceeds to repay Deo.

According to the W-2 forms of Syd Jones and his wife, K. T., they had earned a combined income of $650,000 in 1985. Because this was the last year of the government's 50 percent tax bracket, they had to come up with $325,000 for the IRS. One of the high-end items that Syd received in the division was an emerald that Mel had valued at $240,000. Syd had the stone reappraised. Although he would not say what its true value was, Jones said that he eventually sold the emerald for far less than the taxes he paid on it.

Other than money, the divers contend that the most damaging thing about the end of the hunt for the *Atocha* was psychological. To a man and a woman, they had ridden an emotional roller coaster for years, going months without pay, scrounging for meals, living under the harshest of conditions while working on the salvage boats; then finding incredible riches yet knowing the treasure was not theirs to keep, having to hand it over first to the government, which in turn gave it back to Mel Fisher, who then distributed it first among his numerous investors. They also had suffered the trauma brought about by the deaths of first Gary Borders, then little Nikko Littlehales, and finally Dirk and Angel Fisher and Rick Gage, battling their respective demons for more than a year before finally returning to the water.

Regardless of the accumulation of psychological baggage, the divers pressed on, not giving up, continuing the search despite storms at sea and equally rough circumstances at port.

What sustained them all, said Don Kincaid, was the hunt. "Then again, anyone who says there wasn't a moment when they said 'Fuck it, I'm outta here' is lying. But those who stuck it out, who sucked it up and pressed on no matter the circumstances, were like the early astronauts—they had the right stuff."

It was that unique quality inside unique individuals that compelled them to dive despite knowing their bottom time was almost extinguished, that compelled them to blow another hole despite encroaching darkness, that compelled them to fan away one more layer of sand despite complaints from exhausted muscles. Everything they did revolved around the hunt. But once that had been taken from them, everyone suffered in various ways.

"One guy turned to hard drugs, putting $300,000 worth of cocaine up his nose, a few others sought escape in booze," Kincaid said. "Whatever, all of us were emotionally spent."

According to Kincaid, none of Mel Fisher's divers was prepared for what life would be like once the big prize was found. Had Mel brought in a company shrink to help his personnel through the trauma, maybe that would have helped. But that didn't happen. Instead, the divers were left to their own devices. In essence, almost all of them became self-destructive—touched by insanity in one form or fashion.

"For the longest time, I'd be walking down the street and all of a sudden I'd start crying," Kincaid said. "I ended up buying a 50-foot catamaran, and all I'd do was hide away on my boat. I didn't want to see anyone, talk to anyone. The treasure was found, and I just couldn't deal with it. I'm not alone when I say that one day I woke up and had to ask myself: 'What in the hell do I do now?'"

The Treasure Salvors staff was dealt yet another blow fewer than two months after the division of the *Atocha* treasure when

Mel Fisher on December 5, 1986, sold his company and all future *Atocha* salvage rights to four Atlanta, Georgia, businessmen: shopping center developer Frank Callaway, financier P. K. Ridley, attorney Larry Hyre, and Ronald Barnes. Callaway's group paid Fisher $7 million for the company. For the most part, most of Fisher's longtime employees departed. Only when the stock market crashed late in 1988 and Callaway and his associates lost most of their money, subsequently selling the *Atocha* rights back to the Fisher family, did a kind of normality return to the operation.

Andy Matroci and Kane Fisher shared command of the *Dauntless*, and Mel, by now suffering from a recurrence of bladder cancer, concocted altogether new hunts. He directed his salvage boats to search not only for what he called "the *Atocha*'s missing link"—the vessel's sterncastle, which he claimed contained 35 boxes of church gold and 70 pounds of unrecovered contraband emeralds—but also to scour the ocean's floor near Marathon Key for the wrecks of Spain's ill-fated 1733 fleet.

The problem with searching for the 1733 fleet was that it had reportedly gone down within the state's newly created Florida Keys National Marine Sanctuary, a 2,800-square-mile area set aside in 1990 and maintained by the National Oceanic and Atmospheric Administration. Between January and March 1992, Kane Fisher had found the anchor, cannonballs, and other artifacts from one of the 1733 ships, the *San Fernando*, which sank during a hurricane in an area known as "Coffins Patch."

Diving operations produced little treasure in the years that followed, but then on May 18, 1997, the Justice Department charged Mel Fisher with blowing 100 holes in the search area, each hole 30 feet wide by nine feet deep, which destroyed fragile coral reefs and sea grass. Three months later, Chief Judge Edward B. Davis of the U.S. District Court for the Southern District of Florida ruled in favor of the U.S. government. His injunction banned Mel from using blowers within the nation's largest marine sanctuary, which included Hawk Channel, where the search for the *Atocha*'s sterncastle was being conducted.

After nearly 26 years of fighting yet always losing its court battles against Mel Fisher, the government finally was triumphant. Mel's dreams of finding yet more buried Spanish treasure were shattered, for in order for his salvage boats to continue the search, he first must receive a permit from the National Oceanic and Atmospheric Administration.

18

Death of a Dreamer

Fantabulous. . . . Wow, this is really fantabulous.

—Mel Fisher

Anthony Tarracino may not have known Mel Fisher the best, but among a rapidly dwindling registry of old-time Key Westers, he knew him the longest and observed him the closest.

"Could never say no to the man. Not back when, not even now," said Tarracino, better known on this island as Captain Tony, a self-proclaimed gambler, gunrunner, charter boat captain, and politician. A few months earlier he had celebrated his 85th birthday in much the same way he was observing this day—sitting on the brick ledge in a patch of shade in front of his Greene Street bar, stroking his silver goatee as his milky blue eyes kept abreast of the young maidens walking past.

He gave me a sly look, grinned, and said, "I think I'll just stay right here until 10 o'clock tonight. You know, just in case a stray hooker comes by." And then he laughed, broke into a spasm of hacking, and then lighted another Doral cigarette. He paused as he inhaled deeply and then said, "Don't get into town much any-more. Don't drive; don't have wheels. Hell, I don't do much of anything now except work on my memoirs; folks at CBS are doing a special on me—last of the Key West legends. 'Course, the biggest legend of 'em all was Mel. Bigger than life, bigger than any of the hotshots who've ever called this place home. See, that's why I'm here right now talking with you. I'll go anywhere, anytime to talk about Mel Fisher."

Tarracino is a Key West celebrity, a celluloid blend of Humphrey Bogart: Harry Morgan from *To Have and Have Not*, Rick Blaine from *Casablanca*. He also is arguably the last of the legends on an island that seems to worship the bizarre and all things far from the norm. In this regard it would be hard to find anyone who could better personify rugged individualism and a commitment to marching to a different drummer. His lusty life was set to music in 1985 when Jimmy Buffett recorded "Last Mango in Paris," homage that comes as no surprise because Tarracino gave Buffett his start, allowing him to sing for beers in Tarracino's bar, the oldest in Florida. Long before Buffett sang his tunes in the dimly lit saloon, a host of celebrities frequented the place: Walter Cronkite, Truman Capote, and Tennessee Williams, to name a few. But Tarracino's fondest memories are reserved for Mel Fisher.

It was December 2001 and an old man who had never been far from the sea enraptured me as he sipped his liquor and agonized over the atypical weather—80 degrees with 60 percent humidity. Come to think of it, said the likable raconteur, it was on a day just like this in the summer of 1969 that Mel's station wagon turned the corner of Duval Street and pulled up to the curb. There was no mistaking Fisher, not even then, said the five-feet-six Tarracino: "Biggest guy I'd ever seen, and he wasn't all that famous back then." And there was no mistaking the hugeness of the Fisher clan: "Wife and kids packed door to door in that car." Once Mel had introduced himself, and Tarracino had ushered Deo Fisher and her four children into his saloon to escape the heat, Mel immediately started talking treasure, wondering if there was any truth to the story that Tarracino had stumbled upon a Spanish shipwreck in the southwest channel.

By his own account, in 1959 Tarracino and treasure hunter Art McKee found a cannon and some silver bars in Hawk Channel. "Found the stuff by pure accident," Tarracino said. He lost it the same way, marking the discovery with an old buoy that drifted away. Despite searching for the artifacts for almost two years, he and McKee were never able to relocate the spot.

Tarracino told me this story for one reason, he said. Not to brag about the fact that he might have found the *Atocha* 26 years before Mel did, but to clarify a misconception about Mel. "You see, almost everyone had Mel pegged wrong. We must have spent six hours talking that day. We talked about that Ghost Galleon for about five minutes. Rest of the time Mel talked about his family. Good God, that man was all about family—not treasure."

And that, said Tarracino, was what endeared Fisher to him. Sure, he and Mel became longtime friends, confidants, and drinking buddies. But as Tarracino pointed out, a person's legacy is not determined by the thickness of a stock portfolio or the size of a car or a home. And most certainly not by the number of gold and silver bars he or she might bring up off the bottom from a Spanish shipwreck. Legacy is children.

"I look at Kim and I see Mel; same thing with Kane. And it was the same way with Dirk," said Tarracino. He edged closer, his eyes riveted on mine. "It's all about legacy, understand? You see, Mel's still alive. Yep, way I look at it is that if you have kids, you never ever die."

Tarracino paused to snub out his cigarette and put a flame to another. He struck up a conversation with a pretty brown-haired woman, who in turn had him autograph her T-shirt. Then he turned to me and said, "Did I tell you that Mel's the greatest man I've ever met? My best friend, that's what he was. Our friendship was . . . damn, I sure do miss him."

Tarracino's wife, Shirley, and Deo Fisher also became good friends, using each other's shoulders to cry on in 1973 when Nikko Littlehales died when the props of one of Mel's salvage boats crushed him. They shared their anguish again two years later when

Deo's son Dirk drowned. It was Tarracino who slipped Mel money to buy groceries for his family during the all too numerous hard times of the *Atocha* search; his saloon also was used to help entice investors in the salvage operation. Mel's money was no good, said Tarracino, meaning that Mel and his family drank on the house, which might explain why Mel would often close his financial deals in Tarracino's saloon. But damned if everybody didn't have a good time, said Tarracino, again running gnarled fingers through his goatee.

By his own admission, Tarracino is a hustler and a storyteller, a likable man who sometimes tells outrageous tales to make people laugh. "But I don't have to make anything up when it comes to Mel," he said. "If he liked you, you became family for life. And a family is only as good as its captain. Mel? He was the greatest captain of 'em all."

Tarracino's admiration is endless. Mel Fisher was just a big, beautiful man. And even during the best of times, when treasure was being found, Tarracino said the bloodsuckers were always after him: state lawyers, federal lawyers, insurance people. "And while they were trying to rob him, Mel was giving it away. You see, there is a little piece of Mel in every street person, every hippie, and every down-and-outer in Key West. He was always buying them meals, giving them a few dollars or so to get them through another day. Guy had the biggest heart I've ever seen."

Tarracino closed his eyes and began humming a Buffett song, "A Pirate Looks at Forty," which only seemed appropriate. He smiled and continued reminiscing, saying how, not wishing to be dumped dead into a Dumpster for swindling the Mob on a horse racing scam, he ran away from the New Jersey goons in 1948 and landed in the Keys; how he ran guns to Fidel Castro in the late 1950s but switched allegiance "once the bastard went Commie on us"; how he won the Key West mayoral election by 31 votes in the mid-1980s. He paused at the recollection of the election, grinned, and gave thanks to the 29 hookers who made it all possible.

※

Toward the end of 1997 a little piece of Tarracino died every time he saw Mel. The man he had grown to love and admire had been diagnosed with incurable bladder cancer. It was painfully obvious that Mel was dying. He no longer appeared indestructible, or as tall and exuberant, for that matter. His eyes receded, his cheeks were hollow, and the skin on his once-muscular forearms drooped like jowls. When he spoke, it was in a hoarse whisper.

But Mel always had a smile for his friends, which not even the encroachment of death would let him abandon. So determined was Fisher at holding onto these friendships that, without fail, at noon each day, he slowly shuffled down the half block from his museum and gingerly eased onto a barstool at Tarracino's saloon. And as soon as he had done so, Tarracino mixed a rum and Coke and put it in front of Mel, then stepped from behind the bar and sat beside him. The conversation was limited to days long gone. More often than not, they sat in silence, both peering down a dark road neither wished to travel.

As his condition worsened, Mel leaned on others. One of those who propped him up the most was Pat Clyne, who not only was considered family but also, without doubt, the most loyal of Mel's employees. During the far too numerous tough times, Clyne's fidelity was steadfast. While others came and went, Clyne was in it for the long haul. Mel had taken him under his wing in 1973, hiring the then-26-year-old hard-hat diver as a handyman, then as a treasure diver before making him the company's official video photographer, and finally promoting him to corporate vice president. It was in the latter capacity that Clyne became Mel's personal sounding board. It was not uncommon for Mel to telephone Clyne at 3:00 A.M. to share a dream he had just had, one that pinpointed various lost treasures throughout the world. Clyne laughed and said, "The first words out of my mouth were always, 'Mel, do you know what time it is?' He didn't, so I'd tell him,

I'm on the left, talking with Pat Clyne, Mel's most loyal business associate.

and then he'd tell me all about the dream as if the hour of day didn't matter."

Clyne was Mel's shadow, videotaping his seagoing exploits or capturing the moment when Mel rubbed shoulders with the queen of Spain; Hollywood celebrities Cliff Robertson and Loretta Swit; and television star Johnny Carson, who dived on the *Atocha* wreck site with Mel in 1986. And when Clyne wasn't recording his mentor's comings and goings, he was assisting Mel with the little things—helping with phone calls or writing letters for him—especially during Mel's last days.

In November 1998, Mel's health deteriorated to the point that he was confined to a hospital bed set up in the living room of his Key Haven home. For the first time since beginning the *Atocha* search in 1969, Mel was not sitting behind his desk plotting map coordinates or bantering with his office staff. Complaining that boredom was killing him, he told his wife, Deo, that he wanted to see his office one last time. Clyne said that this would be no easy task. A special hospital lift had to be used to elevate Mel out of his bed; then he was placed into a wheelchair and transported into Key West in a motor home. What greeted Mel when he arrived at the museum brought a smile to his trembling lips—the entire office staff, forewarned that Mel was on his way, had lined both sides of the pathway leading to the museum's front steps. Everyone was cheering and clapping. Each of the women staffers gave Mel a hug and a kiss. No one would admit to having seen Mel brush aside tears.

Mel motioned for Clyne to move closer, then said, "Shouldn't all these people be working?" And then he chuckled, breaking into the biggest smile that anyone could remember.

Once Clyne had wheeled Mel into the museum and down the narrow corridors to his newly refurbished office, Mel's old exuberance took control. He wanted to know where his old charts were, wanted to know if his son Kim had gotten the permits from the NOAA that would enable his dive crews to start searching for the *Atocha*'s missing sterncastle. And speaking of crews, had Kim managed to hire new divers? And what about the old boats? Were the *Dauntless* and the *J. B. Magruder* seaworthy? Kim assured his father that everything had been taken care of, that he should relax and enjoy the moment, that the *Atocha* search was in capable hands. Mel knew this to be true, so he smiled and patted his son's hand. Mel's sigh was one of assurance.

Later, as Mel was wheeled back to the motor home, he told Clyne that this had been one of the greatest moments of his life. Come to think of it, he said, all of a sudden he had figured out what was really causing him so much pain and discomfort. "There's gonna be no more chemotherapy, Pat. No more medicine," Mel said. "My problem's not cancer; it's these damn hemorrhoids of mine. I'm gonna get them taken care of and then I'll be just fine. Yep, I'll be as good as new."

Two weeks later, Clyne sat beside Mel's bed. He held his mentor's right hand in his and fought back tears as Mel slipped into and out of consciousness. It was late afternoon and a glint of sunset streaked through the room's floor-to-ceiling windows.

Clyne had been sitting in the room for hours, silently praying for the impossible, when Mel finally opened his eyes and smiled. After a few painful minutes of strained silence, Mel raised his left arm and pointed with a tremulous finger toward the canal that ran behind his home. "It's out there," he said in a voice barely above a whisper.

"What's out there, Mel?" Clyne asked.

"Treasure . . . treasure's out there," Fisher said.

Now it was Clyne's turn to smile. Yes, he told the man whom he considered his second father, yes, indeed, the *Atocha*'s missing stern was out there somewhere. And yes, someday they were going to find its untold millions in gold and emeralds. And when they did, the credit would be all Mel's.

Fisher painstakingly shook his head. "No, the treasure is right out *there*," he said, again pointing to the canal that ran behind his house. "I dreamed of it just a while ago. All those emeralds, all that jewelry is right out there."

When Clyne asked if Mel meant that treasure was out there in the canal, Mel nodded. But before he could say anything more, his eyes closed and he fell asleep.

The next day, December 15, Kim and Terry Fisher and Clyne motored their fast craft into the Key Haven canal. The trip had been prearranged. Clyne had told Deo Fisher what he and the sons were up to, so when the boats anchored in the middle of the canal, she awakened Mel and opened the curtains of the room's huge windows. It was just like old times, Clyne said. Mel sat back and watched the search from a distance, eagerly anticipating the grand moment of discovery. Everyone exchanged waves, then Kim Fisher and Clyne donned their diving gear, each grabbed a metal detector, then both entered the water. Moments later, Clyne burst through the surface and excitedly waved his arms, followed by Kim, who came up equally as excited. Then the three grown men continued their celebration, acting like little boys. Once the boats were docked, they walked up the back lawn and entered Mel's living room, where he lay trembling in his hospital bed.

"You were right again, Mel," Clyne said as he laid a towel across Mel's stomach and then poured the contents of a diving bag onto the towel—hundreds of brightly colored fake emeralds, sapphires, and rubies. Mel Fisher smiled as broadly as he had on the day 13 years earlier when the *Atocha*'s mother lode had been discovered. And then he laughed. It was a soft, joyful laugh, one that contradicted the disease that had ravaged his body.

"Fantabulous," Mel said. "Wow, this is really fantabulous."

His smile said it all. He knew that treasure had been out there all along. He attempted to express his joy but was racked first by spasms, then coughing. When the spasms subsided, Mel pulled Clyne to his side and whispered, "I'm going to beat this disease, Pat. No more chemo for me. I'm feeling better already."

Mel Fisher died in his sleep four days later.

19

Spirits at Sea

If you gaze long enough into an abyss, the abyss will gaze back
into you.

—Friedrich Nietzsche

It was Father's Day 1999, with calm seas and a clear, blue sky.
Everything considered, a perfect Sunday morning as the pleasure boat *Sea Hawk* navigated through Hawk Channel. Aboard
the vessel were most of the Fisher clan: sons and daughter and
grandchildren plus Pat Clyne. In nearby craft were Don Kincaid
and Mel's extended family, his present-day divers.

Despite the gathering of all her loved ones, Deo Fisher did
not make the trip to sea. "It would have been too painful," she
said, turning away as tears filled her eyes.

Almost six months after he had died of cancer, some of Mel
Fisher's ashes were to be scattered at sea, deposited over the exact
spot where, 14 years earlier, his divers had discovered the treasure-
laden hull of the *Nuestra Señora de Atocha* and a large portion of
her 47 tons of silver and gold.

On the *Sea Hawk*, Kane Fisher bowed his head in silence, then
moved to the boat's stern, his gnarled fingers wrapped around the
copper urn containing his father's ashes. Moments later, Kane gave
them to the sea, depositing what some would call the spirit of the

man, scattering Mel's true essence upon the shimmering waters that had so encompassed his life's work. Red roses were dropped overboard.

As Kincaid watched the roses drift past, he recited from memory some verse from Mel's favorite poem, "Requiem," penned by Robert Louis Stevenson:

> Under the wide and starry sky,
> Dig the grave and let me lie.
> Glad did I live and gladly die,
> And I laid me down with a will.
> This be the verse you grave for me:
> Here he lies where he longed to be;
> Home is the sailor, home from the sea,
> And the hunter home from the hill.

Aboard the salvage boat *Dauntless*, anchored almost three miles away, diver Jim Youngblood watched the ceremony with equal parts bewilderment and fascination. Visitors are rare in this tract of water used only by lobster fishermen and modern-day adventurers, which Youngblood certainly was. The 32-year-old former Marine had walked away from a lucrative job as a heavy-equipment operator in Macon, Georgia, three weeks earlier. "Took a vacation and . . . well, here I am," said Youngblood, a brawny individual whose attitude is as carefree as the lifestyle he now so adamantly embraced.

Youngblood turned to another diver and asked what was going on in the distance, then nodded solemnly when he learned that it was a memorial service for Mel Fisher. Only later, when he surfaced from an unproductive dive and saw the roses drift past the diving ladder, did he feel a chill. Youngblood said that he had grown up loving the water, having seen the *National Geographic* video of Mel's search for the *Atocha* and wishing he could have participated in it. He said he had assumed that Fisher's divers had found everything there was to find years ago. But then he vacationed in Key West and visited the Fisher museum, only to discover that Mel's son Kim was still searching for the *Atocha's* missing sterncastle—that there was an estimated $1 billion in treasure still buried in Hawk Channel. So Youngblood jumped at the opportunity to be part of the adventure. His only regret, he said, was that he did not arrive in time to meet Mel.

The next morning dawned clear and calm. Youngblood was pale and seemed shaken as he pulled on his diving gear. Normally jovial and sometimes very talkative, he said little. Once the day's first hole had been blown, he solemnly entered the water. Fewer than 15 minutes later, Youngblood was yelling for help at the base of the diving ladder: "Silver bar. Someone give me a hand, dammit." Within moments, Captain Robbie Hanna was on the ship's radio, relaying the news to company headquarters.

Indeed, this was cause for celebration. It had been 12 years since a discovery of this magnitude had occurred, and now Youngblood was suddenly a hero. His picture appeared on the front page of the local newspaper as he cradled the 50-pound ingot with the aid of Kim Fisher, president of the *Atocha/Margarita* Expedition, as the Fisher operation is now called, who praised his newest diver's tenacity. Through it all, Youngblood grinned and grudgingly accepted the acclaim. He still appeared shaken.

Two months later, Youngblood was transferred to Fisher's other salvage boat, the *J. B. Magruder*. It was on a late August evening that he joined me at the ship's railing. I was gazing contentedly at a blanket of stars, wondering why the hell I had stayed away from the sea for so long, when Youngblood asked if I had ever heard of strange happenings among those who had searched so long on this treasure trail.

I laughed and jokingly asked, "You mean ghosts and stuff like that?"

Youngblood nodded. It was obvious from the nonsensical glint of his eyes that the subject was no laughing matter, so I kept a straight face and told him everything I could recall about the so-called *Atocha* curse. The most ominous fact was that five *Atocha* crewmen had survived when the galleon sank in the 1622 hurricane, and since 1971 five people had died while searching for her. I told him about Don Kincaid's haunting experience on the *Northwind*, how an unknown voice awakened Kincaid in the middle of the night, twice shouting a warning moments before the vessel flipped over. To me the ocean has always seemed a haunting if not a daunting place. Over the years, divers had told me they had heard mysterious voices and laughter coming from the sea. Doors that had been secured hours earlier would slam shut in the middle of the night. Weird stuff, I told Youngblood, some of which might be explained away by fatigue; some of it due to the lonely nature of a confining ship on the dark expanse of the ocean in the dead of night; some of it due to too many dives and too many days at sea.

Youngblood nodded, as if satisfied with my explanation, but then his eyes fastened on the cross I always wore around my neck. "You're religious, aren't you," he said. Before I could respond, he added, "Well, I want to tell you something. I don't believe in all that hocus-pocus Holy Roller shit. But then again . . ."

Expecting a fistfight, I received instead a truly wonderful story.

Once Mel Fisher's ashes had been deposited at sea, Youngblood said it was impossible for him to think of anything else. How can you idolize a man you have never met? But that was exactly what Youngblood found himself doing. As he dived during that somber Father's Day, he imagined himself in the company of Mel and his crew during that halcyon July 1985 day when they had stumbled on the *Atocha*'s mother lode. In his mind's eye, Youngblood was there on the bottom with Kane Fisher, Greg Wareham, and Andy Matroci, sharing their awe at the sight of that reef of silver bars. And then he pictured himself on the *Dauntless*'s deck alongside Jimmy Buffett, lifting his champagne glass to celebrate the occasion, toasting Mel Fisher, the world's greatest treasure hunter.

Yes, Youngblood said, he was guilty of being a daydreamer. But when you had spent as many days at sea as he had, diving endlessly yet discovering nothing but seashells or an occasional chunk of ballast, there was no harm in allowing your mind to wander.

When Youngblood retired on the evening of Father's Day, he immediately went to sleep. Normally, he said, sleep was elusive. Having read about disasters at sea, especially what happened to the *Northwind* in 1975, Youngblood would toss and turn, then arise and walk about the ship, checking the engines and generators, making sure nothing had gone wrong. Youngblood said it was Marine Corps training—always anticipating and preparing for disaster. But this night was different. Youngblood immediately fell asleep. Then, during the middle of the night, he said some damn idiot woke him up. He felt a relentless tugging on his leg followed by an insistent voice speaking to him from out of the darkness: "*Jim, hey, Jim. Don't give up, Jim. Be persistent. You hear me, Jim? Be persistent. Don't quit on me, okay? Don't quit. Do you hear me?*"

Youngblood rolled over, turning his back to the voice. "Yeah, I hear you," he muttered. "Now let me get some sleep, dammit."

Because he had been half asleep, Youngblood had no idea who had awakened him. Then again, it was no secret among his crewmates that he was getting tired of the daily grind, the monotony of living at sea. Considering the bitching and complaining he had done, Youngblood figured it had to have been one of his buddies concerned that the Georgian might quit the operation and go home.

The next morning, Youngblood approached each member of the crew, asking why the hell they had awakened him in the middle of the night. The crew pleaded innocence, wondering aloud if Youngblood was going psycho on them.

From left, Andy Matroci, Susan Nelson, and Mel Fisher celebrating with champagne. Today's the day!

"Then it hit me. All of a sudden I was covered with goose bumps. Swear to God, it had been the spirit of Mel Fisher who woke me up," Youngblood said. "There's no other explanation. Mel knew I was getting fed up with the operation. But he wanted me to hang in there and not give up. And then I made that first dive and found the silver bar. It was all Mel's doing; he helped me find that treasure—he was giving me a reason to go on, to continue with the search."

Ah, yes, continuing the search—finding the *Atocha's* missing sterncastle. Admittedly, I was as skeptical of its significance as I was of Youngblood's phantom visitor. Pat Clyne, who was now the company's vice president and public relations director, telephoned me in early August 1999, informing me that the search had been rekindled. The Florida Keys National Marine Sanctuary (FKNMS) had finally relented, awarding Mel Fisher's treasure salvors a permit to resume blowing holes in Hawk Channel.

Mel's old salvage boats, the *Dauntless* and the *Magruder*, had been refitted, new crews had been hired, and the search was once again under way.

"You need to get your butt back down here and do some diving, help us find some more treasure," Clyne said.

"Fantastic," I told him. But searching for what? I had been under the impression that Mel's Ghost Galleon had been found. Was I dreaming? Had I not spent all that time at sea in 1985 and 1986, diving and reporting on the discoveries?

Clyne laughed and said he and Mel's son Kim would explain everything just as soon as I arrived in the Keys. "There's treasure to be found," he said. "Like Mel used to always say, *today's the day.*"

20

Keeping the Dream Alive

I was afraid to dream, because if my dreams came true, then I just knew that I would be dead shortly thereafter.

—*Kim Fisher*

Over the course of my numerous trips to Key West to report on the *Atocha* search, I had learned a few statistics about Kim Fisher, Mel and Deo's second son. He was 44 and married. His wife, Lee, and he had two sons: Scott, age two, and Rick, six months. Kim also had three other sons—Jeremy, Sean, and Neko—from a previous marriage. Jeremy, 24, had recently earned a master's degree in electrical engineering from the University of Michigan. Kim had received a B.S. degree in business administration two decades earlier at Central Michigan University. He had attended Florida State University's law school, but dropped out after two years in the 1980s to rejoin his father's treasure-hunting operation.

That was the sum of my knowledge of the keeper of the flame, the new president and chief executive officer of Mel's treasure salvaging operation.

It was August 27, 1999, and I was sitting in Kim's office, which used to be Mel's, kicking myself for having spent almost 13 years away from what had once been my home away from home. From strictly a treasure hunter's point of view, my excuses sounded pretty lame—a regular job that paid me, without fail, on a weekly basis; helping my wife raise our family, which now included not only four daughters but also two sons-in-law and three grandsons. Indeed, I had become suburbanized.

Worse yet, I had not pulled on a wet suit since that memorable day in May 1986, when Donnie Jonas had shown me the wonders of the deep and the treasures it was so reluctant to surrender.

But now, awaiting Kim's arrival, I could feel the familiar flutter moving through my heart, which heralded the anticipation of long-lost riches. Admittedly, it was difficult to squelch the desire to sprint down to the dock and board one of the salvage boats, hell-bent for open water. First things first, for it was necessary to reacquaint myself. Very little had changed in my absence. Sherry Culpepper and Terri Jo Barnes continued to add their collective beauty as well as their skills to the Fisher headquarters; Pat Clyne was as effervescent as ever, speaking glowingly of treasure-finding days gone by and then telling wondrous tales of what the future held: "Just imagine what it's going to be like when we fan away the sand and come face-to-face with all that church gold."

Before I had time to contemplate that, Kim finally left the stockholders' meeting and entered the room. The shock was immediate. I had known him during his fast-track days. Tall and lean and deeply tanned, he had been recently divorced and was a carefree bachelor. When he was not bringing up gold from the *Atocha* or the 1715 fleet, he was tooling about the ocean in a cigarette boat, like one of the stars of *Miami Vice*.

The man standing before me now was the spitting image of his father. Kim had added a few pounds and trimmed his long hair.

But when he spoke, the voice was uncannily like Mel's—same inflection, same soft chuckle, almost the same carnival barker's pitch. Yet, as I would soon discover, Kim, unlike Mel, knew when not to stretch the limits of credibility. He was businesslike without surrendering pursuit of his father's dream, and seemed capable of having dreams and visions of his own. But for now, the *Atocha* still was his goal.

In short, Kim was a more sophisticated version of his father. Identical height and approximate weight, same easygoing smile. Same penchant for deflecting the conversation away from himself, more comfortable speaking glowingly of others. Kim always had been content standing in the shadows of the operation. As such, he had remained a mystery—always friendly as he smiled at inquisitive reporters, yet disappearing when the media sought his perspective. We had seldom crossed each other's path in the old days. Kim was either running his father's operation at Sebastian Inlet or sequestered on the museum's fourth floor, inventorying the loot. Other than one dive together in 1986, a memorable one because Kim found 40 feet of thin gold chain and a 10-pound gold disc, we had never spoken to one another.

Kim preferred it that way.

"Nothing personal, but all I can remember is seeing all you reporters at the dock that day, ready to sell more newspapers at the expense of Dirk's death. It made me angry at the time. I stayed angry for a long time after," Kim said. He paused, as if he were judging my reaction to the professional slap, and smiled when he saw me nod in agreement. And then he said, "But now, of course, I've finally worked through it." The laughter that followed was Mel's.

During the next few hours I would learn many things about this soft-spoken adventurer. Kim made it clear from the outset that he wished me well in my writing pursuit and that he would do anything within his power to make sure that his father's quest of the *Atocha* was told accurately. But when I told him that the story would be greatly enhanced if he lowered his guard and

Kim Fisher, Mel's son and
now the CEO of the *Atocha/
Margarita* Expedition, carrying
on the Fisher search under his
father's favorite motto.

talked about himself, his jaw dropped. The impression I got was
that Kim had never considered himself part of the story. Sure, his
father had passed on his legacy, but there never could be another
Mel Fisher. And yes, even though Kim's divers were making fantastic discoveries along Mel's old treasure trail, some folks were
saying that Mel was still finding treasure, even from the grave.
Kim had no problem with such talk because the title of "the
world's greatest treasure hunter" was his father's epitaph, not
something that could be bandied about.

"But there would be nothing wrong with people thinking of
you as the world's second-greatest treasure hunter, right?" I asked.

Kim smiled, which I interpreted as a good sign—like clear
skies and gentle seas. And before the day was over, he indeed lowered his guard, and a few background gems were brought to

the surface. But the telling was sometimes as painful as Kim had imagined it to be.

As for furthering his education, Kim said that law school was a natural course to navigate; he wanted to have the legal means to fight the government. He grew sick and tired of discovering treasure only to have the state and federal governments try to confiscate it.

"If finding treasure was easy," Kim said, "then everyone would be doing it. But if you are willing to dream, and just as important, willing to pursue that dream, then there surely is a price that will be paid. Unfortunately for our family, we've paid an awfully high price."

Kim made his first scuba dive at age nine on the 1715 fleet near Sebastian Inlet and discovered gold coins and a gold crucifix. Mel called him a natural because it just seemed as if Kim had a knack for finding what others failed to see—an artfully etched gold cup from the Quicksands, ornate jewelry, and gold chains. And when he wasn't diving, he was at Mel's side, watching the grand man's every action, every gesture, listening to the sales pitch as Mel talked total strangers into investing in the *Atocha* dream. Kim was a willing receptacle for his father's advice, the most memorable of which was, "Lawyers are there to help, but not to make business decisions."

In essence, Mel was telling his son to follow his heart, to give substance to his dreams. And what better dream to pursue than scouring the ocean for long-lost treasure?

Live this sort of lifestyle day in and day out well into your 30s and you are tainted for any job other than seeking yesteryear's lost wealth. Anyone can be a lawyer or a writer or whatever. But it takes a special breed of man or woman to sell his or her dreams to a skeptical public. Kim knew he had what it took to live this sort of life. But he was not the sort of individual who could sit back and wait for it to be handed to him. He was more than willing to roll up his sleeves and dig into whatever dirty job his father needed done.

As such, when Mel's diving crews were in hot pursuit of the *Atocha* in June and July 1985, Kim, captaining the *Bookmaker*, did the treasure trail's inglorious work, magging and side scanning. He made several dives with the *Dauntless*'s crew on July 19, recovering copper ingots, silver coins, and barrel hoops, but took his boat to port to refuel that evening, thus missing the next day's exhilaration when younger brother Kane found the mother lode. And once it was found, Kim did not grumble when Mel put him in charge of cataloging the hundreds of thousands of artifacts that would eventually be excavated from the *Atocha*'s tomb. Kim did the grunt work while others gloried in discovery, getting their names splashed throughout newspaper and magazine stories, or their faces shown on television during the five-o'clock news.

"Everything we did, we did as a team," Kim said. "When I look back on Dad's great discoveries—the ships he found off Vero, then discovering the *Margarita* and the *Atocha*—what made the greatest impression on me was the way my father treated people. In his mind, everyone was important. Nothing gets accomplished without other people. If Dad needed something done, something that looked impossible to most people, he would keep asking for help until he finally found someone who said, 'Sure, I can do that.' That's how I came to believe nothing was impossible."

Kim said that his father also taught him a unique way of problem-solving. Mel would envision the solution, then work backward, figuring out step by step how the task could be done. Normally, most people give up once they have bumped into a wall; Mel would look through the wall, his eyes always focused on his goal. Kim said that his mother, Deo, has the same qualities. In fact, "Ma still gives me lots of good advice; a lot of people give me advice. And I listen. You'd be surprised how much you learn by listening."

I asked Kim what he had learned from his older brother Dirk.

The question caught Kim off guard. His face reddened and his eyes clouded with tears. He looked away and took a deep breath, then turned back toward me and inched forward in his chair and absentmindedly moved aside a few pages of correspondence on his desk. The interlude between question and answer seemed like an eternity. Finally Kim made an admission that only his immediate family and a handful of friends knew: he had been a crew member of the *Virgilona* when it rescued the *Northwind*'s survivors and eventually brought the bodies of Dirk, Angel Fisher, and Rick Gage from out of the sunken salvage boat.

"I was out there that day. I can still remember. . . . " Kim looked away. He has always viewed grief as a private matter. And because he wished not to have the wound reopened every time a journalist new to the *Atocha* story showed up at Fisher headquarters, Kim's participation in the ordeal had remained secret. Fellow divers and family honored his wishes. Nonetheless, the memories remain fresh. He remembers waking up that morning and seeing that the *Northwind* was gone. He remembers following the oil slick until the *Virgilona* came across the survivors clinging to a raft. He remembers the call to the Coast Guard and them telling the *Virgilona*'s crew to retrieve the bodies.

"And once we'd done that, I remember crying all the way back to port," Kim said in a voice barely above a whisper. "But most of all, I remember it being the worst day of my life."

Unlike his father's death from lingering terminal cancer, Kim said there was no way to comprehend what happened to his brother. All Dirk had dreamed about was finding the *Atocha*'s cannons. He found them, only to die one week later.

"For the longest time after he died," said Kim, "I was afraid to set any goals; I was afraid to dream, because if my dreams came true, then I just knew that I would be dead shortly thereafter."

That attitude pervaded the company, which is why the *Atocha* search came to a virtual standstill. Overcoming Dirk's death was a slow process. Some of the divers rebounded quicker than others. Kim said he was finally able to move forward once it dawned on him that to abandon the search would be to admit that Dirk had died for nothing, that his death had been a waste.

"We continued searching for the *Atocha*'s mother lode because that's what Dirk would have wanted us to do," Kim said. "And now we're searching for the *Atocha*'s sterncastle because that's what Dad wanted us to do. And when we find it, and I know we will, it will be because of my father. Dad taught me the value of persistence. He believed in his dreams, as do I. He taught me to put aside the negative and move forward."

These words did not come easily for Kim. By nature he thinks long and hard before he speaks. More often than not, if the subject is disagreeable to him, he deftly steers the subject to safer seas. Long ago he became quite adept at avoiding treacherous shoals, which is why he was a good captain. So now he mentally spun the wheel and moved on, guiding us to the *Atocha*'s missing stern. He said that this portion of the 30-year search was not as turbulent as in the past because a truce had been reached with the government after the last court case over the company's alleged environmental damage. Kim and his colleagues were toeing the line. Not that they had broken any laws in the first place, not according to the Constitution of the United States.

Peace was at hand, and the government had shown its good faith months earlier by issuing Kim the permits required for his treasure divers to resume their hunt in Hawk Channel. This brought us to that multimillion-dollar question: What was left out there that necessitated permits in the first place?

Without flinching, Kim categorized the elusive prizes that almost everyone thought had been discovered. First of all, despite four years of salvaging the *Atocha*'s mother lode site from 1985 to 1988, no trace of the sterncastle was found. And it was in the stern area, Kim said, that the Spanish always stored their most valuable cargo—its vast deposits of gold and jewelry earmarked for the king and his court. The stern was where the 38 members of royalty were quartered, and there was no telling how much treasure they were transporting. This was the point in the conversation where I smiled, because not once had Kim thrown out a dollar figure, nor had he mentioned the number of pounds of gold. Had

A jubilant crew showing off sunken treasure. From left to right, the men behind Julie Fisher are Donnie Jonas, Kim Fisher, and me.

Mel been telling the tale, what remained on the *Atocha* would be 300 pounds of gold worth at least $100 million. When I shared this thought with Kim, he chuckled. He had Mel's chuckle down pat. Nonetheless, Kim took the hint and started talking hard figures: According to the ship's manifest, what had yet to be discovered were 297 silver bars, 35 boxes of church gold, 100,000 silver coins, and at least 68 pounds of emeralds, which he estimated at about 160,000 carats.

"As for what all this would be worth? Well, it's only treasure, meaning it's not real money. But I would say what's left out there certainly is worth more than we've already brought up from the *Atocha*," Kim said with a straight face. "I know you'd like a dollar figure, but that's difficult to calculate."

For instance, 19 different experts had valued the bulk of *Atocha* treasure recovered in 1985 and 1986, reaching wildly varying dollar figures. Average these totals, said Kim, and the best guess is $500 million. Monetarily speaking, there undoubtedly was more treasure remaining within the sterncastle than Fisher's divers had found to date. That was factoring in the normal 20 percent in contraband, plus the emeralds that his father said had been smuggled aboard. The emeralds alone would be worth more than everything combined, Kim said, hedging on an exact figure.

He allowed my imagination to calculate a grand total, then said, "Let's just say that there's an awful lot of fabulous artifacts left out there" before he politely excused himself for another meeting.

❀

Pat Clyne was more specific.

"Conservatively speaking, I'd put it at between $500 million and $1 billion," Clyne said, then hedged his estimate with an asterisk: "That's if *everything* is found. Of course, that's a big *if*. The difficulty factor rests with that second hurricane, which tore her sterncastle away from the rest of the ship. In essence she became a huge raft, dumping her contents along a path that extended for at least 10 miles."

Kim Fisher's divers could spend the next 20 years scouring Hawk Channel and still not find all of the treasure.

It is difficult to be in the company of active treasure hunters and not be pulled into their dreams. They will flip the pages of their bible, John S. Potter's revised edition of *The Treasure Diver's Guide*, and point out one stupendous yet undiscovered wreck after another—the *La Victoria* with its estimated $2 million in treasure, or Ibarra's ships with their $1 million in gold. They claim to know exactly where the prize in question went under. More important, they all have irrefutable documentation that places the big *X* on their treasure map. You are wise, indeed, if you contemplate these tales with a firm grasp on your wallet, for when it comes to deep-sea salvage, the ocean truly is bottomless. It has a bad habit of sucking up one's savings. More money has been spent searching for alleged treasure than has ever been brought to the surface.

It is all but impossible, however, to be in the company of an *Atocha* diver and not get delirious with greed, knowing you are on to a sure thing. The man or woman spinning the tale, for instance, is always wearing a gold doubloon or Spanish piece of eight about his or her neck—treasure personally found at the wreck site. The tales, though, are vague about where an artifact was found and about how much loot remained to be found. Loose lips not only sink ships but also scuttle treasure-hunting expeditions. Then again, if you doubt what still lies somewhere in Hawk Channel, simply stroll through Mel Fisher's museum. Surely the friars aboard the *Atocha* or the *Margarita* had more than one bishop's cross in their possession. Only slightly less mesmerizing are the rings set with diamonds and emeralds and the gold chains and the piles of silver coins, gold plates, and solid silver eating utensils. Equally stunning, said Clyne, was that some of this treasure had been found in the past few months.

Naturally, treasure wasn't being brought to the surface by the bucketful, not like Mel's divers did in 1985. But that was only because Kim's divers had not yet found what Clyne referred to as the "Second Coming," the second mother lode. But when they did uncover the *Atocha*'s missing stern, everything that had been found in the past would pale by comparison.

Needing an unbiased observer, I tracked down Don Kincaid. Although Key West was still his port of call, he no longer was a treasure salvor. The 54-year-old maritime scholar said he had finally grown up. He merely sailed for a living now. It's a pleasant, unencumbered way to earn a living, light-years removed from the seemingly eternal saga of the *Atocha*. Nonetheless, to this day he continues to be the most authoritative reference when it comes to the grand Ghost Galleon. Not really wishing to rain on anyone's parade, he said, what remained to be found from the *Atocha* was purely speculation.

"Thirty-five boxes of church gold? The ship's manifest says there were 35 boxes earmarked for the Catholic Church, but we have no way of knowing exactly what was inside those boxes," Kincaid said. "Emeralds? Yes, Mel always talked about a 70-pound box of emeralds being smuggled aboard, but nothing is listed on the manifest."

As for the alleged missing sterncastle, Kincaid spent months diving in the Quicksands between 1971 and 1975, bringing up arquebuses, swords, and daggers, all of which most certainly would have been in the ship's stern area, packed away directly below the captain's quarters. The majority of wondrous gold chains, cups, and plates also were extracted from the area's deep sands. Kincaid said it was obvious to him that they had found not only the stern but also the stern's anchors and the upper-deck cannons in the same area. Then again, perhaps the confusion was a matter of semantics. The divers of yesteryear had a fairly good idea of what they were searching for, based on noted historian Eugene Lyon's meticulous research.

"But what the majority of present-day divers are clutching onto," Kincaid said, "is myth or legend based on theories."

Nonetheless, when it came to the *Atocha*, one of the richest of all treasure galleons that sailed the Spanish Main, legends and myths are as much a part of her as the ravaged timbers that Kincaid so often brushed with trembling fingers. He doubted if anyone would ever know exactly how much treasure was brought onto that ship. More to the point, he said he could punch holes in everyone's theories from here to eternity, but it would not necessarily mean he was right and the others were wrong. After all, despite the lack of documentation for Mel Fisher's emerald theory, his divers discovered magnificent green stones in 1985 and 1986, and today's divers were finding them by the fistful every time they went to sea. Not to mention gold coins, gold bars, and hundreds of silver coins, which continued to be purchased by armchair adventurers for as much as $2,400 each.

"Fact of the matter is they're still finding treasure, even today," Kincaid said. The figurative vault that was the *Atocha* literally seemed to have no end. This is why even today, despite his suspicion that too much fiction was being intertwined with fact and too much credulity was being given to myths and theories, Kincaid would do it all over again. This negated his earlier statement about having finally grown up and grown out of thinking of himself as a treasure hunter.

When I brought this to his attention, Kincaid leaned back in his chair and smiled, then quoted Joseph Conrad, who understood mankind's frailties better than most: "Indeed, there is no way of getting away from treasure once it fastens itself upon your mind."

When I finally tracked down veteran diver Donnie Jonas, he injected a familiar touch of mystery to the present-day search when he told me, "There's no arguing facts. We never did find her keel, and we know the stern hit the big sandbar, the Quicksands, because of all the gold jewelry we found there. Is that where the stern finally came to rest? Maybe, maybe not."

After all, Jonas recalled that one of the *Atocha* cannons and two galleon anchors were discovered in 1984 northwest of the Bank of Spain, on a direct route to the Gulf of Mexico. It wasn't long afterward that a shrimp fisherman discovered an intact 17th-century olive jar in his net while working in 120-foot depths in the Gulf. All of this, said Jonas, leaves today's speculators with the identical information that he and his old-time diving buddies clutched at decades earlier when they searched for the *Atocha*'s mother lode: theories, conjecture, and guesses.

Jonas grinned, then said, "If I had to bet my life on it, I'd say she's still out there in the Quicksands, just like Kim says she is. 'Course, you'll never know for sure unless you go out there and take a look for yourself."

He didn't have to say it twice.

2 1

Bitch Galleon
of the Sea

I found a silver bar on my first trip to sea, and it ruined me.

—*Jim Youngblood*

C hristmas in August—that's how I will always remember my return to sea.

Although 13 years had elapsed since I last made this nautical journey, little had changed, for beneath my feet was the deck of the *J. B. Magruder*. Even she seemed to be celebrating the occasion, proudly skimming through the water with the aid of a new engine, her lustrous new coat of blue paint reflecting the rays of a punishing sun. It took only a few moments to feel the serenity of old, that carefree blanket of peacefulness that enveloped us as we glided toward a seemingly never-ending dream spread before us under a cloudless sky and a fairly calm sea slapping at the ship's hull. Almost the same quest, too, except now, on August 28, 1999, the divers were mopping up in the wake of the glory days of yesteryear.

The names of the captain and crew had changed. Gary Randolph now called the shots from the ship's helm, and Jeff Dickinson and Jim Youngblood carried out Randolph's orders with an assist from Jim Barker, a 43-year-old investor from Larkspur, California. And as an added bonus, joining us were my younger brother Jim and his wife, Mary Martin.

As Kim Fisher had pointed out the day before, everything concerning the *Atocha* search had always been done as a team. That included the compilation of this book. I would not have been here had it not been for my brother. Jim grew up hearing me tell all sorts of tales about Mel Fisher and his *Atocha* divers. Privately, Jim daydreamed about being a treasure diver. Being a realist, however, he pursued a normal life, if working within the political realm can be considered normal. Jim was now 38 and had spent the previous nine years as the top aide for Wisconsin state senator Russ Decker. On a whim, Jim and Mary vacationed two years ago in Key West, actually meeting Mel and some of his old divers. Next thing you know, they said good-bye to Wisconsin's horrible winters and took up residence on this island. They were simply following their fantasies, they said. And that was how they were there in the maddening crowd at Mallory Square a month earlier, during Mel Fisher Day on July 20, and stumbled on Pat Clyne and Don Kincaid. Introductions were made, the foursome hit it off, and that evening Clyne had telephoned me, urging me to join the party at sea.

This was how we found ourselves leaving port aboard the *Magruder*, each of us consumed by treasure fever as we made the three-hour trip to the dive site, which I was told would be halfway up the northwest line that connected the mother lode and the Bank of Spain. I used the time to get acquainted with the crew.

Jim Barker was a veteran diver. He had vacationed in the Keys in 1994, visited the Greene Street museum, and struck up a conversation with Mel Fisher, who promptly escorted Barker to Key West Harbor, pulled up a stool at the Schooner Wharf Bar, and began filling Barker's head with tales about all the treasure that remained to be found from the *Atocha*'s missing sterncastle. One thing led to another, most of which centered on Mel's attempts to induce Barker to invest in the new search; then Mel ordered another round of drinks. "And when the waitress placed my drink in front of me," Barker said, "Mel reached over and stirred it with a gold finger-bar. You know what that is, don't you? It's shaped like one of those breadsticks you get at a restaurant, except it's about nine inches of solid gold. Yes, sir, the man certainly knew how to close a deal."

Barker immediately bought into the operation and spent his vacations ever since in diving on his investment.

The familiar story about Mel's selling techniques rekindled my own memories—only briefly, though, because the old gang was long gone. Donnie Jonas was now a landlord, Don Kincaid a sailing entrepreneur, Tom Ford was working with the U.S. Navy monitoring tactical aircraft, and Andy Matroci was in Guam, running his own treasure salvaging business. "Bouncy John" Lewis still resided in Key West, enjoying the laid-back lifestyle as the chief maintenance engineer for three local hotels, and Keith "Sharkbait" Curry, Angel Fisher's brother, was now a UPS driver in Miami. Syd Jones and his wife, K. T., also had left the operation, four years earlier, to restore and fly World War II fighter planes, working now for Tom Reilly in Kissimmee, Florida. It was a melancholy moment, for I truly missed being in the company of the usual assortment of sea gypsies; seeing them toting AR-15s or a Colt .45 to repel would-be pirates, or hearing Jonas call for a "safety meeting," which was just an excuse for the crew to venture into the wheelhouse for a beer.

Even more disheartening was strolling into the crew's quarters and not seeing the usual assortment of goodies strewn about—gold chains, silver coins, and plastic bags full of emeralds.

On this late August day, times were lean but not quite as mean as I had remembered them. It took little time, however, to feel as if everyone was family. Granted, it was not the dysfunctional family of yesterday, but family nonetheless.

Captain Gary Randolph, 34, was unequivocally in charge of the seagoing operation. Tall, lean, and deeply tanned, he was soft-spoken and polite. Like every other treasure salvage captain I had met over the years, Randolph was not someone who used his position to command respect. He earned it by never asking a member of his crew to do anything he was not willing to do himself. Randolph participated in the daily dive schedule, took his turn at cooking, and helped out with the ship's maintenance. He possessed a Clark Gable–like self-assurance, which helped explain why he was out here at sea instead of sitting behind a computer inside some corporate cubicle.

Equally impressive were Randolph's credentials. A native of New Jersey, he was a college graduate who majored in mechanical engineering, eventually building computers for Charles Schwab. Seeking a relief from stress, he took up scuba diving and promptly fell in love with the sport. It was a natural accompaniment to his long-standing interest in shipwreck lore that had led him to read everything he could find about pirates and their adventures sailing the Spanish Main. Finding treasure was just a dream, however. But then he and his wife, Linda, vacationed in Key West in the summer of 1995, visited Mel Fisher's museum, and learned that divers were still searching for remnants of the *Atocha*. When he inquired further, Randolph was introduced to Mel, who was impressed with the newcomer's diving and computer expertise. Mel promptly put Randolph in touch with Syd Jones, captain of the *Magruder*. Syd and his wife, K. T., were getting ready to leave the operation, and Syd was looking for someone able to take over his duties.

"Of course, at that time I was merely curious about what Mel and his divers were up to, nothing more," said Randolph. "We're at sea and I'm having the time of my life. Then Syd says, 'The job is yours. When can you start?'"

Dumbfounded back in port, Randolph told his wife about the bizarre job offer. Linda was all smiles. Tired of the stress of her duties as the Jersey regional manager for NutriSystems, she responded, "Let's go for it." Two days later, Gary was at the helm of the *Magruder*, and Linda, also a veteran diver, was aboard as a bona fide treasure salvor, diving on the Bank of Spain. Soon she uncovered a chest of silver coins—2,000 pieces of eight that would be valued at $2 million. In December of that year, Randolph discovered a gold coin, a gold chain, and a gold ring. The Randolphs were hooked, and there was no looking back.

But Gary was the first to admit that his adventure did not compare to what Mel's divers experienced in the early days of the hunt. He said he and his crew were disappointed if they didn't find treasure every day, whereas the old hands went years without finding anything. "We're still the new guys, the second generation of treasure salvors," Randolph said. "We're simply following in the footsteps of the old crews."

These footsteps had led all of us to this very spot in Hawk Channel. As Randolph explained, what he and Robbie Hanna, captain of the *Dauntless*, were now doing was filling in the large gaps in the previous search. Unrolling a big chart in the tight quarters of the wheelhouse, Randolph pointed out the clearly marked path of Mel Fisher's prolonged *Atocha* odyssey. At the top left-hand corner of the chart was the location of two recovered *Atocha* anchors; at the bottom right-hand corner was the mother lode, where Fisher's divers had recovered 30 tons of silver in July 1985. The distance between the two points, northwest to southeast on a 165-degree line, was 12 miles; the Bank of Spain lies almost in the middle. Some of the territory had been searched throughout the past 30 years, but only what Randolph considered in "hit and miss" fashion, with far more misses than hits. To date, said Randolph, approximately five miles of the southeast end of the trail had been thoroughly scoured, excavated, and picked clean.

Sounds easy enough, except that it took almost 18 months to complete the task. Before the first new hole was ever blown, Randolph sequestered himself with Donnie Jonas and Syd Jones, and together they pored over Mel's old search-and-recovery charts.

They took the outdated loran readings of the 1970s and Del Norte data of the 1980s and converted them to today's standard Global Positioning System (GPS) reckoning. Confusing, yes, unless you are a computer whiz, which is Randolph's strong point. With the old charts in hand, plus a portable magnetometer on board, Jones and Randolph traveled the 12-mile route, confirming old mag hits and still-unexplored anomalies, diving when necessary, and essentially recharting the entire trail. That done, Jones departed to fly World War II aircraft, leaving the arduous work of blowing holes to the New Jersey newcomer.

What always went unsaid was everyone's belief that the missing stern was tucked away in the 15-feet-deep sands of the Quicksands. But what if it wasn't? This was why every possible inch of the area southeast of the Quicksands had to be rechecked and reexcavated.

"And that's exactly what we did," Randolph said. "In the months and years since, we've narrowed the search to a 60-foot-wide path that extends for seven miles. Not exactly a needle in the haystack; not exactly the easiest job in the world, either. But we're making progress."

Progress on a treasure salvage boat, however, is measured in 30-foot intervals, the approximate size of the craters the boat makes when holes are blown in the sand. On a good day, the captain and crew can move 60 feet up the trail. Over the normal eight-day duration of each excursion to the search trail, each of Kim Fisher's two recovery vessels can cover almost a fifth of a mile if everything goes well. It rarely does. Generators, air compressors, winches, and other mechanical gear fail frequently. And there is the weather. Diving operations cease when waves exceed four feet. When a hurricane strikes, everyone stays in port. Still, this rate of progress reflects a corporate approach that is in stark contrast to earlier years, when the flip of a coin could decide whether to go to sea, or stay in port with a girlfriend or belly up to a bar. Also, drugs and alcohol are not tolerated; periodic urine tests are required.

Dickinson, 41, is Randolph's first mate. Possessed of a quick wit and perpetual leprechaun smirk, Dickinson is a dead ringer for the comedian Gallagher. Dickinson showed his lighthearted side only when the day's work was done. The rest of the time he was a no-nonsense, highly regimented by-the-book diver. Today's dive conditions were less than ideal, he said, with 10 feet of visibility. Then he wasted no time going over the long list of safety procedures—hand signals, what conditions would be like 46 feet below the surface, what we would be looking for and how we would be searching for it, and what to do in case of an emergency.

"No showboating," he said. "I want everyone to stay in the hole where I can see you. Got it?" *Got it.* Dickinson made sure that the dive gear he'd loaned me was working properly, then asked offhandedly, "So, how long's it been since your last dive?"

I grinned and said, "Thirteen years."

Ah, we've got a problem, Houston. The color drained from Dickinson's face, and he quickly disappeared into the wheelhouse. Indeed, I would learn, a lot had changed over the years. Even though I was an experienced treasure diver, I was not a certified *scuba* diver. Big difference, Captain Randolph explained. Not only was it a matter of safety but also liability, so I would not be able to dive until Pat Clyne showed up and assumed total responsibility, personally guiding me to the bottom.

Which was cool, because Clyne eventually arrived via his fast boat and we entered the water, stepping out and turning in midair so that we would immediately find the down rope that led from the side of the vessel to the middle of the blown hole. Without this aid, the strong current would carry us half a mile away before we realized it. No problems, though. We found the hole with little difficulty, then began the meticulous search; one diver scoured the bottom of the hole with his metal detector while the other diver used his detector to scan the sides of the sand berm. Forty minutes later we had one badly abused lobster trap to show for our effort.

Subsequent dives that day produced pottery shards and a piece of skull, origin unknown. Just another typical day of frustration, said Dickinson, who had seen more than his fair share in years past. Before joining Randolph on the treasure trail eight months earlier, Dickinson had worked as an engineer in Saudi Arabian oil fields. It was a sedate life—good pay, no women, no booze. Dying of boredom, he taught himself to scuba, eventually diving on a 13th-century Arabian wreck near Yemen and discovering several hundred pounds of silver coins. Thoroughly bitten by the treasure bug, Dickinson returned to the States, sent out résumés, and finally hooked up with Kim Fisher in December 1998 at a coin show in Reno, Nevada.

Born and raised in Macon, Georgia, Jim Youngblood, a 32-year-old former Marine, had spent the past eight years running an end-loader in a rock quarry, working 14-hour days, seven days a week. Sure, he said, the money was great, but the lifestyle sucked. He kept picturing himself dying at the controls of the big metal beast; plenty of money in his bank account, yet nothing to show for his effort. Then he vacationed in the Keys, answered a help-wanted ad in the local newspaper, and eventually ended up on the *Magruder.*

"I found a silver bar on my first trip to sea, and it ruined me," he said. Now all he thought about was treasure. More to the point, finding one of the eight remaining *Atocha* cannons. Kim Fisher had promised a $10,000 bonus to the diver who discovered one, and Youngblood planned to be the one to collect it. To ensure his success, Youngblood was wearing his lucky diving shorts and lucky fins.

But there were no cannons to be found on this day. Just pleasant diving with pleasant company, which prompted deep reflection as I stood at the ship's starboard rail, watching the orange ball of sun bury itself on the horizon, watching the blue-green water lap at itself, barely hearing the sea because its voice was drowned out by the incessant growl of the twin diesels. With a breeze and a light spray of salt water brushing my face, I stared at the small whitecaps and was mesmerized, for I knew that somewhere far below them was treasure—riches I had actually discovered firsthand, not make-believe stuff. And now I was once again experiencing the frustration of the search, knowing all too well that if you missed a gold or a silver coin by an inch, you might as well have missed it by a mile. I had seen it happen, fanning the sand to my right and coming up empty, only to see another diver fan the sand barely half a foot away and come up with a silver coin. Maddening. Frustrating, too. But it sure as hell beat working for a living.

Out there at sea, where you can barely see the glow of Key West on the horizon, no one cared about anything other than finding treasure. At that corner of an ever-shrinking world, either you could dive or you couldn't. Although I was a member of this special brotherhood, I still found it difficult to believe that I had been away from it for so long. It seemed like only yesterday that I was on this same vessel, almost at the same spot with the Marquesas now a shadowy smear to my right under a blanket of stars and a full moon that cast an eerie reflection on black water; the deck unforgiving to the soles of your feet; the sea unforgiving of your mistakes.

Closing my eyes, I could still hear the old crew telling their favorite stories about Mel Fisher, laughing constantly at his idiosyncrasies. And always dreaming of treasure, truly believing that today would be the day we found it. When I opened my eyes, I knew that nothing had really changed, which was why I thanked God once again for the opportunity to do what few others have actually done, living life by my own set of rules, allowing the kid in me to rule the roost. I pumped my arm in celebration and then found an unoccupied bunk inside the cabin. I collapsed and was fast asleep.

Our second day on the trail proved more successful. Five dolphins circled the boat while the first hole was being blown. It was a good omen, said Dickinson, grinning. Sure enough, Jim Barker entered the water and promptly found a silver coin buried a foot under the hard-packed sand. An hour later, Dickinson and my brother Jim discovered a twisted iron spike embedded in a fist-size chunk of what archaeologists would later determine to be part of the *Atocha*'s decking. The day's fifth hole produced large ballast, but then the bow anchor's line snapped and the search was halted to make repairs. "Just another day in paradise," said Youngblood. Two hours later, the search began again. It was a race against a rapidly dying sun and angry seas, which had steadily increased throughout the day, finally topping off at three-foot swells.

"Adventure is a matter of interpretation," said Youngblood with a knowing grin as he positioned a newly filled tank into his buoyancy control device. Looking back, it was bizarre that he should have said that before entering the water with my brother Jim, who wanted to photograph Youngblood working a blown hole. The plan was to use their entire 50-minute duration posing and taking various shots, which went as scheduled for the first half hour. But then a seven-foot tiger shark cruised between them. Youngblood froze as the blue-gray beast passed inches away. Jim saw nothing because he was checking his camera's lens setting. When he finally looked up to snap the picture, Youngblood's eyes were like saucers. Youngblood rapidly ran his finger across his throat and pointed to the surface. Baffled, my brother reluctantly followed. When they had shed their gear, Jim asked why their dive had been cut short.

Youngblood grinned and said, "Big fish. A *really* big fish."

Only when Youngblood uttered the most feared of all diving's lexicon—"jaws"—did my brother get the point. Neither went back into the water. They had had enough fun for one day.

And then, just as the sun set, Dickinson surfaced at the diving ladder, spit out his mouthpiece, and flashed a mischievous grin.

In his left hand was another silver coin, which elicited a handshake from Randolph. The captain had seen far better days—the gold chain he found on November 4, 1995, for example. And who could ever forget the gold ring with the emerald setting, treasure valued at $800,000, which he discovered near this very spot on January 4, 1997? But two coins were better than nothing. The only problem, said Randolph, was that the *Atocha* continued to tease him and his crew, surrendering only a small portion of her treasure each time, enticing them to return time and time again.

Randolph looked longingly at the sea, then laughed and said, "Yeah, this is not a job; it's a lifestyle."

Later that evening, Jeff Dickinson stood at the ship's rail and stared contentedly into the sea. It had been a fairly good day, he said, but nothing like those of months past when he had found a gold bit and more silver coins than he could keep track of. Now the discoveries had slowed almost to a standstill as the crew had moved farther north on the trail. Just a damn dribble of coins, which prompted Dickinson to imagine what it must have been like for some unfortunate sailor as the hurricane bore down on the *Atocha* 377 years ago. The way his mind's eye saw it, the doomed sailor must have known that someday a handful of eager treasure salvors would be looking for the tons of loot packed into the great galleon's stern.

"So, just to make things interesting," Dickinson said, "that dude had a chest full of coins at his feet. And every five minutes or so he'd flip a solitary coin into the angry ocean, saying, 'She loves me,' then five minutes later he'd toss another coin to the sea and say, 'She loves me not.'"

We shared a laugh, then retired for the evening, knowing full well that we would find the *Atocha*'s missing stern during tomorrow morning's first dive. We did not, though. Nor in the ensuing dives in the days that followed.

※

Eight months later, on April 18, 2000, I was back on the trail, having been properly certified by this time and in the company of Peter Hess, a Delaware lawyer who specializes in admiralty and maritime law. Hess is unique in his trade, a man who actually straps on a diving tank and gets down to the level of those he represents. He is a diver, but not just any diver. The 40-year-old Hess has an affinity with all things historic, which was what had led him to Key West in the first place, working for Dave Horan, Mel Fisher's longtime attorney, long before the *Atocha's* mother lode was discovered. Hess's first dive on the *Atocha* trail was in 1983 with Kim Fisher. In 1985, diving with archaeologist Duncan Mathewson, Hess actually touched the *Atocha's* timbers a few days after she was discovered. Those dives changed his life. So much so that Hess took up mixed-gas diving to reach the extreme depths that held two other elusive wrecks, the *Andrea Doria*, the Italian passenger ship that sank on July 25, 1956, off Nantucket Island after a collision with the Swedish cruise ship *Stockholm*; and the *Monitor*, the Civil War ironclad that battled the Confederate *Merrimac* to a standstill at Hampton Roads on March 9, 1862, before foundering off Hatteras on December 31, 1862. Hess is the only diver who had actually touched three of the four best-known shipwrecks in history. Only the *Titanic* was out of his reach.

On this storm-threatened spring day, however, Hess was in search of what he called the *crème de la crème* of nautical lore, the *Atocha's* sterncastle. Over the past few months, Gary Randolph and his divers had become convinced they were closing on the elusive prize, having discovered three gold bars and numerous gold coins on the ever-shortening trail. And somewhere out there, surely now within his grasp, Hess vowed, were the military accoutrements he longed to see—those 17th-century swords, daggers, and arquebuses that the *Atocha's* conquistadors had carried aboard a scant few days before the *Atocha* sank.

How much of a history nut Hess is became obvious the moment we stepped on the *Magruder's* pitching deck. Soon the lawyer was talking to Captain Randolph about the Spanish army in 1622, then the dominant power in Europe and virtually undefeated on the battlefield. And then the conversation shifted to Spain having revolutionized warfare by equipping its foot soldiers with the arquebus, the forerunner of the musket. Hess said he would rather find an arquebus than gold or silver. All of us had a few laughs at Hess's expense as he pulled on his gear.

"Find an arquebus!" Randolph yelled to Hess as he entered the water.

The lawyer drifted down to the bottom 34 feet below, joining Jeff Dickinson in the freshly blown hole. As Hess moved closer to the sand berm, he saw his dive partner tugging on an elongated object stuck deep in the side of the crater. And that's when Hess's eyes bugged out, for Dickinson was tugging on the iron barrel of an arquebus. Moments later, Hess brought the heavily encrusted weapon to the surface, keeping it out of sight as he neared the dive ladder. All of us on deck could see Hess struggling, battling the heavy chop. Our immediate reaction was that something had gone awry, for Hess had been in the water fewer than three minutes. Only when Hess started up the ladder did we get our first glimpse of the antique weapon. We were too dumbfounded to do anything except grasp Hess's hand and pound him on the back.

Hess's response was priceless: "You asked for an arquebus, so I complied," he said, having the last laugh. And then he handed over the artifact to Gary Randolph, pulled on his mask, and prepared to return to the hole.

Before he did, though, Randolph yelled, "Gold bar!"

Laughing, we all rushed to the side of the ship and waited for him to surface.

22

Life in Paradise

I'd rather be here drinkin' a beer than freezin' my ass off in the
north.

     —*Michael McCloud*, "The Conch Republic Song"

Viewed through the tunnel vision that was my journalistic perspective in 1985 and 1986, Key West was a narrow
strip of sidewalk that led from Mel Fisher's Greene
Street museum to Conch Harbor, where Mel's salvage boats were
docked. Between the two points were various saloons, where most
of my interviews were conducted, and the Half Shell Raw Bar,
which still serves the best fried shrimp in town. While most folks
will tell you that Key West is a good little drinking town with a
bad fishing habit, I was unable to verify that because if I wasn't
interviewing Mel or his divers, I was at sea on the *Atocha* trail.

It wasn't until August 1999 that I saw the community in its
entire sun-soaked splendor, which probably explains why I have
made it a habit to return at least three times a year ever since.
Naturally, diving for treasure also has a lot to do with the sojourns.

Key West was Mel Fisher's kind of town. There was a good
reason for this, the biggest of which is that this community is not
for everyone. It is an adult Disneyland—so laid back that you

The Minimal Regatta at Schooner Wharf in Key West.

swear you are functioning in the comfort of a recliner. It matters not whether you are on foot barhopping, tooling about Old Town on a bicycle, or walking the decks of the catamaran *Stars & Stripes* or the schooners *Western Union* or *America*. No one gives you a second look, no matter how outrageous you misbehave or dress. If a Breathalyzer test were mandatory, the average reading on quite a few citizens here would perhaps register 1.3 shortly after breakfast, at about noon. From that point, the reading would gradually rise to the comatose level, which normally happens shortly after sunset in the company of a maddening crowd that has gathered at the Mallory Square docks. Be warned: When the sun dips into that distant horizon, the cheers and applause have nothing to do with the record number of beers or margaritas you may have consumed; it simply is tradition, a Key West thing.

The proximity of the Spanish shipwrecks *Santa Margarita* and *Nuestra Señora de Atocha* dictated that Mel Fisher and his family call this island home. But it is not a stretch to say that had the two galleons sank anywhere else along the Eastern Seaboard, Mel would have run aground in any other port of call. In Key West he blossomed, being allowed to beg or borrow to keep his salvage boats at sea, and being allowed to be as boisterous as need be to corral investors, but most of all being allowed to be himself. Mel latching onto Key West, or vice versa, was a marriage made in treasure hunter's heaven—the joining of arguably the world's biggest dreamer with a community that abhors the Establishment while embracing all forms of celestial pilots, no matter what their flights of fancy.

Mainlanders with axes to grind don't last long here. You either adapt or the population chews you up, spits you out, and sends you back home.

This is a unique community with an indifferent history, long the home of profiteers of varying degree—salvors, buccaneers, and smugglers, but mostly everyday folks who simply wished to be left alone. This attitude was best characterized during the Civil War. Shortly after hostilities began, a Union naval contingent captured Fort Zachary Taylor. Key Westers responded by drinking a few beers, then shrugged their collective shoulders and gave their allegiance to Abraham Lincoln. A would-be Johnny Reb had to go north to join the South.

Key Westers did a complete turnabout 121 years later when, on April 23, 1982, they seceded from the Union and changed the name of their homeland to the Conch Republic. President Reagan, intent on halting the influx of drugs into the Keys, ordered a roadblock at Florida City, and a thorough search of every vehicle. Before you could say "Make that two reefers," traffic was backed up for 26 miles. The Key West tourist trade was crippled. Infuriated at being treated like a Third World nation, Key Westers seceded and declared war on the United States, then promptly surrendered and applied for $4 million in foreign aid.

The populace created its own flag and declared Mel Fisher its king in perpetuity. Not Jimmy Buffett, mind you. Not Tennessee Williams or Ernest Hemingway, all more universally famous. Key Westers chose one of their own, presumably because this community's everyday party animals could more easily identify with Mel.

The most priceless of the Conch Republic's commodities is anonymity. People come here to get away in one form or fashion. No one ever asks why you had to get away or from whom or from what you are running, for it seems as if everyone here is running away from something. After all, this is the end of the road. And once your roots are firmly planted, you discover that you have run *toward* something far better than anything you have ever before experienced. While everything else is for sale here, peace of mind has no price tag.

Four phrases sum up the lifestyle: "Don't do anything until I get back," "I'm gonna be late," "I'm gonna be real late," or "I just can't make it today." TV's travelwise Charles Kuralt once spent a month here, enjoying a daily beer at the Schooner Wharf Bar. At the end of what he assumed to be his last beer there, he turned to the CBS camera and said this of his newly adopted community and its favorite watering hole: "Key West is the center of the universe. It is a speck of rock in a pastel sea. Palms whisper. Songbirds sing. The place has never known a frost. People spend their days at rest in wicker chairs on gingerbread verandas. Flowers bloom all year and love is free. Without a hint of irony, everybody calls it Paradise."

And then on second thought, Kuralt ordered another beer and missed his flight. At least that is what the locals like to say.

Spend enough time traversing the island at a leisurely pace and you will hear plenty of stories such as that. If you're wise, you will take the journey via bicycle, which is the one surefire way of discarding your accumulation of inhuman indifference. Tooling along on a bike is a juggling act, trying to balance worldly knowledge with a newfound preteen state of mind. The hard part is avoiding low-hanging palm fronds that have a tendency to whack you in the face. But with a little practice you're actually able to pedal, sip a cup of coffee, but avoid getting run over by speeding tourists who still haven't figured this place out.

That cup of coffee, by the way, was purchased at the corner of Margaret and Fleming Streets. I noticed the sign that read "Books, Art & Coffee," failing to notice the big print above it: "Flaming Maggie's." The gentleman behind the counter was friendly enough, the coffee superb. But when I decided I needed some reading material and sought his advice about a good mystery, he smiled and asked, "Gay or straight?"

Did I mention that it's easy to get lost in Key West?

On a bike, you allow your blood pressure to normalize, your cholesterol to flatten out, and you basically do nothing but glide, allowing life to come to you instead of pursuing the unobtainable at 65 miles per hour. You also are able to see what is going on around you. You see that Duval Street is a maze of taverns and clothing merchants; one group sells the same beer at the same price, the other group sells identical T-shirts at the same price. On the other side of the island you see Smathers Beach, where the sand also has a tourist quality to it. Key West is a clump of coral, so sand must be brought in on barges and deposited along the hardtop shore, where the tide gradually pulls it back into the sea.

Pedal your way back toward Mallory Square, tooling northwest down White Street, and you bump into the U.S.S. *Maine* Memorial; hang a left on Southard, then another left on Whitehead, and you bump into Hemingway House. The journey that began 14 years earlier finally ended on Papa's front porch. I toured his home, viewed his writing room and rustic typewriter and even petted his feline descendants, hoping some of the great man's spirit would rub off on me. Although Hemingway viewed the world through a different set of eyes, you still can glimpse what he once saw, for directly across the street is the Lighthouse Museum and its towering beacon to another time and place. And when you have tired of this, simply reverse course up Whitehead and glimpse Mel Fisher's museum, then enjoy some Cuban cuisine next door at the Horny Pelican Café. If you're lucky, Bob Wandras will be entertaining customers. Wandras goes by the moniker "Trumpet Bob." He first came to the Keys in 1952 as a

17-year-old sailor, which makes him an old salt. But from my laid-back perspective, he is ageless on the trumpet.

After hearing Wandras's rendition of "Saint James Infirmary," you can jump back on the bike, hang a right on Greene, and sit a spell with Anthony Tarracino, better known to his friends as Captain Tony. This is exactly what I did on a recent December afternoon, laying the bike down and sitting with Tony in front of his saloon as he kept me spellbound with another of his wondrous stories—what Mel Fisher was *really* doing when his divers discovered those 30 tons of silver bars on July 20, 1985. Tarracino told me that when the good news reached Mel's office via ship-to-shore radio, Mel was among the missing—he was enjoying a drink at Captain Tony's Saloon.

"First of all, one of Mel's office personnel calls, asking if he was there. Mel shakes his head, so I say he ain't there," Tarracino said. "Then the cops call; again I say Mel ain't there. Problem is, no one bothered to say that Mel's divers had found the mother lode and that he was now a fabulously rich man. Finally, the cops came through the door and escorted Mel back to the museum. 'Course, he was pretty shit-face by then." With a burst of laughter, Tarracino added, "Yeah, now that's one story you won't ever hear on that *National Geographic* video."

True enough. The *National Geographic* shows Mel walking up to his museum that day with a bag in hand. "Where've you been, Mel?" someone asks. Mel chuckles, raises the bag, and says, "Bought me some diving gear."

What's truth, what's fiction? On this island it's difficult to sift one from the other. Half the old-timers will tell you that Mel was indeed buying diving gear. The other half swears he was drinking rum on Greene Street. I think Captain Tony's rendition has more of a Key West flavor to it. He agrees, still laughing to himself as I jumped back on the bike and pedaled toward the harbor, taking in all sorts of sights that would be considered obscene anywhere else but here: orange-haired girls, pretty guys holding hands with guys, and rough-looking tattooed people walking around with huge snakes, parrots, or iguanas on their shoulders. All these folks were doing what Jimmy Buffett preached—moving along at three-quarters time.

Speaking of Buffett, Captain Tony said that Buffett enjoys telling Mel Fisher stories rather than talking about himself. In fact, everyone in this community, large and small, famous or infamous, has a Mel Fisher story to tell. If Hemingway were alive today, Tarracino said Papa would be spinning tales about Mel.

Finally I eased into the Schooner Wharf Bar, which Mel Fisher loved for the same reasons as Charles Kuralt did. If you bothered to wear a wristwatch, a rarity in Key West, your clock could have been set by Mel's arrival. At 5:00 P.M. each evening he would pull up a stool and sit with his back to the harbor, an ever-present rum and Diet Coke in hand. Captain Morgan was the brand he preferred, although he was not picky. Nonetheless, Paul and Evalena Worthington, who own this establishment, always kept Mel's preference in stock.

Mel was everything good about this tiny burg of last resort, said Paul. Mel was a chance-taker, a three-time loser, a drinker, and one helluva good sport. Although he had plenty of enemies, he was never one to hold a grudge. And while he was often down and out, looking up for relief, he refused to dwell on the negative side of life. Mel was downright positive that his proverbial ship would eventually come in. And when it did, he would pay all of his divers and staff their back wages, pay off the rest of the bills, then sit back and enjoy a stiff drink or two.

The Schooner Wharf Bar is the gathering place of misfits and mystics, characters and oddballs, shrimpers and pirates and many other movers and shakers of this tightly packed corner of the universe. Even after Mel's death, it is also where all *Atocha* stories begin and end. Until spring 2000, the *Dauntless* and the *Magruder* were docked just a few steps down the pier. The boats are now docked at Stock Island. Before the move, however, when the crews departed during the early morning hours, they were given a resounding send-off from the bar's "Breakfast Club," a unique group of highly trained patrons who proudly wear their T-shirts that proclaim: "If it ain't Bud, it ain't breakfast."

The club still meets daily, and memories remain fresh. Ask any of these gentlemen about Mel Fisher and they will tell you he was always first and foremost a regular guy, someone you could always strike up a conversation with, even if the subject had nothing to do with finding long-lost Spanish treasure. You would say "Hi, Mel" and he would slowly turn toward you, crack a little smile, and then perk up a bit if you were escorting a young lady.

Local singer-songwriter Michael McCloud, who often sings at the Schooner Wharf Bar, has written two songs honoring Fisher: "The Ballad of the *Atocha*" and "Today's the Day." While neither was a commercial success, their composition was not intended to reap financial reward. McCloud simply wanted to honor an individual "who didn't have a mean bone in his body." McCloud's admiration of Mel is best summed up in the *Atocha* lyrics:

> His dreams are born in legend and lore
> In a ghostly Spanish tale;
> Gold and emeralds and possibly more
> As he follows the treasure trail

At the Schooner Wharf Bar, the party atmosphere was in full swing. Margo, Jamie, Vick, Lora, Freddie, Lee, and Bob tried their best to avoid stray dogs underfoot as they waited on tables. Another dude, named Jim, kept the kitchen in order while bartenders Bob, Kelly, Chris, Angie, and Liz kept the flow of bottled beer moving from ice-filled coolers to customers, mainly to Fishin' Jim, my brother Jim, and Lanny Franklin.

My brother was in his full glory. Having spent so many years in Madison, Wisconsin, stuck in the very rump of winter, he now found himself surrounded by new friends and about to embark on his lifelong dream of being a treasure salvor. Very much bewildered, he smiled as he surveyed his new digs, then shouted, "I don't know what this is all about, but it sure as hell doesn't suck!" And then he ordered another round of drinks.

Soon the bar was packed, and Raggs managed to keep the coolers adequately stocked, but only barely. And up there onstage, Michael McCloud paid homage to the insane festivities by singing a little ditty, his "Tourist Town Bar":

> We get bimbos and bozos and bikers and boozers,
> Daytime drunks and three-time losers.
> We get a room full of rednecks and fancy dressed fellows,
> Busloads of blue hairs and dirt bags and sailors

The tourists loved the lyrics, despite their blue hair and red necks. Even the bimbos and dirt bags smiled, while the bikers proudly showed off their tattoos and gave Michael the finger. A good time was being had by all.

Then again, everyone was beyond caring. It was almost 3:00 P.M.

23

The Search Goes On

We're gonna find us some gold.
—*Robbie Hanna*

I had been around the ocean long enough to know that salvage boats, much like combat veterans, need to be pulled from out of the line of fire from time to time and given proper rest and refurbishment. The alternative is never pleasant.

The *Dauntless* was the oldest and most abused of the Fisher nautical warhorses. When she was finally pulled from the water, her most dominant features were rust and a patchwork of welded plates adorning her keel. How desperate she was in need of restoration became obvious when Captain Robbie Hanna, attempting to detect her weak spots, began tapping on her bottom with a hammer. Huge portions of the *Dauntless's* steel plating disintegrated at his touch. What Hanna had hoped to be a four-month job grew to a nine-month ordeal before the *Dauntless* was deemed seaworthy, proving once again that there is far more to being a treasure salvor than diving for gold and silver.

It was nine months of fashioning steel panels and welding them into place, chipping away a two-year accumulation of rust and replacing most of the keel coolers, the wheelhouse, mailboxes, and completely redoing the crew's quarters. Nine months of the grungiest work any sailor could possibly tackle, a curious mix of labor and love: 10 hours a day, six days a week in temperatures that continually hovered at 88 degrees and 80 percent humidity, with just the barest hint of a wind. It was necessary work, for the *Dauntless* would be a floating catastrophe without it. It was spiritual work, for the crew would eventually come to believe it could actually feel the very pulse of the salvage boat. It was inspirational work, for the men came together as one, their personal likes and dislikes temporarily cast aside for the betterment of the whole.

Despite the ever-present specter of the *Atocha* curse, the old boat's refurbishment was completed with only minor casualties. My brother Jim got a taste of what combat was like when a spark from the welder's torch ignited a broom. The ensuing fire caused a nearby emergency oxygen tank to explode, hurling him 10 feet onto his back, leaving him dazed and bewildered but still intact. No harm done. This could not be said for the accident that almost blinded Joe Markovic. Again, it was the spark from a welder's torch that ignited the 7.62 mm AK-47 round hidden deep within a rotted bulkhead. When the bullet detonated, shell fragments became embedded in Joe's right eye. If he had not been wearing sunglasses, which deflected much of the blast, he would have lost the eye. Ironic that Markovic should survive the upheaval in his native Slovakia, only to be almost gunned down in America by a remnant of the Soviet Union.

The *Dauntless* finally returned to the sea on August 15, 2000, working at deepwater depths midway along the northwest-southeast line near the spot where 13 gold bars were found during the Memorial Day weekend in 1985.

After a frustrating start, Captain Hanna and his crew started finding treasure. In methodical fashion, the strikes came fast and

Captain Robbie Hanna leaves the water at the dive ladder of the *Dauntless* in May 2000.

furious: On September 5, gold nuggets and gold flakes were found by Markovic, Mike Piranio, Ray Hopkins, and my brother in 55 feet of water northwest of where the *Atocha*'s main pile was found. Eight days later, the crew recovered three gold nuggets, four gold flakes, and two emeralds. Two days after that, Hopkins and Jim brought three emeralds to the surface. Jim found a gold chain on September 27, then brought up three silver coins within a three-day period in early October. On November 6 the crew picked up the pace by uncovering 23 silver coins, one cannonball, and six musket balls in one hole—$34,000 in silver alone.

Piranio found a gold coin valued at $50,000 on November 15; on January 1, 2001, Hopkins recovered a silver folio used by Catholic priests. Hopkins found a jade sharpening stone on February 17, and then Markovic found a gold bar on the day's next dive. Piranio followed that up with a gold bar on March 2, Markovic found a gold bit 15 days later, and then Piranio found another gold bit on March 19. Not to be outdone, my brother

Jim found a gold chain, six musket balls, and two silver coins on March 28. After the crew found 17 silver coins on April 10, treasure valued at $25,500, Jim telephoned when they had returned to port and told me to grab the next airplane for Miami.

"I'm not trying to jump the gun," he said, "but we're getting closer and closer to the mother lode. We're gonna find that sterncastle any day now. We're on a roll, bro. We've got ourselves a kick-ass captain and crew."

Seeing is believing. The ticket was purchased, the flight taken, and on Monday, May 14, 2001, the deck of the *Dauntless* was rumbling beneath my feet. It had been 16 years since I had last walked her deck, with Kane Fisher at the helm. Now the captain was Robbie Hanna, with whom I had only a passing acquaintance. Hanna is larger than life, big-boned and well muscled, a 36-year-old Harley biker sporting a ponytail. Once upon a time he was a baker at the Key West Pier House, content working in a kitchen for others. But then the Gulf War started and the tourist industry went belly up. When Mel Fisher advertised for experienced divers in 1991, Hanna answered the call and immediately was put under the tutelage of Kane Fisher, working the *Atocha* site plus the 1715 fleet off Sebastian Inlet.

"I'm Kane-trained," said Hanna, who is as soft-spoken as he is mild-mannered. It took only a few minutes in his company to grasp his leadership traits: Discomfort was a given; if there was no pain, there was no gain; what did not kill you only made you stronger. While many old *Atocha* hands seemed to take curious delight in denigrating Kane Fisher, Hanna would hear none of that. Kane took him under his wing and taught him not only how to search for treasure but also how to handle a diverse crew under turbulent circumstances.

"Kane taught me to leave no stone unturned, that you can't be a good treasure hunter unless you want it bad enough," Hanna said. An excellent teacher, he was down there in the hole with you, showing instead of telling, setting high standards by high-minded, unbending example. On the trip to the dive site, he turned the helm over to me, explaining how to follow the GPS computer display, showing the intricacies of turning the wheel to keep his vessel on course. When I screwed up, he said, "Here, turn it like this. It's not like driving a car." Sure enough, within a few nervous minutes I was navigating the craft to his specifications, steering toward the diamond-sparkled horizon. And thoroughly enjoying the newfound success, which he could clearly see. Instead of saying "Well done," he merely smiled.

Hanna also could be a ball-buster. Gentle as he is, his creed was "Let's do it, let's get it done now." Yet he seldom raised his voice. His crew followed him because they wanted to. But God help them if they dug too deeply into Hanna's background. This big bear of a swashbuckler was a classical pianist in his youth. Back then his passion was Mozart, Beethoven, Tchaikovsky, and Rachmaninoff. Today it was ZZ Top and Guns N' Roses.

Ray Hopkins was the boat's chief mechanic. He is 38, almost 16 years removed from the Marine Corps, in which he enlisted shortly after graduating from high school in Alvin, Texas. Tall, wiry, and deeply tanned, Hopkins sported a ponytail, as did Joe Markovic. It took a while before it dawned on me that this crew was much like those I had known in the early days of the hunt— former military, devil-may-care individuals who grew up on the wrong side of the tracks; risk-takers and heartbreakers quick with their fists. Hopkins most certainly fit the bill and did not mind talking about it. He had tried his hand on the rodeo circuit in the early 1980s, lashing himself to the back of wild bulls. Finding it too tame, he took to the water with a passion, working as a hardhat diver for oil companies. Hopkins said he thought the Corps was tough until he found himself working endlessly at depths exceeding 200 feet for hours on end.

So after watching another diver become twisted in knots by the excessive depths and bone-snapping pressure, Hopkins headed to Key West and was introduced to Kim Fisher. Friendly to a fault and sporting an ah, shucks grin, the affable Texan was hired on the spot and assigned to the *Dauntless*. He said he had been in Key West fewer than two days when he realized it was the place he truly wanted to live. And it took him fewer than 10 minutes to realize that hunting for long-lost Spanish treasure was more of an adventure than a job. And once he actually found treasure—gold flakes and emeralds—all he had dreamed of ever since was finding the *Atocha*'s missing church gold. And locating one of those eight missing cannons wouldn't be all that bad, either.

Mike Piranio listened to Hopkins's banter with amusement, like a father tolerating his son's chatter. Indeed, Piranio was close to being a father figure among the crew. After all, everyone said, Piranio, at age 54, was older than dirt. A stretch, of course, but there was no denying that he possessed the saddest eyes I had seen outside of a war zone. The native of Everett, Washington, joined the army in 1966 and soon was handed an M-16 and sent to Vietnam. Foolish the things we do in our youth, Piranio said. An infantryman, he reupped for an extended tour in 'Nam; then, when his time was up, he joined a U.S. civilian engineering company that was intent on winning the hearts and minds of the South Vietnamese populace. The country took such a hold on him that Piranio did not leave until shortly after the 1975 fall of Saigon. And only then did he escape by the skin of his teeth, bringing his Vietnamese wife and extended family on a boat and enduring months at sea before reaching friendly landfall.

Now divorced, Piranio had been a Mel Fisher investor since 1995 and a treasure salvor since 1999. He was Captain Hanna's first mate, a genius when it came to repairing heavy equipment.

And then there was my not-so-little brother Jim. I must give credit where it is due, for he did not make a big deal about the circumstances under which we had been reunited. Since my initial introduction to Mel Fisher in May 1985, I had dreamed of being a full-time treasure hunter. Instead, I must be content to make occasional appearances on the treasure trail—diving and making rare discoveries, but for the most part writing about the high-seas adventures of others.

Then again, Jim said I had the best of both worlds, being able to spend a little time at sea, finding treasure, then departing for the comforts of home. This was true. "Spend too much time out here and you'd be ruined for life—just like me," he said. "I'd go nuts if I had to go back to the real world and its cute little office cubicles and the rest of that corporate crap." Jim laughed, flashed a thumbs up, and added, "Yeah, it's a treasure salvor's life for me, dude."

❁

Indeed. Soon we anchored just south of the Quicksands. It was almost 6:30 P.M., too late to do any serious searching. We would start bright and early in the morning, said Hanna. His plan was to scour a few holes they were unable to search from the last trip; then he would move the boat to virgin ground, farther up the trail than the *Dauntless* has been before, northwest of Captain Gary Randolph's territory.

"We're gonna find us some gold," said Hanna, unrolling a large chart on the wheelhouse's navigation table. He explained the nature of the search, how the *Atocha*'s trail continued to shrink. What remained was basically the width and breadth of the Quicksands. He had felt all along that this was where the bulk of gold, silver, and emeralds from the sterncastle lay hidden. Finding this treasure, however, would be one prolonged pain in the neck. The 15-foot-deep sands were a diver's nightmare, much like trying to sift the Sahara.

We ate, then retired to the crew's quarters, where we watched a video about the sinking of the U.S.S. *Indianapolis*, torpedoed by a Japanese submarine in the latter months of World War II. Not the best of flicks to watch before diving, because 1,100 men went into the water and only 300 survived. Sharks feasted.

I was dreaming of *Jaws* when the ship's main engines woke me at 6:45 A.M. Two quick cups of coffee and a few cigarettes later, the day's first hole was blown. Divers were in the water at 7:30 A.M., finding nothing, not even ballast.

At 11:00 A.M. Hanna moved the boat half a mile farther northwest to an area the crew called "The Gold Trail." Anchors were dropped, then repositioned with the aid of the winches, a hole was blown, and at noon I made my first dive of the day—forgetting everything I had learned, failing to grab hold of the down line, and subsequently being carried away with the current. When I finally stuck my head above water to get my bearings, I was 100 meters behind the stern with no hope of making my way back to the ship. Mike Piranio came to my rescue with the whaler, tossed me a towline, and pulled me back to the hole. Other than my would-be sojourn to Cuba, the dive was unproductive. I managed not to get lost on the second hole of the day, but other than perfect visibility, it produced no results.

While the third hole was being blown, 42-year-old Joe Markovic let down his guard. He talked about being born in Bratislava, about the breakup of Czechoslovakia, and about the European wars. Markovic was a tennis player, so proficient that he taught beginners and professionals for 10 years before the country became divided. While he would prefer to teach the sport here, the language barrier was too much to overcome. So he dives, which was better than waiting on tables or cooking, both of which he had previously done.

Markovic dreams of finding a big gold church cross. As a deeply religious man, he views all crosses as being beautiful. "I have a straight phone line up there to heaven," he said, "so I dream of crosses—magnificent gold crosses." Even as he said this, he did not smile. After all, while treasure was nice, it was not his to keep. His job was to find it; the keeping of it was left to others. And then he politely excused himself and hung a hammock on the starboard side of the boat, connecting it to the upper deck of the wheelhouse and the lower deck's support rail. Climbing into it, he looked down at me and smiled. "Vacation," he said, reclining to work on his tan.

When the third hole on the Gold Trail was finally blown, Jim and Robbie Hanna navigated 30 feet to the bottom and began their search. Near the end of the 40-minute dive, Hanna's detector recorded a hit. Within minutes he was clutching a silver coin.

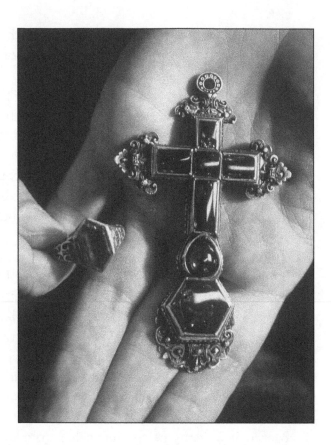

The extraordinary
emerald-studded
Bishop's Cross and
a gold-and-emerald
ring found in a
silver box.

Moving farther along the steep berm, Hanna got another hit and
let out a shout. Jim nodded in acknowledgment and took one last
glance at the barren bedrock in front of him. His job was to scour
the base of the hole—once with the metal detector, and a second
time visually. Satisfied that nothing had escaped his eye, he cut
diagonally across the hole to assist Hanna.

"And I swear to God, that's when my heart stopped," Jim said.

My brother had been in no hurry. After all, finding silver
coins had now become commonplace. The only items that stopped
him in his tracks, not to mention taking his breath away, were
fashioned from gold. Admittedly, he was in the cusp of that daydreaming–deep-diving state—having reached the limit of his dive
time, having found nothing for his efforts, his mind had turned

My not-so-little brother Jim, now a full-time diver for Kim Fisher, with the earring he found.

from treasure to thoughts of a ham and cheese sandwich. So as he swam lazily across the hole, he just happened to look down into a shallow hole in the bedrock. And there, dangling on a coral outcrop, were a pair of gold earrings, each bearing three teardrop pearls. The earrings were attached to one another, just as a lady of evidently royal blood had placed them before being consumed by the sea.

Jim's reaction was customary. He froze, hovering inches from the earrings, afraid to touch them. Staring, his eyes wide, his breath came in short, sharp gasps. When he finally summoned the courage to grasp the exquisite jewelry, he did so with trembling fingers. He gently lifted them off the coral outcrop and placed them in the palm of his hand, then stared again for the longest time, his mind transfixed not only by their beauty but also by the craftsmanship of a long-ago goldsmith. And only then did he shout and pump his fist in victory—one of life's priceless moments.

The ensuing celebration topside was something I had not experienced on this trail since 1986, during the emerald-rush days.

Jim jumping for joy as he received handshakes and pats on the back, everyone whooping and laughing uncontrollably as Jim placed the earrings up to his ear and asked over and over, "What do you think? They look good on me?" Indeed, they did. Both the earrings and the ear-to-ear smile. It warmed my heart to see my brother so thoroughly enjoying himself, without a care in the world. As proud as I was of the entire crew, I was even prouder of my brother, who was proving to be an even better treasure finder than he had been a politician.

During the next five days on the trail I came to admire Captain Hanna and his crew more and more. They worked well together and seldom confronted one another over real or imagined slights. The crew covered each other's backs in the most dangerous of all settings. To top it all off, they were finding treasure at a maddening pace. And they were more than willing to help an inquisitive writer-turned-diver, first by working on my consumption of air, encouraging me to the point that by the third day I was barely consuming 1,500 pounds during a 40-minute dive, then by instructing me how to use the metal detector to scour the base of a blown hole. I finally got the hang of it, yet never did find a piece of eight. Pottery shards and buckets full of exotic seashells, yes, but not one ounce of silver.

Then again, there is more to working at the bottom of the sea than treasure. Trying to keep up with a school of blue runners was almost as big a thrill as watching the rest of the crew find silver coins, which they did with efficiency, discovering 26 before the trip was over—a mere $39,000 in treasure. Not to mention a couple of iron spikes; pottery shards; and those gold earrings, which proved to be the trip's high point. And while this perfect crew was intent on uncovering treasure, I scoured the top of the berm, keeping leery eyes peeled for sharks and finding curious five-feet-long barracudas instead. And every time I came face-to-face with those prehistoric-looking 'cudas, I was scared witless. An eerie moment followed by a comical one—watching Piranio spend at least 20 minutes digging into the cascading sands of the berm, intent on uncovering another silver coin, only to discover a thin Roosevelt dime minted in 1970.

The company was as perfect as the visibility. I had the pleasure of drinking an early-morning cup of coffee with Piranio in the feathery cast of predawn, neither of us talking much as we watched a dolphin leaping close to the boat. I could sit and watch Hopkins attend to the ship's engines, listening as he talked about the intricacies of the big twin diesels. Once I jumped into the whaler with Hanna and skimmed seven miles across Hawk Channel to the aid of Lobster Lee, whose fishing boat was dead in the water south of the Marquesas because of a problem with his starter.

"We're not alone on this sea," said Hanna. "Next time that could be us having a problem. We're all in this together." When the problem was fixed, Lobster Lee and his mate Terry made us a gift of several pounds of grouper; we had a grand feast that evening. Markovic taught me how to cook steak loin the Slovakian way: heavily peppering both sides, then cutting the steak into thin slices, applying Dijon mustard and Worcestershire sauce to each slice, then dropping them in a hot skillet coated with virgin olive oil, cooking them for three minutes on each side. The ship's motto: Work hard, eat hearty.

There also was joy in watching my brother dart about the vessel, emulating a sponge as he soaked up everything about the salvage operation and handling of a boat—eager to learn, eager to work, eager to help his captain and crew.

"I'm a middle-aged man who thoroughly loves his job," Jim said.

But the greatest thrills of all were the dives, each of which began with Hanna's call, "Okay, the pool's open. Today's the day." Then leaping into the water, finding the down line, and slowly dropping to the bottom. Always anxious, no matter how exhausted

A diver displays a gold chain, a gold coin, and emeralds from the Ghost Galleon's tomb.

you might be, hoping and praying under your breath that this would be the moment everyone had been waiting for. Biting back the excitement, yet still feeling the tingle move throughout your body, knowing that with a mere hand fan of the next layer of sand the riches of an ancient kingdom could very well come to light.

And then, all too suddenly, the trip was over. The excitement of the start was replaced by an emptiness that would remain until it was time for me to slip once again into my diving gear.

Treasure has that kind of hold on you.

24

Today's the Day

The question is not whether we will die, but how we will live.

—*Joan Borysenko*

Appropriately enough, it was April Fool's Day, and another diving season approached. As usual, anticipation of discovery made sleep difficult. As soon as I drifted off, I was at the bottom of the sea, fanning away the sand and coming face-to-face with the *Atocha*'s missing sterncastle. Before me are chests filled with gold bars, jewelry studded with diamonds and pearls, and gold-and-emerald crosses dangling from ornate gold chains. But the most breathtaking artifact is an intricately crafted throne, an auspicious piece of gold furniture surely meant for royalty. And just as I'm about to try it out for size, my eyes snap open. It's the dead of night; my breathing is rapid, my hands are shaking, and I'm covered in sweat.

My mind would have been in a far different realm had not the Marine Corps recruiters politely told me thanks-but-no-thanks months ago, that I was far too old to help search out and destroy Afghan terrorists. My newspaper bosses were of no help, either. When I volunteered to cover yet another war, they gave me a sidelong glance, smiled, and said it was a young person's game.

So here I sit with plenty of time on my hands, daydreaming about the *Nuestra Señora de Atocha*, Mel Fisher's queen bitch of the sea, the quest for which he reluctantly passed down to his son Kim. Reluctantly, because no one wishes to die. Surely Mel didn't. But as his second son once told me, all good things pass away, and life goes on. And in this instance, someone *had* to take hold of Mel's dream and continue pursuing it. Me? I've just been along for the ride, a wanna-be treasure salvor with a persistent writing habit who has grown older as the search has grown longer.

A good friend at the newspaper once asked me why I spent so much time at sea diving on another person's dream. I didn't have to give it much thought, in part because I also share Mel's vision. More than anything else, though, I do it because I can. What I cannot do is cross Death Valley in a Conestoga wagon with yesteryear's pioneers. Nor can I storm the beaches of Tarawa with my father or accompany John Glenn on that inaugural space flight.

But I can put my fears aside and give substance to my imagination. When that big Dive Master in the sky refuses to refill my tank, I don't want to depart with a mind filled with a lot of what-ifs.

And what has it gotten me? Adventure for sure, not to mention friendships and the opportunity not only to touch history but also to hear its recital from firsthand participants. Those deep-diving *Atocha* historians proved to be every bit as fascinating as the long-lost treasure they discovered.

Understating the obvious, I was constantly stumbling on characters who told wondrous stories that seemed to have been lifted from an Elmore Leonard novel. Folks such as Kenny "Ding-a-Ling" Lingle, a lifelong Key Wester who joined Mel Fisher's band of merry men in 1971. The then-22-year-old former U.S. Navy torpedoman hired on as a theodolite operator. This meant he was stuck atop a fixed tower secured to the hulk of one of the derelict freighters that had gone aground in the area. From these towers, Lingle would peer through the surveyor's eyepiece, making sure the search boat kept on course. The job didn't pay much, but then again, Lingle didn't need much. He had no debts, no family, no responsibilities to speak of, so he was content to squander his time working for Fisher.

"Other treasure hunters looked upon Mel as being some sort of idiot," said Lingle, who considered himself a pretty good judge of people, the result of a varied lifestyle that included stints as a biker, preacher, strip club manager, bartender, and bouncer. Lingle took an instant liking to Fisher, a sort of down-and-outers' kinship. "Even though people kept pounding on him, Mel just took it in stride. He was a man after my own heart, because he'd just pour himself another drink, hand us a beer, and off we'd go—him saying, 'Today's the day we find her, boys,' and us grinning, truly believing it was going to happen."

Why do the *Atocha* divers continue to search for the galleon's alleged missing sterncastle?

Almost to a man, today's divers say they're still doing it for Mel. And they could care less if their sentiments sound maudlin. In their hearts, at least, the spirit of the man remains strong. Some things never die. Besides, his ashes still linger somewhere out there along the *Atocha* trail. And every time they dive, they are overwhelmed by his persuasive power, repeating to themselves Mel's persistent lexicon, "Today's the day."

Such was and is the power of the man, even from the grave.

I admired Mel Fisher for many reasons, the most endearing of which was his ability to make politicians' knees shake. Mel refused to be intimidated, fighting big government at every turn. What the politicians failed to grasp was the very essence of why Americans are Americans. The government's argument over ownership of the *Margarita* and the *Atocha* boiled down to sovereign prerogative, going back to English common law, which holds that anything washed up on shore from a sunken ship belongs to the Crown. If a peasant found it, he had to turn it over to the Crown, and he might or might not receive a reward. The other part of sovereign prerogative was fornication under command of the king, the right of the first night.

"Since all of the peons out there were under the king's prerogative," Don Kincaid said, "he had the right to deflower any virgin in the land on her wedding night. We had the American Revolution, in part, because we thought that was bullshit."

Kincaid told me that the search for the *Atocha* could very well be the last great treasure hunt in the history of mankind because what the government had tried to do to Fisher was reminiscent of Big Brother in Orwell's book *1984*. In essence, the government wanted to put the Mel Fishers of the world out to pasture. Which is a self-defeating proposition, for without adventurers such as Mel and John Glenn, without mankind's relentless pioneers, you have nothing but a world that subsists on baby food.

So you jump to your feet, pull on your scuba gear, and jump into the water. You don't have to think about it. You just do it. At the same time, you must come to grips with the fact that you're not a one-man or a one-woman show. A treasure hunt functions successfully because of dreamers and visionaries both in and out of the water. For every Donnie Jonas and Jeff Dickinson bringing gold and silver to the surface, there is an eager investor subsidizing the search with a portion of his or her life savings.

In the days immediately after the July 20, 1985, discovery of 30 tons of silver, scores of gold bars, chains, jewelry, and assorted gems nestled amid the *Atocha*'s hull timbers, I spoke with a few dozen longtime investors, all of whom seemed to outdo each other in praising Fisher. Mel was the god of treasure hunting, they said. No one had doubted Mel's ability to find the mother lode. To a man and a woman, the investors had *always* had faith in him. But those platitudes had been given after the fact, after Mel's stick-to-itiveness had made some of them millionaires.

Then there are today's investors, those who continue to help defray the expenses of Kim Fisher's divers in their quest to find the *Atocha*'s elusive stern.

Don and Connie Kiblinger live on a ranch in Strafford, Missouri, which is about as landlocked as it gets. They are in their 50s. Don is a retired engineer, having spent the past 30 years installing conveyor belts in every major post office in the country. Connie is the director of a bank in nearby Ozark. They're doing well financially, so much so that they became investors in the

Atocha/Margarita Expedition. But not because they thought they would get rich or receive a fantastic return on their investment.

"Naturally, we're dreamers, having read *Treasure Island* and fantasizing about pirates and buried treasure," Connie told me over lunch in December 2001. "When you get right down to it, there is a little bit of treasure hunter in everyone. This is our way of being able to actually touch the past, of being an integral part of history."

The Kiblingers travel to the Keys at least twice a year, keeping abreast of the *Atocha*'s sterncastle search while enjoying the sights and the company of newfound acquaintances at a local restaurant. And while Don worked his way through another plate of crab legs, Connie envisioned what it would be like when Kim Fisher's divers finally whisked away the sand, uncovering those 35 boxes of church gold. That moment, she said, would be like *Close Encounters of the Third Kind*, "because it is my destiny to be here."

Destiny presents itself in many forms and fashions. Little did Pat Clyne know that a casual conversation with Mel Fisher in 1973 would lead to personal enrichment, which he values far more than anything he has discovered at the bottom of the sea. Clyne first grew to admire, then to respect, and finally to love Fisher, standing beside Mel through good times and bad. Theirs was a bond that not even death could break. In August 2000, the Russian submersible MIR-1 took Clyne two and a half miles beneath the North Atlantic to the resting place of the *Titanic*. At the behest of the Fisher family, he used one of the MIR-1's arms to place a small receptacle containing some of Mel's ashes on the main bridge where Captain E. J. Smith spent his last agonizing hours contemplating the fate of his "unsinkable" vessel, forever linking one noble maritime legend with another.

And once Clyne had made that journey of a lifetime, he returned to Key West, journeyed into Hawk Channel, pulled on his diving gear, then slipped through the surface to scour the sands along the *Atocha* treasure trail. Because that galleon was Mel's insatiable passion, because finding her elusive stern was among his best friend's final thoughts, Pat Clyne will never cease searching until their shared destiny is fulfilled.

Destiny also had brought Dave Hostie to Key West. At the time I spoke with him, the 41-year-old New England transplant was "the new guy," the most recent diver hired by operations manager Gary Randolph. A commercial diver who specialized in aquaculture, toiling as an underwater farmer, Hostie gave up a job that oftentimes earned him $1,000 a day to become a $300-per-week treasure salvor.

"Can you believe this? I'm actually getting paid to do what every little kid has always wanted to do—find treasure," said Hostie, who, in late November 2001, found a silver coin and a large twisted iron spike at the northernmost boundary of the present *Atocha* trail. The significance of those discoveries could very well mean the missing stern was nearby—or not.

"The only way we're going to know for sure," said fellow diver Jeff Dickinson, "is to dig and dig and dig some more. But we'll find her because we've got the greatest team in the world searching for her. She can't elude us forever."

But she has continued to do just that, despite a string of tantalizing discoveries. Dickinson and Gary Randolph found gold coins and gold bars in February 2001. Then eight months later, my brother Jim discovered 27 feet of gold chains, the biggest discovery of its kind since 1986. They've found gold-and-emerald brooches, gold-and-pearl earrings, a silver tankard, silverware, and hundreds of silver coins, not to mention gold bits and gold flakes and fistfuls of emeralds. Dickinson's discovery of a gold bar on June 23, 2002, raised everyone's hopes that a second mother lode was close at hand. But then the trail petered out.

I share their frustration. It had been my hope that by the time I reached these final pages I would have the privilege of describing the treasures from the *Atocha*'s stern. But treasure hunting cares no more about publishing schedules than it did about the impatience of some of Mel Fisher's investors. I can almost hear

Mel chuckling as he stirs St. Peter's drink with a gold finger bar and says, "Hey, if it was easy, everybody would be out there lookin' for it."

So it is that our tale is left figuratively dangling in the slight breeze that brushes across the surface of Hawk Channel. On and on the search continues, with no end in sight other than within the collective mind of those divers crewing the *Dauntless* and the *J. B. Magruder.*

The truth is that no one really knows if and when the search will finally end. Not even Kim Fisher, who with tongue firmly planted in cheek said, "Maybe it will never end."

Now, there's a curious thought. Maybe our grandchildren will grow up to be *Atocha* divers. Be warned, though, that the job isn't quite as glorious as some of us make it out to be. For $300 a week you have to live at sea, sleeping in tight quarters and eating on the deck of a much-abused salvage boat. You will eat well, but diversions are few. There is no telephone or regular television, but the crew can watch videos each night. Then again, you will most likely be too exhausted to see their endings. The other creature comfort is a library well stocked with Clive Cussler paperbacks—the usual fare about Dirk Pitt discovering various long-lost treasures.

As for the work, to call it monotonous borders on hype—rising at dawn, manhandling anchors and other heavy equipment, then diving on virgin territory. Sure, it has a macho appeal, if you are into that sort of thing. It is the same bravado a fighter pilot, police officer, firefighter, or soldier clings to: being a man among men, or a woman among women, doing what others consider foolhardy or downright stupid. Then again, you will never be among those who ask, "What if?"

And then there is the treasure. Chances are that at first you will only be fortunate enough to see others find it. You will be perplexed, for they were searching right beside you. So how did they find something and you didn't? The days will become weeks, then months, and all you will have to show for your efforts are aching muscles, earaches, shriveled skin on your hands and feet, and a very thin wallet. That and a bellyful of exasperation, for while you are questioning your own sanity, you will see other divers find a few emeralds or a couple of gold bars.

And then, about the time you have convinced yourself that you should return to civilization, apologize to your ex-boss, and plead for your job back, you decide to take one last dive. For some reason, upon entering the water you sense that it seems clearer than you remember. And once you are at the bottom of the freshly blown hole, your body starts to tingle. It is as if you *know* something good is about to happen. You hover, your face a scant few inches above the sand and coral bottom, fanning methodically with your right hand. You scan to the right, then to the left. Slowly at first, then faster, your head swiveling, eyes peering into the feathery cloud of particles. *And then, magic . . .*

Finding treasure, even if it is merely a blackened orb of oxidized silver—that Oreo cookie, the elusive Spanish piece of eight—is truly every bit as exhilarating as anything depicted on the silver screen. Indeed, it is breathtaking, for when you lift it from the bottom, you know that human hands last touched the coin 380 years ago. Had you not been possessed of the right stuff, been persistent to the bitter end, odds are it would have stayed undetected forever. So you pump your fist and thank God under your breath, then continue the search with greater intensity. And when you finally do surface, the cheers and handshakes and claps on the back from the captain and crew will remain with you always. In the blink of an eye you have joined one of the most exclusive clubs in the world; you're now officially a treasure finder, no longer a mere treasure hunter.

As long as you live, those brief moments in the deep and the joyous surfacing will flow unbidden into your dreams and seep into your waking moments, lightening the burden of life's routine.

The coin you found will become one of your most precious possessions, for the first silver coin that a Fisher diver finds is his or hers to keep. This is one of the little trade-offs of the grueling job. Tourists pay $1,500 for them, then take them home to Cedar Rapids or wherever, and place them in lockboxes. You will have yours set in a gold mount and proudly wear it around your neck on a gold chain. And when someone asks about the odd fashion statement, you can relive the moment of discovery all over again, recounting your high-sea adventure.

At least that's how I did it after I found my first coin, on April 18, 2000. In my mind's eye, I will forever be 32 feet below the surface, my dive watch registering 3:17 P.M.

Such is the power of dreams.

Index

Note: Page numbers in *italics* refer to photographs.